RAINBOW WARRIORS

About the author

Despite having been born and lived most of her life in Albacete (in the La Mancha region of Spain), **Maite Mompó** had the sea in her blood. While in her home town, she gained a degree in law, became a qualified English teacher and then worked for a windfarm company. In the late 1980s she started volunteering for Amnesty International's local group and became a supporter of other local NGOs, including Greenpeace. Sailing became her passion thanks to her father's little sailing boat.

In 1997, she started volunteering as a deckhand on the *Zorba*, a 20-meter-long wooden sailing boat used by Greenpeace Spain to carry out an educational project for adults. She moved to Majorca in 2002 to co-ordinate this project and in 2004 joined the Greenpeace International fleet, first as a volunteer and then as a professional deckhand. After sailing a couple of times on both the *Esperanza* and the *Arctic Sunrise*, she arrived on *Rainbow Warrior II* and continued sailing on her until the ship was decommissioned. A few months after that, she began a personal project whose result is the book you have in your hands.

Acknowledgements

This book would have never been possible without the support of dozens of people scattered all over the world. In fact, the best thing about this experience has been sharing this project with all of them.

First, I would like to acknowledge my own family (my parents, brothers, sister and uncle) and my friends, who have always pampered me and given me encouragement. To start with, thanks to my family and also Lluísa Ivars and Ana Ortolá for providing me with a home-office in which to work.

Then, I am deeply grateful to my small team of 'assistants' whose advice was essential in improving what I have written: María José Caballero, Jordi Curell, Lola Mompó and Rafael Ruiz de la Cuesta and specially to Domingo Freijomil. Also here I would like to mention my father and my brother Vicente for all their special contributions.

I also owe a lot to the ones who disinterestedly helped me in the translations from Spanish to English: Brenda Keller, Mariajo Torre de la Osa, Belén Momeñe, David Ransom and Charlotte Cornforth. Then, thanks to Enrique Iniesta for improving my Spanish text.

I would finally like to thank Chris Brazier, my editor, for having such immense patience following me through my chaos and for making so many good contributions to my text; Juha Sorsa, my designer, for his dedication and his maps; and Angie Hipkin for her meticulous indexing.

Obviously, this literary tribute to the life of a ship would have never been achieved without the contribution of all those who dedicated time to telling me stories, giving me information, providing me with graphical material or helping me in some other way. So, sincere thanks go to: Meredith Adams, Sabela Aguiar, Josevi Alamar, Ilai Ben Amar, Pedro Armestre, Carlos Ayllón, Beau Baconguis, Al Baker, Phil Ball, Pep Barbal, Almudena Barrera, Sheena Beaton, Frida Bengtsson, Amanda Bjuhr, Isabelle Bollaert, Carlos Bravo, Dave Caister, Teresa Cano, Ivana Carev, Gloria Chang, Darren Charlesworth, Paloma Colmenarejo, Alain Connan, Gigie Cruz, Miguel Ángel Cuesta, Mario Damato, Arthur Dionio, Sharon Dolev, Jo Dufay, Brad Edge, Paco Escrivá, Simona Fausto, Guillermo Fernández-Obanza (Mito), Faye Ferrer, Sabine Fielitz, Mike Fincken, Brian Fitzgerald, Inés Flores, Sandra Fontanillas, John Frizell, Rita Ghanem, Emilse Garattoni, Conrado García del Vado, Nacho Garnacho, Alessandro Gianni, Pierre Gleizes, Raúl Gómez, Sonia Gómez, Vinuta Gopal, Tim Gorter, Carmen Gravatt, Nili Grossman, Truls Gulowsen, Holly Guy, Madeleine Habib, Emily Johnston, Vj Jose, Rashid Kang, Runa Khan, Pablo Korman, Jun Kwon Song, Rodrigo Lazo, Sihnae Lee, Dima Litvinov, Martin Lloyd, Juan López de Uralde (Juantxo), Ana Rosa Lorenzo, Sebastián Losada, Antón Luis, Óscar Macián, Bustar Maitar, Sven Malmgren, Pilar Marcos, José Manuel Marraco, Ana Carla Martínez, Bunny McDiarmid, Emily McDowell, Stephanie Mills, León Molina, Belén Momeñe, Gonzalo Montón, Raquel Montón, Gianluca Morini, Flavio Nakazono, Susi Newborn, Derek Nicholls, Caterina Nitto, Thijs Notenboom, Sam N'siah, Stephen Nugent, Daniel Ocampo, Celia Ojeda, María Oliver, Marta Orihuela, Grace O'Sullivan, Rémi Parmentier, Edward Patrick, Tapio Pekkanen, Laura Pérez, Naomi Petersen, Manuel Pinto, Ply Pirom, Lalita Ramdas, Sara del Río, Bahadir Riza, Daniel Rizzotti, Dave Roberts, Fernando Romo, Alcedo Rossi, David Roy, Peru Saban, Eva Saldaña, Christian Schmutz, Chariya Senpong (Mook), Dima Sharomov, Kajsa Sjölander, Lesley Simkiss, Andrés Soto, Miguel Ángel Soto (Nanqui), Camila Speziale, Martin Steffens, Joel Stewart, Michael Szabo, Robert Taylor, Wu Ho Tong, Lawrence Turk (Butch), Juan del Valle, Luis Vasquez, Justin Veenstra, Toni Vidan, Frits de Vink, Sue Ware, Tanya Whitford, Peter Willcox, Rex Wyler, and Shailendra Yashwant.

Finally, I would like to thank any others who gave me a hand along the way and are not specifically mentioned and, of course, all those who would have loved to take part in this project but did not have the chance.

RAINBOW WARRIORS

Legendary Stories from Greenpeace Ships

Maite Mompó

New Internationalist

Rainbow Warriors: Legendary Stories from Greenpeace Ships
Published in 2014 by:
New Internationalist Publications Ltd
The Old Music Hall
106-108 Cowley Road
Oxford
OX4 1JE, UK

Designed for New Internationalist by Juha Sorsa.

Printed by 1010 Printing International Ltd, who hold environmental accreditation ISO 14001.

British Library Cataloguing-in-Publication Data
A catalogue record for this book is available from the British Library.

Library of Congress Cataloging-in-Publication Data
A catalog record for this book is available from the Library of Congress.

ISBN 978-1-78026-172-0

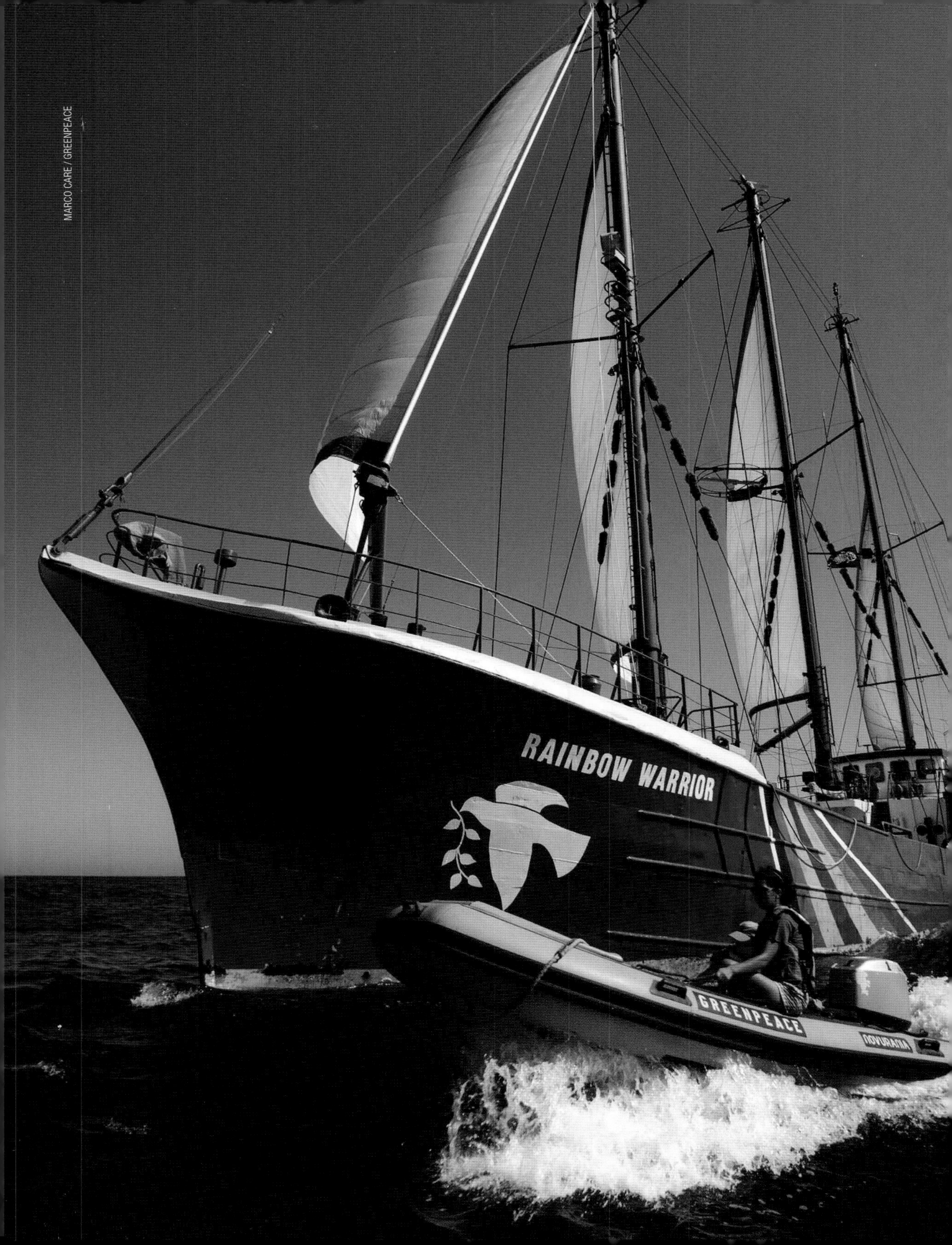

MARCO CARE / GREENPEACE

Contents

Foreword by Susi Newborn 9

Preface by Bunny McDiarmid 11

Prologue 13

1 Beginnings 15
Stories from the past
Birth of a myth
A book called *Warriors of the Rainbow*
The return of a Warrior

2 The nuclear madness 31
Introduction
The day of the two suns
Bikini, the lost paradise (1946) • Rongelap, the dawn of twilight (1954) • Operation Exodus (1985, 2010)
Moruroa Peace boats versus nuclear bombs • The last trip to Moruroa (1995)

3 Between the harpoon and the whale 51
Humans and whales
Whales and the *Rainbow Warrior*
Stories from Norway • A very tough campaign (1999) • Ten years on (2009)
Between the harpoon and the whale (*Arctic Sunrise*, Antarctica, 2005)

4 Poison and hope 69
Introducing Crizel
Toxic-free Asia Tour (1999-2000) Bhopal • Shipbreaking • River and sea pollution • Incineration • Landfills • A clean future
Crizel's story
Hope

5 In defense of forests 85
Introduction
Save or delete? Bloodwood (Spain, 2002) • A question of *Honour* (Spain, 2003)
Paradise on Earth To the beat of drums (Papua New Guinea, 1997) • Riots in Papua (2006) • On the road to Bali (Indonesia, 2007)

6 Expect the unexpected 105
Introduction
Of stowaways and castaways
Running away from Cuba (Caribbean Sea, 1992) • The Djibouti boys (Middle East, 2001) • Mayday in the middle of the night (Western Mediterranean, 2006)
Emergencies on board A hole in the hull (South Pacific, 2005) • Maite alarm (Cyprus, 2006)
Humanitarian missions The Great Tsunami (Indonesia, 2005) • Beirut under bombs (Eastern Mediterranean, 2006) • The story of Chile Willy (Chile, 1996)

7 Prestige 125
Introduction
The great escape (*Rainbow Warrior I*, 1980)
Rise to glory (*Sirius*, 1982)
The oil-tanker disaster (*Rainbow Warrior II*, 2002)
An assault (*Esperanza*, 2004)
The winds that blow these days (*Rainbow Warrior II* and *Arctic Sunrise*)

8 Wars and walls 141
Introductio n
Action against the Iraq War (Spain, 2003)
The voyage of wars and walls (Eastern Mediterranean, 2006) Lebanon & Israel (Lebanon)

• Israel and Lebanon (Israel) • The divided island (Cyprus)• The strength of a wind (Croatia)

9 Pirates! 157
On piracy
Ship pirates • In the pirates' sights (Middle East, 2007) • Navigating pirate waters (in transit, 2010)
Fishing pirates • What gets thrown overboard (Tasman Sea, June 2004 - June 2005) • The sleeping kids (Italy, 2006) • Stories of bluefin tuna (Mediterranean Sea) • The expulsion from Marseilles (France, 2006) • A white lily (Croatia, 2006) • Encounters on the high seas (north of Libya, 2007) • Red hot (south of Malta, 2010)

10 The planet we live on 179
Humanity's greatest challenge (Earth, 21st century)
In the Land of the Long White Cloud (New Zealand/Aotearoa, March 2008)
Sails to be free (Netherlands, November 2008)

The Copenhagen experience (Norway & Denmark, December 2009)
The fingers of humanity (Israel, July 2010)
The story of the Arctic 30 (Russia, September-December 2013)

11 The circle of life................... 209
The last *Rainbow Warrior* missions (East Asia, 2011) • The voyage to Fukushima (Japan)
• The last campaign (South Korea, June 2011)
Of Rainbows and Warriors • Farewell to a Warrior, welcome to a Rainbow • The circle of life

Epilogue 232

Glossary of nautical terms........ 233

Chronology of stories 235

Index.. 236

Foreword

by Susi Newborn

2015 WILL BE the 30th anniversary of the bombing of the *Rainbow Warrior* in Auckland harbor by the French secret service. No doubt the anniversary will be marked in some form by Greenpeace offices around the world. People will remember colleague and crewmember Fernando Pereira, who was killed on board while trying to rescue his camera gear. People will remember how hard we fought to end French nuclear testing at Moruroa, and won. There are so many victories to be celebrated along the road from then to now. It is a history we can all be proud of.

Sadly, the genesis of this special boat with her rainbow and dove, the meme of the Greenpeace organization, her name possibly now even a trademark, is never celebrated by anyone. It even passes me by, and I was the one who named her – after a book of prophecies – and gifted her the rainbow and the dove, from an image in the book.

Let me briefly take you back to 1978, to a smelly backwater basin in London's East India Dockland where a handful of young volunteers worked tirelessly day and night chipping rust off an old Atlantic fishing trawler. We knew then that we were part of something incredibly special, something which would grow, which would inspire and transform others into planet warriors. We had no idea how we would succeed, whether or not we would even come back alive from the higher latitudes of the North Atlantic; we did not really know if our ship would be seaworthy until we set sail on 2 May 1978 and London Bridge opened to let us pass.

Because magic works in special ways, a copy of the book *Warriors of the Rainbow* had been given to me by Bob Hunter, one of the founders of Greenpeace. It had been given to him by a Jewish dulcimer maker who described himself as a gypsy. Bob gave me a copy, years later, in my tiny cabin down below in what was then still the *Sir William Hardy*, during the 1978 conversion. Last year, one of the authors of the book – Iniupiaq elder Willie Willoya – had a diver place a *taonga* (a prized object) from Alaska on the wreck of the *Rainbow Warrior*, in the remnants of that same cabin down below. Later, when he saw the magnificent *Rainbow Warrior III* in Wellington harbor, he exclaimed 'There's my boat!'

Those of us who were part of the very first *Rainbow Warrior* crew firmly believed in nonviolent direct action. We were guided by Eastern philosophies: there were poets, musicians, professional sailors, campaigners among us. We meditated, some of us were Taoists; we were a 'motley crew'. We ran a vegetarian ship, taking turns to cook. We were a tribe unto ourselves: dressed in similar clothes, we even starting looking the same – lean faces, long hair. We listened to Jimi Hendrix while under arrest with machine guns pointed at us. We broke down in front of butchered whales.

In music there is something called 'entraining', the experience of getting in the groove, coming together as a unit, working without ego, being there for each other. There is no need for the spoken word, you just 'do'.

Maite will have experienced this 'entraining' with her crew mates throughout the years she has been at sea on Greenpeace boats. She is certainly much loved and respected by those who know her. During our conversations about this book, she emphasized how the spirit of the original *Rainbow Warrior* is found within all Rainbow Warriors, past, present and future – they all are Rainbow Warrior!

Now, as I reflect on the past 36 years, I feel a sense of incredible pride to have been part of something like this, something that has facilitated a real sea change in the way we view the environment – not as something to be exploited, but something to be valued and preserved for generations to come. This 'greening' of democracy has resulted in a worldwide influencing network of lobbyists, scientists, artists, politicians, even entire governments, working for the benefit of *Pachamama*, not raping her of her strength and beauty.

That the story of the *Rainbow Warrior*, through her continual metamorphoses, had a role in this is a given, and Maite's book will serve as a testament to the years of love and dedication that many people have given to making this world a better place. In the words of Willie Willoya in *Warriors of the Rainbow*: 'Great are the tasks ahead. Terrifying are the mountains of ignorance and hate and prejudice, but the Warriors of the Rainbow shall rise as on the wings of the eagle to surmount all difficulties. They will be happy to find that there are now millions of people all over the earth ready and eager to rise and join them in conquering all barriers that bar the way to a new and glorious world! We have had enough now of talk. Let there be deeds.' Amen to that.

Susi Newborn, co-founder of Greenpeace UK and once a *Rainbow Warrior* crew member

REDSTAR IMAGES

Preface
by Bunny McDiarmid

AS I WRITE this it will have been 30 years since I first met the *Rainbow Warrior* and became part of her crew, part of the Greenpeace story like many others before and after me. If I close my eyes now I can still see the grain in her deck and smell the tar of her seams on a hot day.

The *Warrior* was my first date with Greenpeace and I think that experience is why I am still here today. When I met 'her' in 1984, I had no idea of who or what Greenpeace was, I just really liked what the *Warrior* was going to do and how it was to do it. Her campaign was an anti-nuclear one in the Pacific, part of which involved relocating a whole community of 350 people away from their island home because of radioactive contamination from US nuclear testing 30 years earlier.

It was an extraordinary thing to be part of – to arrive at the doorstep of someone you had not met before, watch them take apart their houses and load their entire lives onto a boat they had never seen before and move to a deserted island 100 miles away that most of them had never seen before. But they did it, because they believed this was the only way to pressure the US government into acknowledging what their nuclear tests had done and to get them to help clean up the mess or nuclear legacy that continues to this day.

The *Warrior* became part of their story and they became part of ours. If you go back to Rongelap today, you will find 30-year-old men named after the ship and songs that tell about the day of two suns and the arrival of the *Warrior* on their beach.

I remember the banner we hung – on the US military base – before we departed the Marshall Islands, which read 'we can't relocate the world'. In the 1980s the biggest threat was nuclear warfare, but that same message is even more poignant today with climate change already affecting millions of people's lives and governments not having learned that we have only one home.

The *Warrior* for me was as much about the people – she tied us all together in a common cause.

The *Warrior* and the origin of her name, which has now been passed on to two more ships in her wake, is drawn from North American Indian prophecies that tell the story of when the earth is sick and Warriors from different places will come together to do something about it. The spirit of that 'doing' is really one of hope that inspires many both inside and outside of Greenpeace. It is still very much alive today and although we are a multinational organization and spread from Beijing and London to Bangalore and Moscow – which makes deciding on the direction the organization wants to sail in a bigger challenge – we still consider ourselves all to be part of a crew.

Our ships are in many ways the best expression of our multinationalism, our collective will and enthusiasm to work together across borders, across different cultural and political experiences, to stop the bad stuff and to start or support the good. Our ships link us together, they make the invisible visible, tell the stories that would otherwise stay out of sight and out of mind. And in many ways they remind us of what we are about.

It was the *Warrior* that most threatened the French government's nuclear-testing programme in the Pacific. When French government agents bombed her in the middle of the night in Auckland in 1985 – killing Fernando, our photographer – she became part of a nation's story, and helped cement New Zealand into being a nuclear-free country.

I have seen three Rainbow Warriors in my time. I never thought that I could feel the same way about the second and third as I did about the first, but I do. When I first walked on board the 'new', the latest *Rainbow Warrior*, I felt it again – that sense that we, all of us, are going to change the world.

Bunny McDiarmid, once a *Rainbow Warrior* crew member and now Executive Director of Greenpeace New Zealand.

NIGEL MARPLE / GREENPEACE

Prologue

AUGUST 2006. With my nose pressed against the window of the taxi, I could finally see her three masts emerging at the end of the long dock. My heart raced a little. I had already sailed on the two other Greenpeace International ships (the *Arctic Sunrise* and the *Esperanza*) but this was my first time on the *Rainbow Warrior*. For me, this legendary sailboat represented a great symbol of struggle and hope, which I had been following since childhood.

As the taxi left, I found myself alone in front of the ship. I walked towards her bow holding my breath, gazing at the rainbow, her own name and the white dove with olive branch. When I came to her pointy bow, a smile spread across my face and I finally remembered to breathe. Then I stepped away a little to take in the whole view of her – the silhouette and the masts reaching for the clouds. 'How beautiful you are!' escaped from my lips. Feeling very happy, I finally made my way to the entrance. As my feet stepped on her main deck, I knew for certain that this ship would be very important in my life. And so it has turned out.

During the following five years, my life revolved around the *Rainbow Warrior*. The people whom I lived with on board – both crew and guests – became my brothers and sisters of the sea. I have often been asked what was my best experience sailing with Greenpeace. The answer has always been the same: 'The wonderful people I have had the great privilege to meet.'

In August 2011, the ship was transferred to another organization and, under the name of *Rongdhonu* (rainbow in Bangla), began a new phase of her life as a hospital ship in Bangladesh. The day after the ceremony, which took place in Singapore, I said goodbye to 'my' *Rainbow Warrior*. However, in some ways, I have never completely left the ship because on land I then embarked on a paper journey in which I have explored the ship's whole life. My final destination, one might say, is the book you hold in your hands.

The ship had by 2011 been serving environmental and pacifist causes for 22 years. Her decks and bulkheads had been the silent witnesses of every conceivable situation, from states of high stress and danger to tremendous fun and total relaxation, from confrontation between crew members to the most extraordinary camaraderie, from the incredible sadness that death brings to great stories of love and friendship... Days of storms and high waves followed by days of swimming in totally calm oceans, and weeks of frenetic campaigns followed by others of mere maintenance and routine, getting rid of rust, painting, cleaning and so on. Actually, each trip was itself a great adventure!

This book rescues from oblivion just a small portion of all that has been lived aboard or around the second *Rainbow Warrior*. The rest of her stories will perhaps come to light another time in other books or will remain in the subjective memory of those who lived through them. My ultimate intention has been to pay tribute to the spirit of the *Rainbow Warrior*, to the people who have lived on board her and to the ship herself (on behalf of all those who have ever served Greenpeace). I have tried to show the positive influence the ship has had, forging links with organizations and local communities, and uniting thousands of people who are 'sailing' in the same direction – that of putting an end to the major environmental damage that our planet is suffering.

I once read that 'The ships that have known the taste of adventure fall in love with the seas of ink and they nicely sail on paper'.* I invite you to take part in this special journey on board a warrior who carries a rainbow on her shield.

* *Mundo del fin del mundo*, by Luis Sepúlveda

'The rainbow is a sign of the union of all peoples, like one big family. Go to the mountaintop, child of my flesh, and learn to be a Warrior of the Rainbow, for it is only by spreading love and joy to others that hate in this world can be changed to understanding and kindness, and war and destruction shall end!'

Eyes of the Fire's words to her great-grandchild
(from the book *Warriors of the Rainbow* by William Willoya and Vinson Brown)

1 Beginnings

This chapter is dedicated to the memory of Bob Hunter, Marie Bohlen and Fernando Pereira

Stories from the past
Birth of a myth
A book called *Warriors of the Rainbow*
The return of a Warrior

Stories from the past

THE 55-METER length schooner was a kind of floating museum. 'The objects that surround us are important. In the same way as they tell the story of the ship, they also tell the story of Greenpeace. We mustn't forget that...' How many times did I repeat these or similar words throughout my years as a deckhand on board the second *Rainbow Warrior*?

When I joined her for the first time, the ship had already been the Greenpeace flagship for 17 years, meaning that she had visited countless countries and navigated all the world's oceans and many of its seas. The ship was thus home to numerous gifts and special items, ranging from paintings and drawings to a wooden dolphin or particular portholes. So many people had come and gone on the ship over the years that some of the information relating to these objects had been lost, changed or even 'reinvented' while being passed from one person to the next. During my third trip on the *Rainbow Warrior* I started a project to be carried out in my free time. I ended up loving it: researching the origin of any object that represented a significant part of the ship's story. I began with the most urgent tasks – documenting the parts of the ship that we used to show the public on open days, including the three decks (main, bridge and fore decks), the wheelhouse and the hold. Then I continued with the relics in the living quarters.

During this process, which took several trips, I came across some truly marvellous stories. It would certainly have been a great shame if all these had fallen into oblivion.

What had started off as something of a hobby ended up becoming part of my job during the last journey of the second *Rainbow Warrior*, as I was put in charge of making an inventory of the 'historical' objects. In August 2011 this ship was given to an organization called Friendship, which was to convert her into a hospital ship serving the needy who live on the coasts of Bangladesh – and still sails the Bay of Bengal in that guise.

A few months later I also took on the task of moving the most important items onto the third *Rainbow Warrior*, including some (such as the bell of the wheelhouse) that had belonged to the legendary ship that began the saga. Without doubt, the third *Rainbow Warrior* needed to acquire the baggage inherited from its ancestors before beginning its own run and forging its own character. The chosen objects would be keys opening the door to the past – a past made up of dreams, defeats, legends, adventures, fights and victories. Thousands of stories unfolding in a miniature universe called *Rainbow Warrior*.

The *Rainbow Warrior*'s bulkheads and decks were the witnesses to countless secrets and tears, friendships and disappointments, fears and joys. Here, a group of children from South Korea looks at the photographs in the main alleyway

SIHNAE LEE

Birth of a myth

'I am on the most famous ship in the world!' a Norwegian volunteer proclaimed as he entered the *Rainbow Warrior*'s mess with a broad smile across his face. It was January 2009.

'Well, I think you're exaggerating a bit,' I replied.

'Really? Tell me another one more famous.'

I thought about it. Of course the *Titanic* was famous worldwide but it had been under the water since its doomed first voyage. And the *Queen Mary* was very well known, but mostly in the Anglo-Saxon world. 'You're right,' I had to admit. 'Wherever you go, you will find someone for whom the name *Rainbow Warrior* rings a bell. You couldn't say that about any other ship.'

So we were on board a sort of floating, living legend. However, she could not boast the title of 'legendary ship' purely on her own merit, but rather as something shared with her predecessor.

Over the seven years that the first *Rainbow Warrior* took a leading role in the environmental fight on the oceans, the ship had already climbed up several rungs in worldwide fame – thanks mainly to the television images that had shown her saving whales and seals, and obstructing the dumping of nuclear waste out at sea. In 1984, Greenpeace decided to send the ship to the South Pacific to participate in the campaign against the nuclear tests that France was carrying out on Moruroa atoll. Before this, she was to stop in the US port of Jacksonville, where the ship would be provided with two masts. In the middle of March 1985, a brand new *Rainbow Warrior*, converted into a sailing boat, unfolded her five sails and set off to the Marshall Islands to accomplish what would be her last-ever mission: evacuating the entire population of Rongelap, victims of the nuclear tests that the United States had carried out three decades earlier.

When the ship arrived in Auckland on 7 July, around 30 vessels came to greet her. The people in the New Zealand/Aotearoa office had spent months organizing a flotilla of boats that would escort the *Rainbow Warrior* to Moruroa and seeing her arrive was the realization of a dream. Once the ship was in harbor, the activity became almost

C DEES / GREENPEACE

The original Rainbow Warrior under full sail in January 1985 after being refitted in Jacksonville, Florida.

frenetic. On the evening of the third day, while a meeting with the skippers of the flotilla was taking place in the hold, some friends were in the ship's mess enjoying Steve Sawyer's birthday celebration. Steve was a campaigner from the US who was later to become Director of Greenpeace International. By 11.30pm the only people on board were a small group having their last drinks in the ship's mess and a few crew members who were in bed asleep.

It was 12 minutes to midnight when a tremendous explosion shook the *Rainbow Warrior* and plunged her into darkness. The engineer Davey Edwards cried 'It's the engine room!' and set off running only to see, to his astonishment, that water was pouring in through an enormous hole in the hull. At that moment, the captain, Pete Willcox, who had been shaken awake by the huge jolt, joined Davey and immediately shouted for everyone to be woken.

Confusion reigned. Most of those on board got hastily off the ship, which had started to keel over. While the doctor, Andy Biedermann, checked all the cabins and so rescued the cook Margaret Mills, chief mate Martini Gotje went off to his cabin in search of his partner, the second engineer Hanne Sorensen, to whom he had said goodnight a while before. Someone heard the ship's photographer

Fernando Pereira saying 'She's sinking! She's sinking!' Despite this, he decided to go to his cabin and rescue his cameras. Then came a second blast, this time right under the feet of those who were still on board. Pete gave the order that no captain wants to give and that no crew member ever wants to hear: 'Abandon ship! Everybody out of here!' Only two minutes had passed since the first bomb had exploded.

From the quayside, the survivors watched, astonished, as the *Rainbow Warrior* began to sink, releasing thousands of oxygen bubbles as she went down. Then Davey spoke, and his words made everybody's blood run cold: 'Fernando is down there.' Panic mixed with desperation took hold. Both Fernando and Hanne were missing. To everyone's relief, Hanne appeared shortly afterwards, having decided just before the explosion to go for a walk. Fernando, however, never made it out of his cabin, which the second explosion had turned into a death trap.

The crew members, who were totally in shock, were taken to the police station at the port. At first the authorities were convinced that the explosions had occurred due to the crew's negligence. The harbor chief summoned Steve and Pete to ask them harshly how and when they were going to

PIERRE GLEIZES / GREENPEACE

The damage inside the *Rainbow Warrior* done by the French secret-service bombs on 10 July 1985.

was immediately overwhelmed by the amount of support offered by the locals. A few words dreamed up by David Buller turned into a slogan that gave people the strength to overcome the situation they were facing: 'You cannot sink a Rainbow.' Once it had been confirmed that this had been an act of sabotage, the main suspicions fell upon France. Although the French embassy in Wellington flatly denied that its government was involved, just a few days later French secret-service agents Alain Mafart and Dominique Prieur (the only two members of the team who had not yet left the country) were arrested. The inquiries advanced as every New Zealander who had witnessed anything suspicious came forward to inform the police. With these arrests, what was known as *'L'Affaire Greenpeace'* began – and it was to cover many pages with ink for months, particularly in the two countries involved (see box).

In strategic terms, the French government had made the worst possible move. Far from achieving its purpose of destroying the organization by sinking its ship, the attack gave wings to Greenpeace worldwide and proved to be a landmark moment in the organization's history. The number of supporters suddenly increased (except in France, where the opposite happened and it took years to revive support and rebuild the national office) and the working dynamics of Greenpeace changed dramatically.

The French had also thought that killing some activists would intimidate the others (the bombs exploded without warning and were scheduled to go off at a time when crew members were certain to be sleeping). Certainly, the first *Rainbow Warrior* never reached Moruroa but a few of her crew members did, joining other vessels that same year and in the years to come. So it was that the deckhand Bunny McDiarmid embarked on the *MV Greenpeace* – an ocean-going tug newly acquired and refitted by Greenpeace, which was to have as its first mission taking the *Rainbow Warrior*'s place leading the peace flotilla to Moruroa. Three other crew members were on board another of the flotilla's boats, the *Vega*: captain Pete Willcox, deckhand Grace O'Sullivan and veteran Chris Robinson.

get their boat off the bottom of his harbor. Once there was a bit of daylight, however, police scuba divers confirmed that it was sabotage: the plates of the hull had been blown inwards by bombs placed on the outside.

New Zealand/Aotearoa woke up deeply shaken by the news that the first and only act of terrorism in the country's history had taken place, and that the target had been an eco-pacifist organization. The news crossed borders and was broadcast by the main television channels around the world so that a few hours later, millions of people were watching, with total incredulity, images of the half-sunk *Rainbow Warrior* in an Auckland dock.

After the bombing, the ship somehow no longer belonged just to Greenpeace but also to New Zealanders. The organization's local office

If the various feats performed by the ship

Murdered photographer Fernando Pereira

Fernando Pereira

In the mid-1970s, Fernando Pereira left his native country, Portugal, in order to avoid having to fight in the dictator Salazar's colonial war in Angola. He settled in the Netherlands, where he married and had two children. Fernando joined Greenpeace in 1983 because he wanted to help raise people's awareness of important environmental issues through his photographs. It was a tragic irony that someone who had fled from war and enrolled on a 'peace boat' should have been killed by a bombing. He had celebrated his 35th birthday on board the *Rainbow Warrior* shortly before arriving in Rongelap, just a month before he was murdered.

Margaret Mills, the *Rainbow Warrior*'s cook, wrote a poem for him, from which these lines come:
'He should be famed not for dying
but for living.
For how he used his life
and for caring.
He did not give his life,
they took it.'

L'Affaire Greenpeace

On 10 July 1985, the Rainbow Warrior is bombed.

In early August, two French weekly magazines accuse French agents of the sabotage. President François Mitterrand orders an investigation. The resulting report, issued at the end of the month, exonerates France of any responsibility.

On 17 September, *Le Monde* states it as likely that the operation was carried out under the orders of Charles Hernu, the Defense Minister, and Admiral Pierre Lacoste, Head of the Direction Générale de la Sécurité Extérieure (DGSE). Two days later, Hernu resigns and Lacoste is dismissed. Shortly thereafter, Prime Minister Laurent Fabius recognizes that DGSE agents sank the boat acting under orders.

On 4 November, the French agents Alain Mafart and Dominique Prieur plead guilty in Auckland's High Court and are sentenced to 10 years in prison.

In 1986 and 1987, France is forced to offer financial compensation to Fernando Pereira's family and also to Greenpeace (for the loss of the ship). New Zealand also receives money but in exchange agrees to transfer the two prisoners to the French military base on Hao atoll. Mafart and Prieur are finally released in May 1988, return to their military careers and are both promoted.

This picture was created by artist Stanley Palmer in 1985 after it became clear that the French government was responsible for the attack on the first *Rainbow Warrior*. It is based on the famous 1898 letter *J'accuse!* by French novelist Emile Zola.[1]

This silk-screen print of the second *Rainbow Warrior* by Joe Petro was commissioned by Sebia Hawkins, who was responsible for the Pacific Campaign. This edition was specially made for the crew and given to the ship in New York, in October 1989, during the ship's maiden journey.

aboard vessels that share the same special name, which derives from the book that helped mark the beginning of Greenpeace as a movement. It is a small book with a yellow cover containing dreams and prophecies of a time when humans of all races will join together and when love will end all wars and destruction – the rainbow being the symbol of this multicolored union of warriors.

A book called *Warriors of the Rainbow*

In the summer of 1969, Robert ('Bob') Hunter, a Canadian journalist and writer, was sitting on the front porch of his farmhouse when an unknown and rusty pickup came rattling up to park just outside his door. The driver got out and gave him a book with these words: 'This book will reveal a path that will affect your life.' The strange character turned around, got into his vehicle and left. Bob stared at the book he had in his hands. It was entitled *Warriors of the Rainbow* and its front cover showed a Native American man in the company of an eagle and a buffalo. The authors were William Willoya and Vinson Brown. Bob took a look at it and saw that it contained Native American prophecies but also references to the Bible, Buddha and Krishna, among others. He read no further and simply placed the little yellow-covered book on his bookshelf.

That same summer, the United States announced that a series of nuclear tests would be carried out at Amchitka, an Aleutian island that belongs to Alaska. The first of these tests generated strong protests in Canada that even led to the border between the two countries being blockaded. Despite this, the US government announced that a second test, to be called 'Cannikin', was to be held in the autumn of 1971. In the city

WARRIORS OF THE RAINBOW
Strange and Prophetic Dreams of the Indian Peoples

WITH FOUR PAGES OF COLOR

William Willoya and Vinson Brown
Naturegraph Publishers

throughout her life had already given her a mythic quality, those two bombs gave birth to the legend. Four years later, another ship refitted and renamed *Rainbow Warrior* took up the baton left by her predecessor, bringing the legend up to the present first with her continuing protests against nuclear testing in Moruroa (until victory was achieved) and then with all the other campaigns in which the ship was involved over its many years in the service of Greenpeace. Twenty-six years had passed since the terrorist attack when a third boat, this time built by the organization, replaced the second *Rainbow Warrior*.

Thus, the legend has continued sailing the seas

REX WYLER / GREENPEACE

The *Phyllis Cormack* was not only a pioneer in the fight against nuclear testing. In 1975, displaying the Kwakiutl totem on its sail, it was the first Greenpeace ship to confront whalers.

of Vancouver – located on the Canadian west coast, close to the border with the US – a small antinuclear and pacifist group composed of people from both countries made it their goal to send a boat to Amchitka. This way, the crew members would be able to protest against the test just by 'bearing witness', a tactic commonly used by Quakers[2] as a way of expressing their disagreement with unjust or objectionable events – several members of the group were Quakers, including Marie Bohlen, who had come up with this brilliant idea. The group called themselves the 'Don't Make a Wave Committee', referring to the high risk of an earthquake and a tsunami following a nuclear explosion.

The 'Don't Make a Wave Committee' meeting had just finished when Irving Stowe made his usual V sign and said, 'Peace'. The youngest member of the Committee, Bill Darnell, responded: 'Make it a green peace'. Then Jim Bohlen said: 'That sounds good. If we ever find a boat, that's what we'll call it – *Greenpeace*.'[3]

On 15 September 1971, an old halibut seiner cast off from Vancouver. Although it was called *Phyllis Cormack*, in honor of the owner and skipper's wife, it had been renamed for the trip as *Greenpeace*. The ship hoisted a triangular green sail in which the

word 'Greenpeace' was written between the symbol for peace (see Chapter 8) and that for ecology (a circle divided in half by a line, symbolizing the Earth and the Equator). Though no-one was aware of it, that first trip of the *Phyllis Cormack* marked the beginning of an adventure that was to last for decades, as this tiny peace movement grew into the international organization Greenpeace.

In addition to several members of the organizing committee, there were on board a few sympathetic journalists whose mission was to inform the public about the events that took place during the journey. The young Bob Hunter was one of those. The night before the ship's departure, Bob finished his packing and went in search of books to take with him on the voyage. As he pulled out one or two, *Warriors of the Rainbow* fell on to the floor and, rather than place the book back on the shelf, Bob put it in his bag.

Just three days after the *Phyllis Cormack* had sailed from Vancouver, the crew were invited ashore by the Kwakiutl people in Alert Bay to accept a 'blessing' and a gift of salmon for the trip. Once ashore, it was explained to the crew that the wishes of all the Native Americans of the west coast went with them. This brief visit greatly impressed many of the crew, especially the youngsters. As soon as the boat set sail, Bob pulled out the little yellow-covered book that the stranger had given to him

REX WYLER / GREENPEACE

The crew of the *Phyllis Cormack* on board ship. Clockwise from top left: Hunter, Moore, Cummings, Metcalf, Birmingham, Cormack, Darnell, Simmons, Bohlen, Thurston and Fineberg.

and passed it around. The following day, while making their way through beautiful channels, sounds and inlets, rainbows repeatedly appeared in the sky, increasing their feeling that they were living through a magical moment.

The journey to Amchitka was to turn into an odyssey. They did not know when the bomb would be detonated, they met very rough weather which knocked out most of the crew members for days, and disagreements between crew members started to arise. Finally, on 30 September, the *Phyllis Cormack* was arrested by a US Coastguard and charged with a customs offense. The ship was required to withdraw to clear customs on an island far from Amchitka. Two days later, after a long argument among crew members, it was

decided that, in view of all the difficulties that lay ahead, it was best to retreat. The Greenpeace ship was never physically to reach the island but, apart from having delayed the test, the trip proved to be a significant achievement in and of itself. The expectations raised by their courageous attempt had been spectacular, public protests and demonstrations expanded (including more border blockades), and there were even threats of strikes and boycotts aimed at the US.

On the way back to Vancouver, the boat stopped again in Alert Bay. Around a large fire and surrounded by large totem poles, a sacred brotherhood ceremony was held and the crew members (who were all men) were made brothers of the Kwakiutl people. The prophecy that opens *Warriors of the Rainbow* came into Bob Hunter's mind. The old grandma Eyes of the Fire tells her great-grandson that a day will come when the Native Americans will awake, gaining back their spirit, and will teach the whites to live in peace and harmony, turning hate into understanding, and bringing an end to the wars and destruction that ravage the planet. Those who pursued this path of brotherhood/sisterhood would become 'warriors of the rainbow', as the rainbow symbolized the union of all the people. Barely a decade earlier, the ceremonies and rituals of the native peoples were still banned by law in Canada. Now it seemed that the crew of the *Phyllis Cormack* were witnessing this prophecy beginning to materialize.

A crowd of supporters welcomed the *Phyllis Cormack* in Vancouver on 30 October. Although the opposition against the nuclear test had grown dramatically – not only in Canada but also in the US – the nuclear test was carried out on 6 November. However, shortly after, the US government announced that this would be the last bomb to be detonated at Amchitka.

In June 1976, the *Phyllis Cormack* and the *James Bay* were moored at a dock in Vancouver. Both

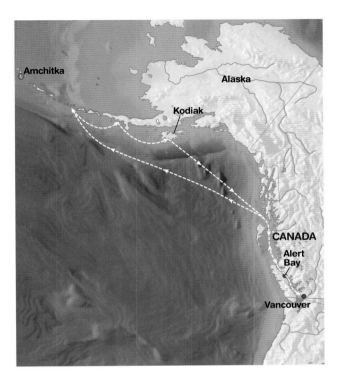

Greenpeace boats flew the United Nations flag, had a rainbow painted on each side of their hull and were about to set sail for a second campaign in defense of whales. People were gathered listening to a series of farewell speeches. The last of these was delivered by Fred Mosquito,

Robert Hunter, who had become the President of Greenpeace, addressing the crowd at the launch of the second Greenpeace whale campaign in 1976. Cree elder Fred Mosquito is standing with him.

REX WYLER / GREENPEACE

MARRINER FERRERO / GREENPEACE

The brand new *Rainbow Warrior* sailing on the Thames by Tower Bridge in London in 1978.

a Cree medicine man, who had unexpectedly appeared at the last minute. He told the audience about the prophecy of the warriors of the rainbow (shared by his people with others), which speaks of the union of the human family to protect the Earth. Mosquito said to the crew members: 'You are the Warriors of the Rainbow.' The prophecy had crossed the path of Greenpeace once more.

The next time the little book sneaked into the story of the organization, it happened on a different continent. In May 1977, the small group of people founding Greenpeace Limited in the UK had a very clear priority in mind: to find and buy a boat that would be 'fast enough to keep up with the whalers'.[4] Denise Bell and Susi Newborn, who were the first people to step onto the deck of the *Sir William Hardy*, sensed immediately that this was just the boat that they were looking for. There was

only £2,000 in the organization's bank account but they made an offer of £42,725. Thanks to small private donations and with the special help of World Wildlife Fund Netherlands, they were able to buy the ship.

When Bob Hunter – who had by then become the first President of Greenpeace – came to meet the newly acquired vessel, he gave Susi a copy of *Warriors of the Rainbow*, telling her that they had to have the book on board, as wonderful things had happened thanks to it. The book began to be passed around and, when the time to name the boat arrived, Susi proposed 'Rainbow Warrior' as a neat combination of the two key words. And when they had to decide what to paint on the hull of the boat, Susi went to the book again, opening it right on the page containing a drawing with the Warriors of the Rainbow rising after the Great Spirit, symbolized by a white dove. After that, there could be no doubt about which symbols should be displayed on a boat bearing that name.

On 2 May 1978, a boat passed under Tower Bridge in London displaying on its dark-green-colored hull the word 'Greenpeace', with a rainbow painted on both sides. The name *Rainbow Warrior* was inscribed on her bow along with a white dove carrying an olive branch, and on her stern the Kwakiutl totem (see Chapter 3) was painted. No-one could have imagined the future that awaited this boat.

If the *Sir William Hardy* already had a small place in British history as the first diesel/electric-powered ship built in the country, renamed as the *Rainbow Warrior* the ship would become part of world history. Chosen by the intuition of two women who knew nothing about boats, she was to become one of the most successful ships in the Greenpeace fleet.

The return of a Warrior

The horns of the several boats there began to sound in mourning for a ship that was starting to descend into the deep sea. Dozens of people had arrived at the place to give a final farewell to the first *Rainbow Warrior*. Going underwater bow first, then her central section and wheelhouse, the mythical ship finally raised her stern towards the clouds – like a whale that shows its tail – before disappearing beneath the dark waters. The downed warrior was to find its final rest at Matauri Bay – a beautiful place dotted with small islands in the northeast of the North Island of New Zealand/Aotearoa – following a traditional Maori burial ceremony. The Greenpeace Board had decided, among the different options under consideration, to let the boat become a reef so that she would continue to protect the life of the oceans and a local *iwi* (tribe) had then offered this place to the organization.

BRIAN LATHAM / GREENPEACE

The first *Rainbow Warrior* is laid to rest in the ocean, off the Cavalli Islands in Matauri Bay, New Zealand/Aotearoa on 12 December 1987.

ROGER GRACE / GREENPEACE

The first *Rainbow Warrior* has turned into a reef full of marine life.

Before coming to Matauri Bay, a long and painful process had taken place on board the *Rainbow Warrior*. Anything that might be either toxic or reused had to be taken off the ship. The two masts and the propeller were removed as well. As the boat became ever more 'naked', her appearance instilled more and more sadness into those who witnessed it. After being put up for auction, countless pieces and objects ended up scattered

In this photo, taken in December 1988, some of the major changes to the ship are already visible. The bow was extended to enhance its capacity as a sailing boat. In addition, the accommodation at the stern was rebuilt, while the wheelhouse became smaller and was also moved a few meters backwards.

JAN A. MADSEN

across the country that had witnessed the end of the ship's seafaring life, so becoming part of other boats and homes.

The bombing of the *Rainbow Warrior* marked a turning-point in the history of Greenpeace as an organization. On the one hand, people who were part of the relatively small group that made up the active Greenpeace in 1985, especially those who had had direct contact with the *Rainbow Warrior*, were desolate at what had happened to their ship and their friend. On the other hand, events began to escalate and it was necessary every day to handle situations that had never arisen before. The name *Rainbow Warrior* became famous worldwide and the number of supporters dramatically increased in a few months (I include myself here). Suddenly, the organization was also able to count on much more money, which was to make it possible to launch new campaigns. From the bombing of the ship onwards, Greenpeace would never be the same.

One of the things that had to be settled was, of course, what to do with the *Rainbow Warrior* itself. This was a complicated issue, as the ship was not 'just a boat'. She also had huge symbolic value. So discussions as to what should happen began. Fearing that a ship that had been badly injured by two bombs could never again be fully trusted as a seaworthy vessel, and also fearing that to recover

UNKNOWN

Deckhands armed with needle guns and iron brushes to get rid of the rust. In the photo, from left to right, Naomi Petersen, Phillip Pupuka, Mariana Aspinall and Sue Ware.

her would be too expensive, it was finally decided that a replacement should be found for her and that the first ship should become a reef. This decision hurt many of those who felt that the boat had such a distinctive character and particular beauty that it could not be equalled by any other. There were also many who regarded it as impossible to replace the ship as a symbol.

Time would prove that it was possible to replace the ship – but not only that. In some strange way the spirit of the first boat was transferred to the next one along with the name. By the same token, this spirit must be now settling in the third *Rainbow Warrior*.

So in the midst of this maelstrom that was raging around Greenpeace after the bombing in 1985, it was also necessary to find a boat that could take on such a special role, which was never going to be an easy task. The search was placed in the hands of a broker who eventually found in England what the organization had requested: a North Sea trawler (trawlers being seaworthy vessels with hulls that are easy to steer) that was long enough to be equipped with masts. The boat awaiting its destiny had been built in 1957 (two years after its predecessor) in Selby, England, and had been named *Ross Kashmir*. It was part of the fishing fleet of a large company. Although it was originally powered by steam and was 44 meters long, later

on it was converted to diesel and had its hull lengthened to 55.2 meters (in order to enlarge its hold). In the end, the fishing boat was converted into an oil rig stand-by vessel and renamed *Grampian Fame*. When Greenpeace acquired it in late 1987 – a purchase partly financed with the compensation received from the French government – the ship was essentially a hull with an empty interior.

On 21 December 1987, the *Grampian Fame* arrived in Hamburg in order to undergo its metamorphosis. The rebuilding of the ship took almost a year and a half, in which Greenpeace acted as project manager and had to face a few unexpected complications – the main ones being the rig manufacturer and the piping company going bankrupt.

In November 1988, the deckhand Sue Ware joined the team working on the ship, which included Pete Willcox and Bene Hoffman (both from the original *Rainbow Warrior*) as well as several engineers and technicians. Sue, a New Zealander, had come directly from the Southern Hemisphere summer to land in the bitterly cold winter of northern Germany. When she arrived, the future *Rainbow Warrior* was out of water, in dry dock. When the mate, Naomi Petersen, turned up shortly after Sue, the first thought that crossed her mind looking at it from the outside was that there

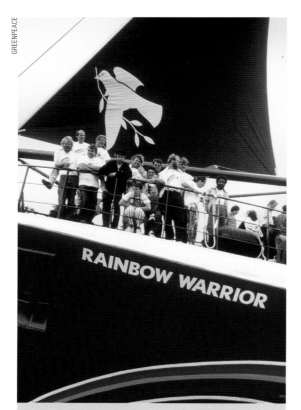

GREENPEACE

Many of those involved in the conversion stand at the bow at the launch of the second *Rainbow Warrior* in Hamburg – and most of them were also to be crew members on the maiden journey. From right to left: Phillip Pupuka, Mariana Aspinall, Karsten Petersen, Jan Madsen, Peter Willcox, Liliana Trumper, Maike, Naomi Petersen, Nick, Sue Ware, unknown, John Brouwer and Bene Hoffman.

was still a long way to go before the ship was able to go anywhere.

The amount of rust that the old trawler had accumulated seemed to be endless. The team of deckhands spent weeks of that winter doing practically nothing apart from needle-gunning and sanding what were to become the cabins and stores located below the main deck. The arrival of spring increased the pressure as the date set for the ship's launch approached.

Enthusiastic volunteers from the Greenpeace office in Hamburg started to show up, willing to help and to contribute to the hard labor. Their appearance represented a great relief for most of the crew members, in both physical and psychological terms. Working against the clock for so long had given rise to some tensions on board and this 'fresh air' coming from outside somehow relieved the enormous stress. Everything had seemed to be progressing slowly but then suddenly things started to happen very fast: the masts were in place; the navigation equipment was installed in the bridge; the varied equipment was set up in the radio room; the furniture and accessories for the cabins arrived... At last the crew were able to move on board the *Rainbow Warrior*, and the ship became a home.

To make her as environmentally friendly as possible, the new *Rainbow Warrior* was provided with, amongst other things, three masts (approximately 40 meters high), two new diesel engines (much more efficient), a heating and hot-water system that used waste heat from the engines, and a sewage treatment system. In addition, satellite equipment for communication and navigation was installed, as was a crane for launching the inflatable boats and loading or unloading heavy material.

All the cabins, the radio room, the library, the toilets and showers, the galley and the ship's mess were built on the main deck and the space of the former fish hold (reconverted to a storage area and theater for videos and slide shows) was reduced to allow space for more cabins and storerooms. The five portholes in the living quarters on the main deck were relics: made of bronze, they had belonged to the original *Rainbow Warrior*.

The launch of the second *Rainbow Warrior* finally took place on 10 July 1989, on the fourth anniversary of the bombing, and the ship began a promotional tour of a number of European countries. The maiden journey was also used to test all the systems and equipment. Her innovative Indosail rig was a unique model designed by the

ANON

On her maiden journey, **Rainbow Warrior II** was approaching Belgium when she met a search-and-rescue helicopter doing maneuvering exercises. The crew agreed to allow someone to be winched down from the helicopter to the ship's deck as part of the pilot's training – not an easy task avoiding the masts and shrouds! – but also because the person in command wanted to buy a Greenpeace T-shirt. The exercise was carried out and the helicopter crew members were given T-shirts for free.

German Peter Schenzle, who had been inspired by looking at small radio-controlled model sailboats. The two central gaff sails were rectangular, and the foresail (the jib) was mounted on a mobile boom system that pivoted on the foredeck. The old fishing boat responded splendidly to the novel rigging that turned her into a sailing ship, though there were some teething problems that required improvements after this experimental trip.

In each port the ship visited, the *Rainbow Warrior* was received with great excitement and enthusiasm, and there were always volunteers willing to help with whatever was needed, including guiding the numerous visitors around the ship.

As the *Rainbow Warrior* was sailing in the Bay of Biscay towards La Rochelle, in France, something unexpected happened. On a night of calm sea and perfect visibility – a rare event in itself in these waters – the ship collided with a Spanish fishing boat. Neither altered course to avoid it: on board the Greenpeace ship, the second mate who was on watch thought that, because they were under sail, they had the right of way, while there was nobody in the bridge of the fishing boat. As a result of the collision, the anchor of the *Rainbow Warrior* was pushed up inside the hosepipe, and a hole was ripped open in the side of the Spanish boat so that its galley became visible. But both ships then continued on their course as if nothing had happened. Everybody was very concerned on board. They expected the story to cause a great stir in the news, this being the first time a Greenpeace ship had visited a French port since the bombing of the first *Rainbow Warrior*. However, instead of making an insurance claim or any other complaint, the Spanish fishing crew never said a word. Later on, the answer to this silence was revealed: they had been fishing illegally.

The ship then crossed the Atlantic Ocean to the United States. In New York, Pete Willcox disembarked and Joel Stewart debuted as Greenpeace captain. The first campaign of the second *Rainbow Warrior* took place in the Tasman Sea, working in support of the international ban on driftnets. However, it was with her first mission to Moruroa that the new *Rainbow Warrior* actually began writing her own story (see Chapter 2).

It is true that the sterns of the first and second *Rainbow Warrior* were very similar and they were also alike in being trawlers built in the same country at around the same time. Beyond this, any physical comparison between them seemed to be impossible. The personality of the first one, a classic fishing boat in which the interiors were preserved (wooden inner bulkheads and decks, for instance), could not possibly be matched. The new ship had been rebuilt according to practical criteria so as to accommodate as many people as possible; this made it a bit like a hotel, though certainly one with a hippie touch. However, it was just a matter of time: over the years, the second *Rainbow Warrior* was to build her own unique character.

The arrival of a newly built third incarnation of the ship, in September 2011, means that the *Rainbow Warrior* legend will continue years into the future. But if the spirit of the original ship was revived after the terrible attack, the same could not, of course, be said for the life of Fernando Pereira. I cannot help but end this opening chapter with a poem dedicated to Fernando by someone called Pip. This is inscribed on a plaque that was displayed in the main alleyway of the second *Rainbow Warrior* and is now on the third ship.

Poem in memory of Fernando Pereira, which has been displayed in the main alleyway of both *Rainbow Warrior II* and *Rainbow Warrior III*.

Monsieur,
  You thought you sank The Rainbow
  but you cannot sink a dream.
  May it always be your nightmare
  on your conscience never free
  for the Warrior lives for ever
  you cannot change what's been.
  How can you chain a spirit
  rising endless from the sea?
  You'll never sink The Rainbow
  or what it all stands for.
  It's a symbol of our future
  that will live for evermore.
(In memory of Fernando Pereira)

1 In the letter Zola blew the lid off rampant French anti-Semitism; a Jewish army captain called Dreyfus had been unjustly accused of spying and of causing France's defeat in the 1870 war with Germany. 'Frog' has been used as a pejorative term for the French since the 18th century by the British (who in return have been called 'rosbifs' in France). 2 Quakers are members of a family of religious movements known as the Religious Society of Friends.

The first Quakers lived in mid-17th-century England. They defined themselves as 'religious witnesses for peace' and nowadays continue to campaign for pacifism, social equality, integrity and simplicity. 3 As Robert Hunter tells it in his book *The Greenpeace Chronicle,* reissued in 2011 with the title *Warriors of the Rainbow* to commemorate Greenpeace's 40th anniversary. 4 The quotation comes from Susi Newborn's autobiography *A Bonfire in my Mouth.*

> 'Only two things are infinite, the universe and human stupidity,
> and I'm not sure about the former.'
>
> Albert Einstein

2 The nuclear madness

This chapter is dedicated to the memory of all victims of both civil and military nuclear madness

Introduction
The day of the two suns Bikini, the lost paradise (1946) • Rongelap, the dawn of twilight (1954) •
Operation Exodus (1985, 2010)
Moruroa Peace boats versus nuclear bombs • The last trip to Moruroa (1995)

CLOSE YOUR EYES for a moment. Now think of a small island in the Pacific... What image comes immediately to mind? I bet it will be a kind of paradise, with palm trees fringing white sand beaches and transparent turquoise waters over coral reefs. You cannot really avoid this heavenly image because this is what we have always seen in films, magazines and travel brochures. And it is hard instead to conceive of a Pacific island as hell. Yet this is what some of the islands were turned into thanks to nuclear tests conducted in the region by two far-distant countries – the US and France.

During the five decades of the 'Cold War', the major powers took part in a mad arms race in which nuclear weapons occupied a privileged place. For the people of the Pacific islands, this nightmare began at the end of the Second World War.

In 1947, the United States – immediately after agreeing with the UN Security Council that it would govern the Trust Territory of the Pacific Islands[1] – announced the establishment therein of the 'Pacific Atomic Grounds'. It specified the islands in which the nuclear tests would be performed, though these had already started the previous year with the detonation of two bombs on the Bikini atoll.[2] Over the next 16 years, there were a vast number of tests.

The inhabitants of Bikini (and also Enewetak Atoll) were moved to other islands before testing began, though they were promised they would be able to return. They lost their home forever. Some years later, their neighbors on the atoll of Rongelap were not 'rescued' from the radioactive fallout. The Rongelapese lost not only their homes, but also their health and that of their descendants. God was not the one throwing them out of paradise, but rather other humans who were supposedly learned and civilized – 'developed', as we say in Western culture.

Four years after the US ended its tests, the Pacific nuclear nightmare moved to French

FERNANDO PEREIRA / GREENPEACE

Blue lagoon. Our images of paradise are dominated by palm-fringed vistas like this one, in Rongelap, which is now lost to the people born there.

Polynesia, on the other side of the Equator. In 1966, France decided to perform a series of atmospheric

---

Trusteeship: 'The administration or government of a territory by a foreign country under the supervision of the Trusteeship Council of the United Nations'.[3]

The US played the role of wolf rather than shepherd when it came to the people of the Marshall Islands. Between 1946 and 1962, 105 atmospheric nuclear tests were conducted in the Marshall Islands, including of high-yield hydrogen bombs.

In 1990, the UN ended the Trusteeship and the Marshall Islands officially gained independence. However, the islanders are totally dependent on the US for medical and financial assistance in dealing with the consequences of nuclear testing.

---

nuclear tests at Moruroa and its sister atoll of Fangataufa after the independence of Algeria meant that it could no longer conduct them in the Sahara desert.

At the time, the world was fixated on the terror aroused by the Cold War and the constant threat of nuclear confrontation. There was also great concern,

---

As a result of the US nuclear tests, the incidence of cancer, leukemia, thyroid dysfunction and birth defects have all increased significantly in the Marshall Islands.

'Ivy Mike', the first hydrogen bomb ever detonated, completely destroyed Elugelap Island, in Enewetak Atoll. In Bikini Atoll, three islands have been deleted from the map and the detonation of 'Bravo' caused a crater that is easily visible on a satellite image.

---

as there is still today, at the idea that any country could make nuclear weapons. After years of hard work, a large number of countries (including acknowledged 'nuclear weapon states' the US, the Soviet Union and the UK) signed the Nuclear Non-proliferation Treaty (NPT) in 1968. Surprisingly, France headed in the opposite direction.

The Nuclear Non-proliferation Treaty

Born in 1968, the Treaty aimed to prevent the spread of nuclear weapons and weapons technology, promoting cooperation for the peaceful uses of nuclear energy – with a long-term goal of eliminating nuclear weapons entirely. The signatory states that did not already have nuclear weapons agreed never to acquire them.

A total of 190 countries have joined the Treaty (including the five nuclear-weapon states: the United States, Russia, the United Kingdom, France and China). India, Pakistan and Israel (all assumed to have nuclear capability) have not signed it and North Korea has withdrawn from it.

France faced international opposition to its tests from the beginning and did not sign the NPT until 1996. In 1995, France resumed testing after a three-year moratorium, and opposition grew within its borders. It conducted a total of 41 atmospheric tests and 138 underground tests in French Polynesia in flagrant disregard of the health implications for inhabitants of the region and the concerns of nearby states such as Papua New Guinea, the Philippines, Japan, New Zealand/Aotearoa and Australia.

According to the Australian Nuclear Science and Technology Organisation, there will be a serious danger of radioactive leakage over the next 1,000 years because the volcanic base of the Moruroa and Fangataufa atolls has been weakened by successive tests.

The question is not just how such terrible things could have happened but also how the US and France could behave as they have with total impunity. If I had been asked as a child where I would escape to in the event of a nuclear war, I would have seen the idea of seeking refuge in one of these small paradisal Pacific islands, far from major continents, as definitely the best bet. Now that I know what has happened there, I have naturally changed my mind and might see another planet as the only option.

The first bomb detonated by the US on Bikini atoll in 1946 was codenamed Able. It marked the beginning of nuclear testing in the Marshall Islands and was similar to the one dropped on Nagasaki in Japan the previous year.

ANON

Total number of nuclear tests conducted[4]		
United States	1032	1945-1992
Soviet Union	715	1949-1990
France	210	1960-1996
China	45	1964-1996
Great Britain	45	1952-1991
India	3	1974 and 1998
Pakistan	2	1998
North Korea	2	2006 and 2013

FERNANDO PEREIRA / GREENPEACE

A cemetery on the now-abandoned island of Rongelap. The inhabitants of Bikini, Rongelap and other Marshall Islands were expelled from Eden – and not by God.

The day of the two suns

Bikini, the lost paradise (1946)

Everything started with a big lie. The US governor of the Marshall Islands told the inhabitants of Bikini Atoll that they had to leave their home for a while 'for the good of all mankind and to end all world wars', not giving any further explanation about the experiment to be carried out. Feeling overwhelmed before such a responsibility towards the rest of humankind, Juda, the atoll leader, answered: 'Everything is in the hands of God.' The following day, a navy ship took the 167 inhabitants of Bikini to the uninhabited Rongerik Atoll, 128 nautical miles away. The US government promised the islanders that they would come back home a couple of months after the tests had taken place. The islanders believed this. They had lost their paradise forever without even being aware of it.

The first two tests, in 1946, were part of the so-called Operation Crossroads, which investigated the effect of nuclear weapons on naval ships. To

Bikini Atoll used to have 23 big islands (with Bikini itself, the largest one) and several small islands surrounding a central lagoon of almost 600 square meters.

make room for the 95 ships of all kinds, coral reefs were dynamited. Some of these ships carried thousands of animals, including pigs, guinea pigs, goats, rats, mice and insects, because information was wanted on the effects of radiation on living beings. With the exception of the 10 per cent that died immediately, these animals were to suffer dreadful agony.

The same year the first atomic tests were conducted in Bikini Atoll, a French designer launched a daring new swimsuit design. Louis Réard foresaw that his two-piece swimsuit would have an 'explosive' effect in a society not used to seeing so much of a woman's body and so he named it 'bikini'.

Of all the nuclear tests carried out in Bikini Atoll, the greatest atrocity was Bravo, the first hydrogen bomb ever detonated by the US and the biggest ever tested – a bomb 1,000 times more powerful than the one that incinerated Hiroshima. On 1 March 1954, Bravo was exploded, creating an enormous 'mushroom' cloud, so that daybreak brought two suns to the inhabitants of Rongelap Atoll, 150 kilometers southeast of Bikini. The US military knew that the westerly winds forecast

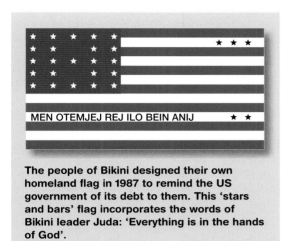

The people of Bikini designed their own homeland flag in 1987 to remind the US government of its debt to them. This 'stars and bars' flag incorporates the words of Bikini leader Juda: 'Everything is in the hands of God'.

Infamous heritage

Between 1946 and 1958, 67 nuclear weapons were tested in Bikini. The combined power of all of them was equivalent to 7,000 times the force of the Hiroshima bomb.

In 1963, the US signed the Partial Test Ban Treaty, which banned nuclear tests in the atmosphere, in outer space and under water, and so no further tests were conducted on the Marshall Islands.

In 1974, three families came back to the atoll to try and recover what had been lost. They had to be evacuated four years later due to the high levels of radiation in their bodies.

In 2010, UNESCO named Bikini Atoll a World Heritage site because 'through its history, the atoll symbolizes the dawn of the nuclear age, despite its paradoxical image of peace and of earthly paradise'. Yet what this statement glosses over is that, before the testing, Bikini was not just an image: it genuinely was an earthly paradise.

would take the nuclear fallout towards inhabited islands. In this case, the living beings on which to study the effects of direct radiation would be humans.

Rongelap, the dawn of twilight (1954)

With the first light of dawn, a sun appeared in the west. This sun, that would change their lives forever, was beautiful as it came dressed in red, green and yellow. Shortly after, the real sun began to emerge in the east. Then a kind of smoke filled the sky and a strong but warm wind swept across Rongelap, as in a typhoon. After the wind, the sound of a great explosion was heard. A few hours later, a fine ash started to rain down, covering

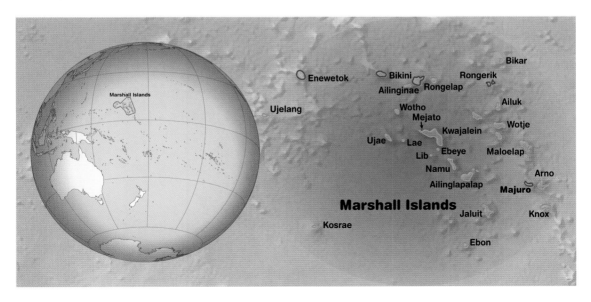

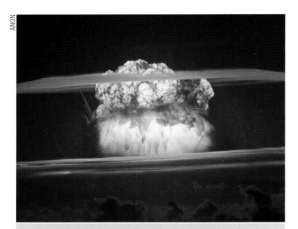

ANON

Castle Bravo was the codename given to the bomb exploded on Bikini atoll in March 1954. It was the most powerful nuclear device ever detonated by the US.

In 1956, the Atomic Energy Commission of the United States regarded the Marshall Islands as 'by far the most contaminated place in the world'.

everything and adhering to adults' and children's bare skin. They thought that the four planes seen flying overhead had dropped the powder. The 'white rain' continued into the night, forming a layer of powder more than two centimeters thick and dissolving into water supplies.

The following day, many of the inhabitants of Rongelap were already suffering severe diarrhea, nausea and vomiting and had sustained severe burns to their skin, eyes and mouth. The wells had turned yellow and John Anjain, the mayor, advised his people to drink only coconut water. A seaplane arrived in the afternoon. Two people came out of it, took some readings of water and soil using some strange machines and, 20 minutes later, left without a word.

On the morning of the third day, a navy destroyer arrived and told them that they should immediately leave their island or their lives would be in danger. The Rongelap natives left with only the clothes on their backs and spent some months in an atoll farther south. There, they began to receive medical 'help' from doctors who confessed they had no idea how to treat their burns and the pains they were suffering from, since this was a 'new disease'. Finally, they were moved to an island in Majuro Atoll, even further from their home. The US 'assistance care' continued there.

Three years later, in 1957, the people of Rongelap were returned to their island after being told that the little radioactivity remaining would not cause them any harm. They were completely unaware of the existence of a report by scientists at Brookhaven National Laboratory, which openly said: 'The habitation of these people on the island will afford us most valuable ecological radiation data on human beings.' The former paradise had become a big secret laboratory in which its own inhabitants were the guinea pigs, and in whose language words such as 'radiation', 'radionuclides', 'cancer' and 'poison' were unknown.

Women began to have a high number of miscarriages and gave birth to creatures that did not resemble human beings: some of them, according to John Anjain, 'looked like monkeys, some like octopuses, and some like bunches of grapes'. The children born with no bones started to be called 'jellyfish babies'.

John Anjain lost his son, just a young boy, in 1972. He decided to go to Hiroshima and Nagasaki to request help from independent doctors. Once in the Marshall Islands, these doctors could not visit the atoll, since they were immediately repatriated to Japan by the US government.

In 1974, one-third of the people who were rained on by the nuclear fallout had developed some type of cancerous tumor and, two years later, 20 out of 29 children who were under 10 years of age when Bravo was detonated had developed thyroid cancer.

In 1985, 95 per cent of the population born between 1948 and 1954 had contracted thyroid cancer and a high proportion of children suffered from genetic birth defects.[5]

Operation Exodus (1985, 2010)

Nail by nail, piece by piece, the Rongelapese people patiently dismantled their homes and put all their belongings together. They took all of their possessions, everything but the thing they wanted most: their island. On 17 May 1985, the *Rainbow Warrior* arrived at Rongelap Atoll. A few months before, Greenpeace had received John Anjain's call for assistance. The mayor had approached his own government and the US but they had always answered that the atoll was safe. Faced with his people continuing to become sick, he thought their only hope of survival was to abandon the place that had been their home for more than 2,000 years.

People from Rongelap had been constantly shuttling between hospitals all over the US. They were subjected to many tests and treatments but nobody wanted to tell them what diseases they were suffering from. In conditions of total secrecy, doctors and laboratories were conducting all kinds of experiments on them, including thyroid and genetic experiments, as well as bone-marrow transplants.

On the morning the ship arrived at Majuro, the Marshall Islands' capital, captain Pete Willcox saw the green flash – an optical phenomenon that occurs shortly after sunset or before sunrise, when, for no more than a second or two, a green spot or ray is visible above the sun – and took it to be a good omen.

When the *Rainbow Warrior* reached Rongelap it was welcomed by the whole community. A group of women sang songs while others held up signs indicating their concern for their children's future. For these people, forced to leave their land, this was not just a material but a spiritual tragedy – according to tradition in the Marshall Islands, land and spirit are fundamentally connected. Even so, people opted to move to another island in the hope that their children could have some sort of future. Their new home, the uninhabited Mejato island, was not the 'paradise' they had left behind and food was not so abundant but at least the community could stick together.

The *Rainbow Warrior* moved over 300 people, their belongings and more than 100 tons of construction material. The evacuation lasted for 10 days and three trips were made between Rongelap and Mejato, which were separated by a distance of 120 nautical miles. The crew of the *Rainbow Warrior* found the experience of sharing the sorrow of these victims of the nuclear madness deeply touching. This was the last-ever mission of the first *Rainbow Warrior* and the photos of Rongelap

Women officially welcome the *Rainbow Warrior* to Rongelap – even though it means the departure from their homeland is imminent.

FERNANDO PEREIRA / GREENPEACE

were the last ones crew member Fernando Pereira would ever take. In Auckland, both the ship and the photographer were to meet their tragic fate, as described in Chapter 1.

Five years after the evacuation of Rongelap, in June 1990, the second *Rainbow Warrior* – then practically brand new – paid the islanders a visit in their new home of Mejato. Amongst other things, the ship transported a group of Rongelapese people to another island, where they had to go through a medical examination. Mejato was a much poorer island in every way, and the community was finding it difficult to survive. Every three months, if you were lucky, a ship arrived to deliver supplies, including canned food from the US Department of Agriculture. 'They were wonderful people but it was devastating to see the state they were in,' said the ship's cook, Belén Momeñe.

In 1996, the US Congress allocated $45 million for Rongelap to be cleaned up and rehabilitated so that people could live there again. About 200 acres of land – under a square kilometer – have been decontaminated as six inches (15 centimeters) of soil have been replaced by clean coral sand. The worst of the radioactive elements, Cesium-137,[6] has been neutralized so that vegetables planted there can now be grown and eaten without risk. That, at least, is what the Lawrence Livermore National Laboratory, in charge of carrying out the project, says.[7] Houses, a small power generator and a desalination plant have been built. Rongelap now has a new town hall, library, church and schools. It even has a paved runway and a port for large ships, hotels and facilities to cater for those hypothetical tourists who might come here for the diving. All of this was put in place so that the exiled islanders could finally return to their ancestral land.

The Rongelapese had been dreaming of going back home since the day they had to leave but what would life be like there now? Their living space would be restricted to just the rehabilitated

---

Martin Steffens was the electrician aboard the *Rainbow Warrior* on the ship's 'Fisheries Tour' around several Pacific islands in 2004. The ship was in Majuro, the capital of the Marshall Islands, in July when Rongelap's mayor, John Anjain, died. Martin read about his death in a newspaper that reprinted an interview with the mayor from 1981, and he was so moved that he keeps the copy of the newspaper to this day. John Anjain's life spoke volumes about the tragedy of Rongelap's people and their treatment by the US government. Anjain said that his saddest experience of all was watching his son dying of leukemia in Washington.

Packing up the old life and waiting for the new. Inhabitants of the radioactive atoll of Rongelap preparing to be transported by the *Rainbow Warrior* to their new home on Mejato island.

FERNANDO PEREIRA / GREENPEACE

200 acres of the atoll. Given that this space was far too small for them to grow sufficient food for their needs, they would continue to depend on ships supplying canned food. Apart from this, there were other important questions. Where would the inhabitants resettle as the population grew? And what about the long-life radioactive elements other than Cesium-137– more than a dozen of them – that had been dispersed on the island?

Greenpeace returned regularly over the years to see how the Rongelapese were doing. Bunny McDiarmid, a deckhand in 1985, has revisited people many times and ties remain strong. She last retured in 2010, 25 years after Operation Exodus. 'Once you've seen the effects of nuclear testing with your own eyes,' she says, 'you can't pretend it doesn't exist – you've got to do something about it.'

Today, the Rongelapese are scattered over three different islands: Mejato, Ebeye and Majuro. Many live in what is effectively a concrete urban slum. In particular, the Marshallese have long fought the US over conditions on Ebeye, home to the Ronald Reagan Ballistic Missile Defense Test Site.[8] Workers on the Base, who were once spread over many islands, live now in Ebeye, which has become one of the world's most densely populated places.

During Bunny's most recent visit a group of Rongelapese women sang for her one afternoon, while practising for a church recital. She could not stop the tears streaming down her cheeks. Set to beautiful melodies, the women sang of the impact of nuclear testing on them and of all the illnesses that have afflicted them. Yet although the story was sad, the singing was not, which reflects the general attitude of the Marshallese people – they are resilient survivors who do not spend their time raging against those who have done them this wrong. In the Rongelapese native language, the word 'enemy' does not exist.

A few months later, the Rongelapese community received an ultimatum from the US government: from 1 October 2011 on, only those moving back to Rongelap Atoll would continue receiving financial compensation. The deadline has long passed but the Rongelapese have still not returned. Jelton Anjain, the son of the former mayor, explained why in 2012 (see box).

Seeing the funny side. Children on Rongelap before the mass evacuation.

Why we cannot go home

'We were given until October 2011 to move back but our people are still uneasy about going back as we know the islands are still not clean. The US calls this relocation a necessity due to its budgetary difficulties. But if the scientists are saying that these islands are safe to go back to, why are they urging our people to "consume 30 per cent local diet from the land and 70 per cent imported food"? This statement alone clearly indicates that the islands are still contaminated.

'Now they say it's a "legal and economic necessity". Our lives are worth more than their money, our lives are worth more than their legal system. We have a right to live a full and healthy life as human beings... The Alap association of Rongelap, which I represent, does not support this resettlement at the moment, for we all know the islands are still not livable. We do not want to risk going back and have our people get sick again just like we did when the US told our people back in 1957 that the islands were safe to return to after three years of exile. We surely don't want to take that risk again.'

Jelton Anjain

Desolation. The first *Rainbow Warrior* after its bombing by French secret-service agents in 1985.

Moruroa

Peace boats versus nuclear bombs

I was 18 years old and I remember vividly watching the news on television: the *Rainbow Warrior*, the Greenpeace flagship, had been attacked. The TV images showed the ship tilted and half-submerged by a wharf in the New Zealand/Aotearoa city of Auckland. The rainbow and peace dove at the bow of the boat were still forlornly visible. The death sentence on the ship – and on crew member Fernando Pereira – had been passed because Greenpeace had announced that the ship would go to Moruroa to prevent the French nuclear tests planned for 1985.

France had already been detonating bombs at Moruroa and Fangataufa for five years when, in 1971, those who started the Greenpeace movement went to Amchitka aboard the *Phyllis Cormack* to stop US nuclear tests.

The following year, Ben Metcalfe (one of the *Phyllis Cormack*'s crew) sailed part of the way to Moruroa with Dave McTaggart (later the co-founder of Greenpeace International) and three other volunteers on board the *Vega*. This was McTaggart's small sailing boat – just 12 meters long – which had set out from Auckland with the intention of stopping the scheduled French tests. What they managed to achieve was a delay in the testing of almost one month. The odyssey ended when a French minesweeper rammed the *Vega*, causing it serious damage. The ship was repaired just in time to return a year later.

In 1973, France announced that a hydrogen bomb would be detonated. World opinion had begun to oppose nuclear tests and boycotts of French products started. On this occasion, a peaceful international protest flotilla was organized of about 25 ships from many different Pacific Rim countries. This was arguably the first time in history that warships took part in a protest for peace of this kind (one from Australia and one from New Zealand/Aotearoa). For a variety of different reasons, the *Vega* was alone when it crossed the 12 nautical-mile line and entered Moruroa territorial waters. French commandos

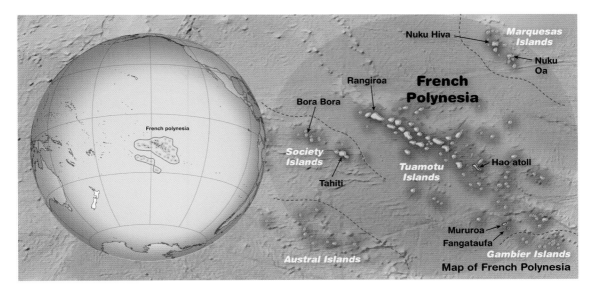

Nuku Hiva

Marquesas Islands

Nuku Oa

Rangiroa

French Polynesia

Bora Bora

French polynesia

Society Islands

Tuamotu Islands

Hao atoll

Tahiti

Mururoa

Fangataufa

Austral Islands

Gambier Islands

Map of French Polynesia

stormed the boat and beat up the two men on board. Dave McTaggart was knocked unconscious and almost lost his right eye. Crewmember Ann-Marie Horne fooled the military and hid the photos she had taken of the assault. They were published in at least 20 countries a few days later, causing an international scandal. The version of the arrest given by France was totally different from what had happened. The French government was then forced to make public, at the UN General Assembly in November 1973, its intention not to conduct any further atmospheric nuclear tests. From that moment on, tests would be underground.

The *Vega* returned to Moruroa in 1981 and 1982. On the second trip, the boat managed to stay inside the island's territorial waters for seven days before being boarded. The French kept the sailing boat under arrest for a whole year before finally sending it to Auckland on a cargo ship.

David and Goliath. The small yacht *Vega* played a big part in opposing French nuclear testing in the Pacific. It is seen here in November 2013, confronting the oil-drilling ship *Noble Bob Douglas* in the Tasman Sea, off Australia.

OIL FREE SEAS

NICK TAPP / GREENPEACE

Three years later, fresh from her trip to Rongelap, the *Rainbow Warrior* was in Auckland preparing to go to Moruroa for the first time. It was close to midnight on 10 July when the first bomb lodged under the ship exploded. The second bomb killed Fernando Pereira. In a few days it was known that the attack had been carried out by the French secret service. The response of Greenpeace to this was not at all what the French government had expected. It sent to Moruroa not only the *MV Greenpeace*, but also the *Vega*, with Pete Willcox, the captain of the *Rainbow Warrior*, on board as skipper. The determination of the activists and crew members to resist the French nuclear tests had only been reinforced by the bombing and the murder of their comrade.

* * *

On 10 July 1989, the fourth anniversary of the bombing, the second *Rainbow Warrior* made its maiden voyage and, after an exhausting tour around Europe and the US, headed for the Pacific. First, she visited the former inhabitants of Rongelap and, on 26 November 1990, arrived in Papeete, the capital of Tahiti. The people of French Polynesia had been protesting for many years against the nuclear tests being conducted on their territory. This first trip to Moruroa was not about trying to stop any bomb detonation but to check if radioactivity was leaking from the broken coral reef. Three years before, the world-renowned marine biologist Jacques Cousteau had spent several days in the atoll and, despite the restrictions, had been able to take images of a large crack in the coral crown. He had also collected plankton samples that turned out to contain traces of Cesium-134 – though the French government continued to deny that there was any leakage.

Sailing outside the 12-nautical-mile limit, the *Rainbow Warrior* began taking samples of plankton. Three warships escorted the ship day and night, circling around. Finally, Greenpeace announced that the organization had found traces of radioactivity in plankton. This announcement completely changed French behavior: the next time the *Rainbow Warrior* sent her rigid inflatable boat, the *Avon*, to take samples, its five occupants (both crew members and scientists) were arrested for five hours. The following day, when they attempted to take more samples, they were not only arrested but also deported. The *Rainbow Warrior* was forced to abandon her mission.

Display of unanimity. The *Rainbow Warrior* crew wearing 'Stop Nuclear Testing' T-shirts near Moruroa in January 1990.

LORETTE DORREBOOM / GREENPEACE

DANIEL BELTRÁ / GREENPEACE

The French military's nuclear-testing site in Moruroa, pictured in 1995.

Russia proposed a global moratorium on all types of nuclear tests in 1990. The UK signed up to this in 1991 and the US in 1992. However, France and China continued testing until 1996, when the Comprehensive Nuclear-Test Ban Treaty was finally signed.

Although the 'Cold War' was over and the rest of the planet was moving in a different direction (three out of the five nuclear powers had already agreed a moratorium on testing), France continued with its nuclear policy. In 1992, President François Mitterrand – who had personally approved the sinking of the first *Rainbow Warrior* – announced that his country would perform a series of underground tests at Moruroa Atoll. Greenpeace's reaction was immediate. The organization announced that its flagship would go there. The ship would take scientists on board again, but this time, the aim was to enter the area where the test was to be

performed and establish a 'Peace Base in the Pacific', so as to prevent the tests with their presence.

Several French warships 'welcomed' the ship. As soon as the *Rainbow Warrior* stepped over the 12-nautical-mile exclusion line, a thrilling chase began, which lasted for about half an hour. The ship was only half a mile from the atoll lagoon when she was boarded by French commandos. The scientists and all those on board except those necessary to sail the ship were immediately deported. Two days later, the ship was free to go.

During the arrest, a big international uproar had taken place. A few images, this time video ones, would unmask France again. The *Rainbow Warrior* was carrying a small device called a 'squisher' that allowed the radio operator to send live images of the assault to the Greenpeace office in London. Although nowadays, when we are accustomed to video footage from mobile phones, this is quite

RANDI BAIRD / GREENPEACE

Warship ahoy. The French frigate *Lafayette* shadowing the *Rainbow Warrior* at the 12-mile exclusion zone around Moruroa in March 1992.

STEVE MORGAN / GREENPEACE

Pacific outrage
The French President, Jacques Chirac, did not anticipate the reaction to his nuclear-testing plan.
For the first time, protests began to spread within France itself, while at the same time anti-colonial
sentiment was growing in French Polynesia, including calls for independence. Citizens were outraged
as bombs were detonated within their territory without consultation and concern was growing about
environmental damage and the possible radioactive contamination of the islands. In the Cook Islands
and Tahiti the biggest anti-French demonstrations ever took place. The photo shows demonstrators in
Rarotonga, where a quarter of the 8,000 population marched in protest in June 1995.

commonplace, in those days this was a totally revolutionary technology. In a few hours, the main news bulletins around the world were showing the French commandos boarding, breaking the windows of the bridge, shouting and launching teargas. A tremendous wave of indignation went around the planet. As an immediate result, France received such a storm of protest – both domestically and internationally – that President Mitterrand had to cancel the testing program and announce that his country would join the international moratorium proposed by Russia.

It seemed that the battle for a nuclear-free Pacific Ocean had been won. However, this optimism did not last long.

The last trip to Moruroa (September 1995)

Shortly after becoming French President in 1995, Jacques Chirac announced the end of the moratorium on nuclear testing (which had barely lasted for three years). Between September 1995 and May 1996, eight tests on the Moruroa Atoll were to be performed. It was enough to leave thousands of people across the globe breathless. The ghost of nuclear war had returned to haunt them once again. The crew of the *Rainbow Warrior* knew that if the ship sailed to Moruroa the French commandos would seize them again but that did not matter: they felt they had to make every effort and try, by all possible means, to impede the detonation of the first bomb, which had been announced for 1 September 1995.

On 9 July, almost exactly 10 years after the sinking of the first *Rainbow Warrior*, her successor ship crossed the invisible line and entered the territorial waters around the atoll. The French response was immediate. French commandos boarded the ship and entered the living quarters below using a blowtorch and spreading teargas. Stephanie Mills, head of Greenpeace's anti-nuclear campaign, made a dramatic live radio broadcast during the terrifying assault. In between coughs, the last thing heard from her was her scream when the commandos entered the radio room. She and the others with her got out through a porthole to escape the teargas, hauling themselves up onto the bridge deck, only to be caught there by the commandos.

Despite the aggressive French response in July, Greenpeace was determined to frustrate the testing program and, when the *Rainbow Warrior* returned the following month, she was packed with 37 people on board. In addition to the crew and Greenpeace volunteers, there were also journalists and some special guests, celebrities both from France (such as José Bové, later to become a member of the European Parliament for the Greens, and the Catholic bishop Jacques Gaillot) and from Polynesia (such as Oscar Temaru, who subsequently became President of French Polynesia). The ship sailed from Papeete, Tahiti, on 24 August. The next day at dawn, those on deck who were looking for the sun's arrival were gifted with a fleeting glimpse of the green flash. On the third day of sailing, about 20 nautical miles from the Moruroa atoll, the *Rainbow Warrior* stopped to meet two other boats: the *Vega* and the *Bifrost*, which had been in the area since July. The *MV Greenpeace*, coming from Europe, was to join them a few hours later. It was a curious meeting of boats in the middle of the Pacific, as there were also four French warships – circling endlessly around the small eco-pacifist fleet – together with a submarine that had been accompanying the *Rainbow Warrior* for days.

At dawn on 29 August, the boats belonging to the international peace flotilla began to appear on the horizon. They had left Auckland on 6 August, 50 years to the day after the US had dropped a nuclear bomb on the city of Hiroshima. The flotilla consisted of around 30 boats from countries as diverse as New Zealand/Aotearoa, Chile, Australia, Germany and the US. They all stayed on the outer edge of that invisible line that marked the 12-nautical-mile limit.

That summer of 1995, as well as being the 10th anniversary of the sinking of the *Rainbow Warrior*, was the 50th anniversary of the dropping of the atomic bombs on Hiroshima and Nagasaki by US aircraft. The two bombs instantly killed some 200,000 Japanese citizens, while more than 200,000 died afterwards as a result of the lethal overdose of radiation.

Wrapped in darkness on a night of strong winds and rough seas, the *Rainbow Warrior* crew began launching the inflatables into the water at 2am on 1 September, the date designated by the French for the detonation of the first bomb. At the same time, someone with a very special mission was being lifted up the foremast. At full speed, the inflatables – crewed by 13 people – drove into the 12-mile zone with their bows facing the entrance to the lagoon. Three more had left the *MV Greenpeace* heading in the same direction and all were escorted from the air by *Tweety*, the Greenpeace helicopter.

At around 4.45am, the *Rainbow Warrior* crossed the line at full throttle in pursuit of the small boats, two of which had just entered the lagoon of the atoll. Half an hour later, the first French commandos arrived in a big inflatable and, after hanging a ladder on starboard side, started to board the ship. These men were the 'élite' of the French Special Forces. Most of them were physically huge and all were dressed in black from their helmeted heads to their boots. However, despite their intimidating appearance, the first invaders' entry to the vessel could hardly be described as 'elegant' – their ladder slipped away so that the third man fell on top of his two companions, and the three of

DANIEL BELTRÁ / GREENPEACE

Invading army. French commandos on board the *Rainbow Warrior*, having made a hole in one of the engine-room ventilation hatches, gain access to the interior.

them ended up forming a small mess of arms and legs on deck.

Everything happening on deck was being filmed and Tim Gorter, the radio operator, was sending live images of the assault to the 'outside' world from the radio room. Also from there, Stephanie Mills was on the phone describing to Reuters what the cameras were showing and what she could hear. A group of commandos approached the bridge deck. Using spray paint, they covered the windows of the wheelhouse so that the person steering could not see. One of the commandos broke a window to launch a teargas canister inside. Derek Nicholls put his anti-gas mask on and continued at the helm of the ship – all the windows had been reinforced with steel bars on the inside to stop the invaders accessing the wheelhouse through them.

Nevertheless, the commandos found a way through – they made a hole in one of the engine-room ventilation hatches, located behind the wheelhouse, and crawled through that. While some of the agents were boarding the ship, others were dedicating themselves to crushing and cutting all the wires up to the antennae. One after another, the ship was losing all her means of contact with the rest of the world. The last message issued was

the desperate pan-pan or state of urgency signal launched by Tim.[9] Shortly after that, commandos made a hole in the door of the radio room and entered, removing the three people there by carrying them like sacks of potatoes: one agent picking up the ankles and the other the wrists. The commandos that had accessed the wheelhouse pushed Derek aside. He was the chief mate but they thought he was the captain. When they tried to change course and stop the engine, they found out that the ship did not obey. They had to go down to the engine room again and manually stop the engine. The *Rainbow Warrior* was about eight nautical miles short of Moruroa when it eventually stopped going forward and began to drift.

As they were arrested, each of the ship's occupants were carried to the bow, which then became a small prison. At six in the morning, it was known that three of the inflatables had managed to enter the lagoon and that two divers were immersed in it. More or less at the same time, the news was given that the entire crew was in custody, except for the most important person of all: the captain. Where the hell was Jon Castle?

Hours were passing and it was obvious that the French were not able to make up their minds. They

DANIEL BELTRA / GREENPEACE

The *Rainbow Warrior* under arrest inside Moruroa's 12-nautical-mile exclusion zone in January 1995.

tried to convince several crew members (who also wore a beard, like Jon) to sign a paper saying that they were the captain, something that they all flatly denied. After noon, they finally decided to tug the ship, but after an hour the rope pulling the *Rainbow Warrior* broke with a loud crack. It was then replaced by a steel cable, much more appropriate for towing in high seas. At the beginning, an agent followed any crew member who went inside for food or to the toilet but, as time passed, things became more relaxed. At midnight, the commandos took all the journalists and guests to the atoll. The reduced crew left on board could not

MIKE FINCKEN / GREENPEACE

This is the device that, when connected to the bridge controls by ship electrician Manuel Pinto, enabled captain Jon Castle to steer the ship from the crow's nest.

believe what they were seeing when they woke up the next morning to find that the *Rainbow Warrior* and the *MV Greenpeace* (which had also entered the forbidden boundary and had been assaulted from a helicopter shortly after the flagship) were being towed in circles right beside Moruroa.

It was not until nearly noon that the commandos, alerted by a radio news broadcast, began to pay attention to the foremast, looking up at the crow's nest, and realized that the captain, Jon Castle, was up there. The last section of steps up to the crow's nest had 'disappeared' and, not knowing how to force Jon to come down, the commandos hit upon the idea of using the ship's fire hoses. Fortunately for the captain, instead of high-pressure water spouting from the hoses, the water came out without much force – a crew member had opened the valve to divert water into the anchor's chains. When Jon saw that the soldiers had discovered him and that they intended to use the powerful hoses of one of the French ships, he knew it made no sense to continue. He shouted from up high that he wanted to go down. However, he said he would only accept being 'rescued' by his own crew, who finally brought him down sitting in the bosun's chair. In total, the captain had spent 33 hours hiding on the small platform and he left there with his whole body numb. Just before the assault on the wheelhouse, Derek had disconnected the

This photo of the *Rainbow Warrior* and the *MV Greenpeace* going to Moruroa together on the second voyage in 1995 was displayed in the ship's mess. Thanks to it and also to the holes on the inside part of the wheelhouse windows (to position the steel bars that made it more impregnable), the story of this epic journey was told again and again to the visitors and guests of the *Rainbow Warrior*.

At present, it is displayed in one of the alleyways of the third *Rainbow Warrior.*

instruments there, and for more than half an hour after that, Jon had been steering the ship and dodging the military boats, thanks to a device with a few small joysticks.

Using the same halyards, a commando came up to see what else was in the crow's nest. The whole crew burst into laughter when they heard him shout from the heights: *'Mon capitaine, les contrôles sont ici!'* ('Captain, the controls are here!'). The French finally understood how the ship had been steering herself, as if by magic, until they had managed to stop the engines manually.

Once the captain had been captured, the two Greenpeace ships were towed to Hao Atoll, where they remained until March 1996. The activists on the inflatables were arrested and deported. The French government finally relaxed, believing that they were now free to detonate the bomb. They were wrong once again...

A few hours after the Greenpeace ships left the waters of Moruroa, in the early hours of 3 September, a small inflatable with two occupants and towing two kayaks, left the yacht *La Ribaud*, located about 15 nautical miles outside the exclusion zone. The British activists Al Baker and Matt Whiting – dressed as French Legionnaires – left their boat outside the atoll then dragged the kayaks to the lagoon, paddled for a couple of hours,

and then hid themselves in the bushes. A few hours later, they separated. While Matt went deep into the inhabited part of the atoll and stuck dozens of stickers saying 'Non!', Al began to set off distress flares sporadically, as a distraction, constantly moving his position. Shortly before four in the morning, Matt was arrested in a very violent way (a gun was placed against his forehead, he was beaten and told that he was to be killed). Al decided to hand himself in at 7am. After being interrogated, they were placed in different cells. Three hours later, the activists felt as if the floor dropped and then came up and then dropped again and they heard a strong explosion that seemed to come from afar. The French had made the terrible test after evacuating their own citizens to a 'safe' place but leaving the two activists in the danger zone. They were deported to the UK two days later.

At the end of January, Chirac announced that the two last scheduled tests would not be performed. Even so, the *Rainbow Warrior* and the *MV Greenpeace* were detained for over a month more. It took almost six months before the crews could finally access their ships. It was then they noticed that, in addition to all the damage caused in the assault, many objects had disappeared and the computers and radio equipment had been subtly sabotaged.

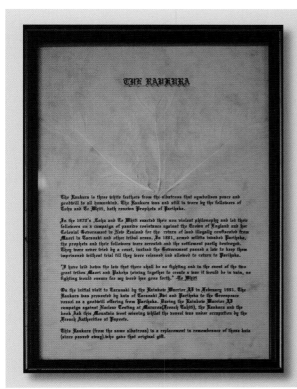

The Raukura is three white feathers from the albatross that symbolizes peace and goodwill to all humankind. The Raukura was and still is worn by the followers of Tohu and Te Whiti, both renown Prophets of Parihaka.

In the 1870's Tohu and Te Whiti erected their non violent philosophy and led their followers on a campaign of passive resistance against the Crown of England and her Colonial Government in New Zealand for the return of land illegally confiscated from Maori in Taranaki and other tribal areas. In 1881, armed militia invaded Parihaka, the prophets and their followers were arrested and the settlement partly destroyed. They were never tried by a court, instead the Government passed a law to keep them imprisoned without trial till they were released and allowed to return to Parihaka.

"I have laid down the law that there shall be no fighting and in the event of the two great tribes Maori and Pakeha joining together to create a war it would be in vain, no fighting would ensure for my word has gone forth." Te Whiti

On the initial visit to Taranaki by the Rainbow Warrior II in February 1991, the Raukura was presented by kuia of Taranaki Iwi and Parihaka to the Greenpeace vessel as a goodwill offering from Parihaka. During the Rainbow Warrior II campaign against Nuclear Testing at Moruroa(French Tahiti), the Raukura and the book Ask this Mountain went missing whilst the vessel was under occupation by the French Authorities at Papeete.

This Raukura (from the same albatross) is a replacement in remembrance of those kuia (since passed away).iwi gave that original gift.

Raukura

Raukura are the three white feathers of the albatross of Parihaka, New Zealand/Aotearoa. They symbolize peace and good will to all humankind. They were worn (and still are) by the followers of Tohu and Te Whiti, the Maori leaders who, in the 1870s, embraced the philosophy of nonviolence, and led a campaign of passive resistance against the illegal occupation of their land by the British. Parihaka was the center of this movement and became the largest Maori city of its time. It is located at the foot of Taranaki, a huge extinct volcano that dominates the southwest coast of North Island.

In February 1991, the elders of the *iwis* (tribes) of Taranaki and Parihaka, gave the Raukura and the book that tells of this epic nonviolent fight, *Ask that Mountain*, as an offering of good will to the *Rainbow Warrior*. However, both of these disappeared (along with many other things) when the ship spent months in French custody in Papeete (Tahiti) after her second trip to Moruroa in 1995.

A new Raukura was delivered to the ship to replace the first one and was lodged in the ship's mess until it was transferred to the third *Rainbow Warrior*.

Victory

In 1971, Greenpeace began its life as an eco-pacifist movement with the *Phyllis Cormack*'s trip to Amchitka, Alaska, to try to stop US nuclear tests.

In its struggle against the madness of the nuclear era, Greenpeace lost a person and a ship when the French government bombed the *Rainbow Warrior* in 1985. The victory against nuclear testing finally came in 1996, with the signing of the treaty that established a total ban. It brought an end to 25 years of active campaigning, though Greenpeace continues to work towards the end of the nuclear industry and the destruction of all nuclear weapons.

The stupidity of the US and France lasted only a few years, but its radioactive legacy will remain in the Pacific forever. There are currently about 20,000 nuclear bombs in the world – enough to end life on the planet 40 times over.

1 The Trust Territory of the Pacific Islands consisted of around 2,000 islands scattered along some 7,800,000 square kilometers (3,000,000 square miles). 2 An atoll is a small ring-shaped coral reef that includes a coral rim encircling a lagoon partially or completely. 3 Collins English Dictionary. 4 According to UN data. However, other sources provide different figures for some countries – and reported recent tests are not included in the figures. 5 According to the Brookhaven National Laboratory. 6 Cesium-137 is one of the isotopes that has caused major damage to health after the Chernobyl disaster – it remains in the environment and in the food chain for 300 years. Cesium-137 impregnates the ground and plants absorb it through their roots. It is soluble in water and highly toxic in tiny amounts. 7 Lawrence Livermore National Laboratory belongs to the Department of Energy (the agency that controls the cleaning effectiveness) and was in charge of making the 'Dose Assessment and Radioecology Program'. See nin.tl/1fpI5Jr. 8 Eleven of the 100 islands comprising the Kwajalein Atoll are leased by the US from the Marshall Islands government. Radar, optics, telemetry and communications equipment on eight islands provide instrumentation for ballistic missile and missile interceptor testing, and space operations support. 9 Three calls of pan-pan is used to signify that there is a 'state of urgency' on board a boat or aircraft but that, for the time being at least, there is no immediate danger to anyone's life or to the vessel itself.

> 'From space, the planet is blue.
> From space, the planet is the territory
> Not of humans, but of the whale.'
> Heathcote Williams

3 Between the harpoon and the whale

Humans and whales
Whales and the *Rainbow Warrior* Stories from Norway • A very tough campaign (1999) • Ten years on (2009)
Between the harpoon and the whale (*Arctic Sunrise*, Antarctica, 2005)

Humans and whales

Around 50 million years ago, some creatures who had been living on land decided to embark on a great adventure that would affect their entire future evolution: the conquest of the oceans. To change their terrestrial environment to a marine one was a huge challenge but they took it in their stride, slowly adapting themselves to their new home, generation after generation, gradually making profound changes to their bodies. Through this evolution, unparalleled on the planet, cetaceans became the guardians of the oceans, contributing enormously to the expansion of life under water. And years passed by, thousands of years, millions of years...

On the African continent, around six million years ago, groups of hunter monkeys abandoned the trees and, in order to survive in their new environment, began to stand up straight. Since Homo Sapiens became the only human species on the planet – which occurred some 25,000 years ago – we have not experienced even one major physiological change: the extraordinary evolution of humans has been merely cultural.

Iconic: the flukes of two humpback whales off the Canadian coast.

51

Maori people arrived in Aotearoa (New Zealand) in large canoes after travelling across thousands of kilometers of the Pacific Ocean. A legend says that the people of the east coast of the North Island are descendants of a man who came on the back of a whale that had rescued him after his canoe had capsized. In Maori mythology, the whale is a guardian spirit, who looks after the people from the sea.

Dave the Dolphin
Given as a gift by a group of German volunteers, this wooden dolphin lived at the bow of the *Rainbow Warrior* and eventually became her most iconic object. It seems that the name comes from the biblical story of David and Goliath, the Dolphin representing Greenpeace fighting the economic interests that produce huge environmental damage (Goliath).

In recent years, people touring the boat would be told the 'true' story of Dave, who had insisted on helping and being part of the crew of the ship so much that the sea god Neptune transformed him into a wooden dolphin to be placed on the bow with the important mission of indicating to the *Rainbow Warrior* where she had to go.

Dave the Dolphin is now leading the voyages of the third *Rainbow Warrior* from her bow.

An Inuit story tells how the Great Spirit created the whale as its final and finest creation. Then he realized that people would need it to survive in such a harsh and cold environment. Consequently, the whales would come every summer to be sacrificed by humans who would show them their respect by taking only as many as they needed. It was so hurtful for the Great Spirit that, to avoid watching it, he put a thick mist between the sea and the sky.

According to the mythology of ancient Greece, when Dionysus, the god of wine, discovered that pirates planned to sell him as a slave, he scared them so much that they jumped overboard. Dionysus took pity on them and decided to turn them into dolphins. This is why they save lives and accompany castaways: the former pirates want to make amends. In this culture, the cradle of European civilization, dolphins were seen as messengers of the gods and to kill them was punishable by death.

Humans have always maintained a special

What are whales?
• Whales are not 'big fish' but rather mammals that spend their entire lives in the water – the only ones to do so, along with the Sirenia.[1]
• They descend from terrestrial animals – the Archaeocetos – that had four limbs and cows, for example, have the same ancestors.[2] Evidence of whales' evolutionary past is visible in the finger shapes in their pectoral fins.
• Nowadays there are around 80 species of cetaceans surviving, presenting so many varieties that their classification is very complicated. Usually when we talk about whales we are referring to the largest cetaceans (in contrast to the smaller 'dolphins' and 'porpoises'). However, the most accepted division is between Mysticeti (the baleen whales) and Odontoceti (the tooth whales).[3] Anyone considering baleen whales to be the 'authentic' ones will soon find that some other tooth species are also known as 'whales', such as the sperm, the beluga (or 'white whale') and the beaked whale, not to mention a couple of Delphinidae: the pilot and killer whales.

Coming up for air: a sperm whale resting on the surface off the coast of Samoa, in the Pacific. There is a school of thought that sees cetaceans as 'non-human persons' because of their high level of intelligence and self-awareness. In February 2014, India banned dolphin shows on exactly those grounds.

relationship with cetaceans, fundamentally based on the admiration and respect that these very developed and intelligent beings instilled. For thousands of years, whales were only sacrificed for the sake of the survival of a community and the most common method was simply making use of those animals that were beached on the coastline.

It was like this until in one part of the world, western Europe, the relationship between humans and whales changed and what had formerly been subsistence turned into business. And when business turned into big business, human greed almost destroyed the whales completely.

Commercial whaling was initiated by the Basque people[4] in around the eighth century. But it was not until the mid-18th century that the hunt became such a merciless war that even females with calves were killed. It is sad that history does not even recognize the invaluable contribution

of whales to what is considered to have been a great leap for humanity: the industrial revolution. Without whales, industrialization would not have been possible, as the list of products obtained from them is almost endless, starting with fuel and oil to run the machines, and including oil and wax for lighting, food, clothing and accessories, furniture, detergents, creams, insecticides, fertilizers, vitamins, and insulin.

In 1946, when it was obvious that the hunting was turning into extermination, the 14 most powerful whaling countries created the International Whaling Commission (IWC) in order to 'provide for the proper conservation of whale stocks and thus make possible the orderly development of the whaling industry'.[5] Although the aim was to protect the economic interests of its members, for the first time it was decided to protect certain species (Grey, Greenland and Right

The big slaughter

Since the explosive harpoon began being used, almost one million sperm whales, half a million rorquals, a quarter of a million humpback whales and hundreds of thousands from other species have been killed. Just one example of whaling madness: between 1830 and 1845, the whaling industry in New Zealand/Aotearoa was born, expanded and disappeared after killing all the whales in the area.

whales, considered 'commercially extinct'). For the rest of the great whales, the relentless slaughter continued.

It wasn't until the 1970s that a strong world movement against whaling was born, given the imminent risk of losing the largest beings on Earth forever. Greenpeace was an essential part of the expansion of this movement. Finally in 1982, the IWC agreed on a global moratorium on commercial whaling that came into force in 1986. This moratorium constitutes one of the greatest conservationist achievements of the last 30 years.

We cannot, however, claim final victory just yet: around 20,000 cetaceans have been hunted since the moratorium took effect. Humans have also generated new threats that decimate their populations, such as collisions with ships, intensive fishing of other species, by-catching in nets, ingestion of plastics and toxic products, destruction of marine ecosystems as well as climate change. In addition, certain modern forms of sonar[6], especially those used by the military, have caused massive numbers of cetacean deaths all over the world.

Sometimes, in a conversation about 'whales', someone wields the argument that, beyond being 'cute', there is no strong reason not to kill them. Why should a whale have more right than a cow not to be eaten? Leaving aside the ethical question of the suffering and cruelty involved in the way they are hunted, the answer is simple: we have so much to learn from cetaceans that to use them as expendable goods seems, at the very least, stupid. It would be as if extraterrestrials came to Earth and hunted humans to make steaks, sausages, lamps, creams and clothes.

Whales do not need telephone, internet or satellites to talk to each other, they simply sing. Nor do they need a compass or GPS to navigate or to know where they are, and their own biological sonar allows them to know in detail the size, shape, distance and movement of everything that surrounds them.

The songs of the great whales travel thousands of kilometers through underwater acoustic channels created by differences of salinity and temperature in the various water layers.

They eat only what they need to survive and in precise relation to the amount of food available, without undermining the resources on which they feed. They spend more than three times longer having fun than searching for food. No case was ever documented of a cetacean suffering from a serious pathological illness or cancerous tumor until well into the second half of the 20th century, coinciding with the onset of dangerous toxics.

Finally, the number of cases in which cetaceans, especially dolphins, have saved lives is very high: in shipwrecks, in shark attacks, in preventing ships from grounding.

International agreements on protection of whales

• **The global moratorium on commercial whaling agreed by the IWC, in force since 1986.**
• **Article 65 of the Law of the Sea states that 'States shall co-operate with a view to the conservation of marine mammals and in the case of cetaceans shall in particular work through the appropriate international organizations for their conservation, management and study.'[7]**
• **All large whale species are recorded in the Convention on International Trade in Endangered Species, Appendix 1. Because they are considered endangered species, it is absolutely prohibited to trade in them.**

Wanton destruction. A dying whale, harpooned by the *Yushin Maru* ship of the Japanese whaling fleet in the Southern Ocean in 2005.

JEAN PAUL FERRERO / GREENPEACE

Bodies on the line. Greenpeace activists in an inflatable try to obstruct the Icelandic whaling ship *Hvalur 9* in 1978. The first *Rainbow Warrior* is just visible in the background.

Whales and the *Rainbow Warrior*

In 1975, members of Greenpeace decided to take on a new cause: to stop the killing and save the whales from extinction. To access the places where whaling fleets were operating, a ship would be used and, as a new tactic, the whales' defenders would stand directly between them and the whalers on board small inflatable boats. The first images of activists putting their lives at risk to prevent the deadly harpoon attacks travelled the world. There is no doubt that the impact of all these images greatly contributed to mobilizing public opinion against whaling.

In 1978 the first mission of the newly bought and refitted *Rainbow Warrior* was to stop Icelandic whalers who were killing fin whales, a species whose stocks were severely depleted. In the years that followed, anti-whaling campaigns in Iceland, Spain and Siberia alternated with other campaigns until 1984, when the ship was equipped with sailing rigging. At that point the *Rainbow Warrior* headed to the South Pacific, where she was to meet her tragic fate in Auckland (see Chapter 1).

When the second *Rainbow Warrior* began to sail the seas, the international ban on commercial whaling was already in effect. However, this in no way meant that the moratorium was being respected. The ship did not work in defense of whales until 1999 in Norway.

In 2003, Iceland unilaterally set a whale quota, thereby bypassing the international moratorium. That same year, the *Rainbow Warrior* visited Iceland in support of the country's emerging and successful whale-watching industry. During the days spent in Reykjavik, the ship and its crew were the objects of a curious peaceful protest: demanding respect for their cultural values, a group of teenagers staged a whalemeat barbecue in front of them. The young people were invited to visit the *Rainbow Warrior* so that a dialogue could be opened up and, on the last day, some of them asked to embark.

In mid-March 2005, the *Rainbow Warrior* arrived in South Korea for a month-long tour working alongside the Korean Federation for the Environment Movement (KFEM). The highlight of the visit was a protest that lasted several days and managed to paralyze the building of a whale and dolphin meat processing plant in Ulsan. In South Korea, it is permitted to sell the meat of dolphins and whales found dead in fishing nets. The high prices reached for this meat have led to figures of 'accidental' catches skyrocketing and it has become known as 'the lottery of the sea'. Using the argument that whaling is necessary on scientific grounds to find out if whales are destroying fish stocks, the country puts more pressure on the IWC meetings each year. As one KFEM activist put it: 'Complaining that whales are depleting the fisheries is like complaining that woodpeckers are causing deforestation.'

The second *Rainbow Warrior* could never confront the Japanese whalers operating in the Southern Ocean because her hull was too thin to allow her to navigate through the ice in these latitudes. It was the end of 2005 when, aboard the *Arctic Sunrise*, I travelled to the Antarctic Whale Sanctuary[8] and became a direct activist in defense of whales. Later in this chapter I will recount an episode from that trip that illustrates how tough such campaigns can be.

Stories from Norway

Legend has it that the minke whale owes its name to a Norwegian whaler called Meincke who, in the 19th century, killed one of these, mistaking it for a blue whale. After that, other whalers began sarcastically to call these small whales 'Meincke's whales'.

It was precisely their 'small' size – about 10 meters long – that prevented them from being

---

Greenpeace and whales

• In total, 10 Greenpeace vessels have been used so far in specific campaigns in defense of whales, the *Phyllis Cormack* being the first one in 1975. Before the global moratorium on hunting took effect in 1986, Greenpeace ships confronted the fleets of the Soviet Union, Iceland and Spain. Since then it has tried to prevent hunting in Norway, Iceland and South Korea. In the Whale Sanctuary in Antarctica, different ships have stood up to the Japanese fleet on nine occasions.

• In addition, over the years, several of the organization's ships have worked to protect dolphins and porpoises, both collaborating on research projects and denouncing the activities that cause the deaths of high numbers of small cetaceans (including tuna fishing and the use of driftnets).

• Finally, Greenpeace International and national offices work both inside and outside the whaling countries. The activities are varied, ranging from participation in the IWC annual meetings to protests at embassies, from collecting signatures to denouncing the illegal trade in whale meat. There are also several other Greenpeace campaigns that occasionally report on cetacean mortality (such as fishing, toxics, climate change, marine reserves and pollution).

Whales painted by volunteers in the *Rainbow Warrior* engine room.

MIKE FINCKEN

chased during the great slaughter of the 19th and 20th centuries. When the populations of the larger species reached their commercial exploitation limit, however, eyes turned towards the minke whales. In 1993, Norway decided to ignore the global moratorium, choosing the minke as its victim, and thousands of these whales have lost their lives since as a result.

A very tough campaign (1999)

The *Rainbow Warrior* arrived in Oslo on 3 May 1999. Although most of her crew were experienced in direct action, they knew that this time they would not come between the harpoon and the whale. This time the ship would be in Norwegian waters as an international observer of the hunting – collecting information and standing as a planetary symbol against whaling. But the *Rainbow Warrior* also had no less important a mission than the opening of channels of dialogue with the Norwegian public, most of whom supported whaling on the grounds that it was culturally important. To that end, the ship visited some small ports as well as the capital. Once back in the open sea, however, the flagship met with the *Sirius*, which had a very different mission: its crew would be the ones actively trying to stop the hunting.

> Every year since 1993, the Norwegian government has allocated a number of whales to be killed within its Exclusive Economic Zone.[9] In 1999, the quota was 753 minkes.

It took them many days to locate a whaler and, when they finally found the *Villduen*, it was being escorted by a coastguard. As the *Rainbow Warrior* put the media boat in the water (which had been especially prepared for the campaign and was dubbed the 'Popemobile' by the crew due to its shape), the *Sirius* lowered the two inflatables that would aim to hinder the whaling. The coastguards also lowered inflatables and so a relentless persecution of the activists immediately began, with small boats zigzagging like bees around the four ships.

At full speed, a Greenpeace inflatable went along one of the *Rainbow Warrior*'s sides and its pursuer along the other side. When both passed the bow of the ship, they met each other and the coastguard boat rammed its rival, landing on top of it. Mark Hardingham, a British activist, was thrown from the inflatable and fell unconscious into the water. He was rescued by his colleagues but it was soon

A minke whale in the North Sea. Minke whales can spend up to 20 minutes underwater and can swim at almost 40 kilometers per hour.

CRIS TOALA OLIVARES / GREENPEACE

Ålesund

NORWAY

Bergen
Oslo

Stavanger

Aftermath of a collision: injured activist Mark Hardingham is rescued by colleagues in action against the Norwegian whaler *Villduen*.

animals' destruction nor to their disposal. The country not only violated international agreements on the protection of whales but also permitted its whalers to discard nine-tenths of their slaughtered prey with total impunity.

The outrage of discards

Millions of tons of fish and other marine animals that are of no commercial interest are 'discarded' and returned to the water dead. If only a part is wanted, as with the whales in Norway, the rest of the animal is wasted.

evident that his condition was serious and the coastguard helicopter took him to the nearest hospital in Stavanger. It was some hours later that news reached those on board that, aside from a blow to the head, Mark had two severe fractures in one of his arms, a fractured pelvis and a back injury. Mark remained in intensive care for a few days, was in hospital for many more and had to spend months in rehabilitation. The terrible question of whether the accident could have been avoided remained in the air.

Contrary to the desired effect, when disproportionate force is used against nonviolent people who are guided by strong conviction, these people become neither discouraged nor frightened. The following day, the *Sirius* inflatables returned to the water loaded with activists willing to put themselves at risk in protecting the whales, despite being very affected by what had happened to their colleague. Once a whale had actually been harpooned, the 'action' boats left, leaving only the 'Popemobile' to film the butchering of the animals on deck, and to record the fact that 90 per cent of each body was thrown overboard. The environmentalists felt double outrage!

The Norwegian government had sent two more coastguards to 'protect' the whaler. Although the drivers of their inflatables were now much more cautious, they did not stop their constant hassling. Norway did not want to have witnesses to these

One day, on board the *Rainbow Warrior*, it was decided to organize a boat training session so as to give the crew some practice. When they were notified, the coastguards replied that there was no problem as long as the inflatables did not enter the 'forbidden' perimeter set around the whaling ship. The environmentalists were practising on

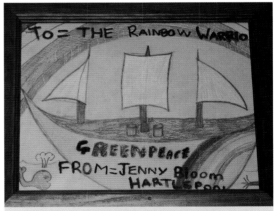

In 2002, the *Rainbow Warrior* did a research tour around the United Kingdom in co-operation with 'The Whale and Dolphin Society'. A school was meant to visit the ship in Blackpool but the port authorities did not allow them entry. Very disappointed, the children decided to make drawings dedicated to the *Rainbow Warrior* and send them to the ship. The crew members selected and framed the best two, which found a place on the ship's office bulkheads. This is one of them.

LUIS VASQUEZ / GREENPEACE

Bloody business. The crew of the *Villduen* flense a dead minke whale in the North Sea. Flensing involves removing a whale's blubber or skin.

the sea for a while when the inflatable crewed by Madeleine Habib (the chief mate) and Amanda Bjuhr (the cook) was boarded and the women were taken to a coastguard. Amanda was aware that she had only half-prepared dinner and eventually managed to gain permission to radio the *Rainbow Warrior*. There ensued a long call that thoroughly perplexed the Norwegians who were listening, as Amanda issued her detailed instructions about meal preparation to the captain, Derek Nicholls, who was patiently writing things down at the other end. As their boat-suits were confiscated as evidence, Mad and Amanda ended up wearing coastguard tracksuits during the several days they spent under arrest. On the Greenpeace ship they

On land, Greenpeace found out that the two largest whalemeat warehouses were full and even had pieces dating back to 1986. It was clear that the Norwegians were reluctant to eat whalemeat. Norway's defense at the IWC talked about 'small-scale traditional whaling', concealing the fact that most of the whalemeat and blubber gathered was exported to Japan and Iceland. Did the oil-rich Norwegian economy really need the sacrifice of whales?

were really missed – especially Amanda! At one point Derek even joked by hinting at a deal with the Norwegians: 'If you give my cook back, I will give you two deckhands in return.'

Although the *Rainbow Warrior* had to leave Norway due to her other scheduled commitments, the *Sirius* remained in the area looking for more whalers. A new chapter of this whaling campaign was begun. After many days of searching, the whaling ship *Kato* was intercepted exactly one month after the accident in which Mark Hardingham had been injured. Shortly after the *Sirius* arrived, two coastguards – the eternal bodyguards of the whaling industry – appeared. The Greenpeace boats defended a whale from the *Kato* for as long as they could but eventually the harpoon reached its prey. Seeing that the defense was at an end, the Greenpeace boats had already moved away when the whaler's captain fired three shots at them, one of the bullets puncturing the sponson of one of the activists' inflatables. However, in this version of a Hollywood western, the sheriff arrested not the shooter but rather the defenseless activists, whose ship was also detained and towed to Stavanger.

In the course of barely one month, those taking direct action in the inflatables had seen their lives

JOHN CUNNINGHAM / GREENPEACE

Under arrest. Four of the Greenpeace activists in the custody of Norwegian police after the anti-whaling action in 1999.

seriously endangered twice and, in addition, had been threatened with knives, thrown into the water and seen a harpoon shot over their heads. On top of all this, the campaign faced totally unexpected legal and economic consequences: a large bail had to be paid to release the *Sirius* and, later in October, Stavanger's county court sentenced three activists, Mark Hardingham included, to individual fines. The last straw was the massive support of Norwegian public opinion for their government on the issue. Support for Greenpeace in Norway decreased so quickly that the office in Oslo was left with almost no staff and just a handful of volunteers.

In recent years, the Norwegian government has argued that the killing of whales is justified on the grounds that an uncontrolled population would threaten valuable fish stocks. This reasoning widely ignores the fact that cetaceans have never emptied the seas of fish – not even when there were millions of them – while commercial fishing, in just a few years, is sweeping away not only commercial species but everything that lives in the planet's waters.

Ten years on (2009)

Despite the bitter cold, almost everyone was on deck. We were sailing with the four sails unfurled amid spectacular scenery and with music by the Norwegian composer Edvard Grieg blasting from the bridge, courtesy of our captain, Mike Fincken. The *Rainbow Warrior* was heading north, ploughing between the islands and fjords of continental Norway. It was mid-March 2009.

The reason for the new visit to the Nordic country was not related to whaling in any way. We were campaigning for the establishment of marine reserves that would fully protect the valuable and unique coral reefs off the Norwegian coast. To that end, it was necessary to mark the boundaries of future protected areas and it was paramount, once again, to win the backing of the Norwegian public.

The natural beauty helped us to overcome the slight bad taste in our mouths left by our experiences in Bergen – a beautiful city justifiably recognized as a World Heritage Site. There we had presented our campaign to the media and the public, and we had also carried out the last technical adjustments on the sophisticated underwater camera that we were going to use.

While many citizens of Bergen welcomed us and were greatly interested in knowing the condition of

The relationship between the destruction of coral reefs and the reduction of marine animal life is direct: coral provides a home, shelter and food for many organisms.

the Norwegian coral, there was a small group who were not very happy about our presence in the city. Some of them had sporadically expressed their anger from the dock, launching insults that often were accompanied by spittle and urine as well as eggs and a variety of garbage. As we were leaving, we found out that they had chained one of the bow mooring lines to the dock. We had to abort the maneuver and, in an emergency situation, come alongside again, moor back and disembark to cut the chain.

Ten years after the bizarre anti-whaling campaign, the *Rainbow Warrior* and her crew discovered that not enough time had elapsed for some locals' animosity to Greenpeace to have been forgotten.

While the Norwegian government blames whales for the shortage of fish, the natural habitat for fish is being destroyed by its own trawlers. In 2009, it was estimated that about 50 per cent of Norway's coral reefs had already been ruined by fishing trawlers.

This wooden whale used to be in the mess of the second *Rainbow Warrior* and is now on the third ship.

After several days of uninterrupted work filming a wide area of coral reefs, a storm forced us to seek refuge in the nearest port: Ålesund. Only four degrees latitude south of the Arctic Circle and placed at the entrance of a large fjord, this beautiful city is surrounded by breathtaking landscapes. Ålesund is also one of Norway's main fishing ports – and the more isolated and distant these ports were, the more supportive of whaling they tended to be.

[Left] Crew members Sven Malmgren, Jocke Schullstrom and Pelle Petersson operate the underwater camera photographing coral. [Above] This *Lophelia pertusa* species forms part of the largest-known cold-water coral reef, discovered in Norway in 2002.

Wind power: the second *Rainbow Warrior* sailing in Norwegian waters north of Sognfjorden in 2009.

The berth we had been given was in the city center and the *Rainbow Warrior* was right in front of the entrance to a disco-club, with just the wharf and a two-lane road in between. It was a Friday evening and, in the knowledge that alcohol fuels extreme feelings, it was decided to have two people rather than one on watch during the night.

That night, I was on duty from midnight to 4am with Jari Ståhl, the Swedish video camera operator who was travelling with us on that tour. On guard in the wheelhouse, we watched the shore closely. For hours there was a steady trickle of incidents involving drunken men. Many came to insult us, invariably either throwing objects at the boat or spitting at her. As sneaking on board was quite a simple operation – the main deck gunwale was very low and at the same height as the wharf – several men managed to step on board. When we emerged and exchanged words with them, though, they left by their own volition. Undoubtedly the favorite activity of the night was to come and piss up against the hull, expressing their opinion about the organization in a very graphic manner.

It was not until after three that we had the biggest fright. Because they arrived from along the quay, we only realized the three men were there when they were right beside the ship. Astonished, we watched as they lifted and threw the stern springline into the water. Rushing out of the wheelhouse, we saw them doing exactly the same with the next mooring line they passed by. Jari asked them to stop lifting the lines and one of them stood in front of him and began to shout abuse so loudly that he woke a few of the crew. Jari was challenged to a fight on the quayside but simply tried to calm the man down.

There are times when being a woman has its advantages. Mired as they were in their argument, I took the opportunity to leave the ship. Although I passed scarcely a meter from the Norwegian, he simply ignored me and I also behaved as if he were not there. I was then able to put the two spring

MAITE MOMPÓ

The Kwakiutl Totem
The orca crest of the Kwakiutl, a Native American people from Canada, was adopted as a symbol when Greenpeace decided to campaign in defense of whales. The design was borrowed to create what was going to be the movement's totem, the Greenpeace flag: two orcas joined together in the circle of life with the Greenpeace ecology and peace emblems inside it. The *Phyllis Cormack* was carrying the totem on its sail when it and the *Vega* departed from Vancouver in April 1975 for the first anti-whaling campaign. On its way back to Vancouver, the *Phyllis Cormack* stopped and the flag with the Kwakiutl symbol was presented to the tribe which accepted it with due ceremony.[10] Since then the totem has been present in most of the Greenpeace ships.
     The orca is said to protect those who travel away from home, and to lead them back when the time is right. In this symbolic sense, cetaceans have accompanied the Greenpeace ships on their travels ever since that first voyage to defend them.

roused people to report what had happened and from that moment the watch continued with four people instead of two.

The next morning, the port authority granted us another berth where we were not so accessible and the problems virtually stopped. From then on, as a precaution, we were the ones chaining the ropes to the dock and then unlocking them to leave port. Two days later, the *Rainbow Warrior* was again collecting images of coral reefs. Finally it was decided to come back to Ålesund and open up the ship to the public. It was fascinating to observe how the initial simple curiosity of many visitors turned into real interest after learning about our campaign, and how they then looked at us in a different light. To round off the campaign, we went to Oslo, where we had a nice welcome and many visitors who were supportive, which greatly helped to erase all the bad experiences from our minds.

Over 12,000 signatures calling for the protection of coral were collected during the campaign. Partly as a result, the number of protected coral reefs has increased – as has the degree of their protection.

We left Norwegian seas without having sighted any of the animals responsible for the animosity towards us – the minke whales would not make their seasonal arrival in these waters for a few more months yet. In 1999, we in Greenpeace realized that the best way to help and save these whales is simply not to talk about the situation inside Norway.

Nowadays
The vast majority of the Norwegian population prefers to eat beef or chicken rather than whale. The government continues to find it very difficult to export whalemeat. Even if whaling still happens, the activity is in decline, with a decreasing number of animals being slaughtered. In addition, increasing numbers of Norwegians regard killing whales as unnecessary and think that a whale-watching industry should be developed instead.

---

lines back in place. Tired of not getting the desired response from his 'opponent' and seeing that his two companions had already walked away, the guy finally left. With the help of the long hook, Jari and I immediately started to recover the four remaining mooring lines that were floating in the water. We were very lucky that there was a slight wind blowing towards the dock: in that period of several minutes nothing had been holding us to land. In a different situation, the boat could have been in serious trouble. After securing the boat, we

Between the harpoon and the whale (*Arctic Sunrise*, Antarctica 2005)

That day, the *African Queen* scudded quickly over the small waves of the Antarctic Ocean and I felt like a jockey on the back of a galloping horse. We were attempting to follow the unpredictable movements of a desperate whale, trying always to keep our boat between the determined pursuer, the Japanese ship *Yushin Maru 2*, and the defenseless victim, a huge adult minke whale. My 'horse', the inflatable boat, was like a runaway as it zigzagged and broke suddenly, accelerated and broke yet again, then a few seconds later changed direction and accelerated at full speed. We were in pursuit of this magnificent being that was feeling death circling and yet was unable to understand what was happening: its ancient intellect did not know the concept of 'enemy' because for millions of years its kind had not had any.

The second inflatable boat, the *Orca*, was stuck to the bow of the whaler, shooting into the air a stream of sea water so as to block the vision of the harpooner and therefore limiting his capacity to shoot (the harpooner is always male, and are regarded as heroes by many Japanese, akin to modern *samurai*). We had been protecting the whale for more than an hour, sharing with this animal an increasingly pronounced fatigue, when our companions on this mission called us by radio. Their engine was giving them problems and they had to return to the *Arctic Sunrise*. The three of us who were on the *African Queen* exchanged looks to decide what we were going to do – for safety reasons, there always has to be a minimum of two boats in an action. It was a unanimous decision. We were incapable of abandoning this whale.

So we stayed alone between the harpoon and the whale. Hunter, prey and protector entangled in a desperate struggle for survival, tiny dancers in the

In your face. Greenpeace activists in the Southern Ocean use a modified fire pump to obscure the view of the harpooner on the Japanese whaler *Yushin Maru 2*.

KATE DAVISON / GREENPEACE

immensity of the Antarctic sea and sky.

Holding tight, sometimes seated, other times standing, I followed the animal with my eyes so as to be able constantly to signal with my free arm to Texas Constantine – who was at the wheel of the inflatable – where the whale was or where it was reappearing. At the same time, I also had to indicate to him the position of the whaling ship. Like an owl, my head was turning constantly without losing sight of all that surrounded me. My inner voice never stopped encouraging the mammal: 'Don't give up. Keep on running. Come on, come on...'

Suddenly the whale disappeared under the waves. A terrible feeling gripped my body. Where would it appear this time? Instants later, my eyes, staring into the black sea that extended before me, saw on our starboard bow the whale re-emerging with a majestic jump that took its immense body out of the water. Close, very close to us. We were so close that I felt its eye staring at me and my heart leapt. I completely forgot where I was and what I was doing there. From my wide-open mouth escaped a loud 'Wow'. Out of the corner of my eye I felt rather than saw something pass over my head. A loud bang sounded that froze my blood and paralyzed my body. 'Boom.' The whale could not finish drawing the arc of its body in the air. It did not get to show its tail. It collapsed into the water.

I shut my eyes tightly in a crazy attempt to erase from my mind what was happening. That big boom had changed a sweet dream into a horrible nightmare in a second. 'Please... Be dead!' I thought immediately, knowing that the harpooner's shot had not erred. Now my own survival was at risk. If this whale had only been wounded, its giant tail would cut us into pieces.

When it crashes against the skin of a whale, the grenade at the tip of the harpoon explodes and the harpoon opens, anchoring itself in the thick layer of fat. If the animal manages to survive, it tries to get rid of the harpoon by beating its tail with fury and trying to submerge. The agony can last for many long minutes.

Our inflatables had been many days ruining the hunt and the Japanese were becoming nervous about not reaching their government-established quota. I suppose the killing of this whale after so much effort meant for the crew the delight of a small win over Greenpeace, and for the harpooner in particular, a sweet sense of victory. For my part, it was hard to realize that our lives were worth less than a fistful of yen. One slap from a wave could have raised up our boat, one false move from the harpooner at the trigger, and we would have received the impact of the grenade.

Tenths of seconds that feel like hours, minutes suspended in slow motion in which thoughts fly through your mind at the speed of light. So many extreme emotions and so many conflicting feelings.

A sharp pull returned me from this unreal state in which time stood still. They were trying to recover the rope to bring the precious prey to their bow. Like a spinning top, our boat did a 360-degree turn. They were dragging us sideways, along with the lifeless body of the whale now stuck at our port side. Its huge V-shaped mouth was open, completely dislocated, and through it we could see its stomach, floating like an immense white bubble over its inner organs.

Finally the whalers stopped pulling and we had a bit of respite. We had to free ourselves from the rope, which was not an easy job, given that we had a dead body weighing more than 10 tonnes hanging from the other end. If our big outboard engine had been hooked, we could have had a serious problem. Suddenly, without warning, the whalers tightened the line again. I felt a sharp push and Texas fell abruptly on top of me. But a moment later he was gone. I shouted his name and sat up looking for him. I looked at the stern and then I saw him: the rope had hooked underneath his arms and dragged him so that he was now hanging halfway between the bow of the whaler and the corpse. The water beneath him was completely red.

Like a monkey, Texas started climbing down the rope to reach the water and swam as far as he could away from the whale. While we started moving towards him to pick him up and pull him out of

Clear as day. On 20 January 2006 the crews of the *Arctic Sunrise* and the *Esperanza* form a message with their bodies on the Antarctic ice.

the icy Antarctic waters, the hunter took its prey. Once we began to move away from the whaling ship, I exploded. I couldn't hold back the flow of insults that escaped from my mouth – nor did I want to. The crew of that ship had put our lives at serious risk twice: if all three of us had fallen into the water, would we have been able to endure until someone came to rescue us?

It was hard for me to get to sleep that night and for many of the nights that followed. I closed my eyes and I saw the eye of the whale. And although many years have passed, I still hold that image very clearly in my mind. I doubt it will ever leave me. That look of bewilderment pierced me to the soul.

That was our last action to try to stop the slaughter of whales. The confrontation had become far too dangerous as the tension between us and the whalers had grown daily. We were totally exhausted and on top of that we were running out of fuel. Before leaving the area, we went ashore in Antarctica to send a message to the world, with our bodies forming the letters: 'Help End Whaling.'

When I am asked how I came to work on Greenpeace ships, I always have to go back to the moment in which the idea came into my head. I was just an 11-year-old child but I remember watching the Greenpeace inflatables standing between the harpoon and the whale. That was when I made my decision: some day I will be there with those people defending the whales. The ship where those whale saviors came from was the first *Rainbow Warrior*. How could I forget it? I had immediately fallen in love with that ship, with her name and everything she stood for. And 26 years later I had fulfilled my pledge.

Nowadays

• Since 1987, Japan has followed its so-called 'scientific whaling program' with the slaughter of thousands of whales. Most of these attacks have been launched in the Southern Ocean despite the fact that it has been a Whale Sanctuary since 1994. In addition, about 20,000 dolphins and porpoises have been killed every year by Japanese ships.

• However, in March 2014, the UN International Court of Justice ordered Japan to stop hunting whales off Antarctica and, a few days later, the Japanese government announced that it would abide by this ruling. This means that, for the first time in over 100 years, whales will not be hunted in Antarctica.

• In 1993, Norway openly resumed commercial whaling of minke whales, first with the argument that this was 'small-scale traditional whaling' and, more recently, that whales threaten their valuable fish stocks.

• Iceland kept killing whales until 1989. Then the country resumed the activity in 2003, in order to carry out a 'scientific program' whereby mainly minke whales but also a small number of fin whales (which are endangered) have been killed.

• In July 2012, South Korea announced its plans to resume commercial whaling, also under the guise of 'scientific whaling'. In 2013, however, after a big Greenpeace action in the country, and the delivery of a petition signed by thousands around the world, the Korean government seems to have shelved these plans.

• In the Faroe Islands (owned by Denmark) there is an annual slaughter of about a thousand Delphinids (mostly pilot whales).

• Several indigenous groups have permission from the IWC to hunt whales under the 'Provision for aboriginal subsistence' in several countries (including the US, Russia, Greenland and St Vincent and the Grenadines).

• All the species that used to have great commercial value are now considered either threatened or seriously endangered. The vaquita (a porpoise in the Gulf of Mexico) is the next whale at risk of becoming extinct.[11]

1 Sirenia, being the only marine herbivorous mammals, are also called the 'sea cows'. Nowadays there are four species living: a species of dugong and three species of manatees. 2 Whales are therefore related in evolutionary terms to the *Artiodactyla*: that is, hoofed herbivorous mammals that are even-toed, including cows, deer, pigs, goats, camels and hippopotami. 3 Among the Mysticeti are the rorquals, the right whales, the grey whale and the humpback whale. None of these escaped commercial hunting. Odontoceti are very varied in size and cover sperm and beaked whales, narwhals and belugas, along with around 34 species of oceanic dolphins and six species of porpoises. 4 The Basques live between the southeast of France and the north of Spain, around the western end of the Pyrenees. Their origin is unknown and their language, Euskera, is not related to any other in the world. 5 With the passage of time, the International Whaling Commission has changed a lot and nowadays is dedicated to the protection and conservation of not only whales but also the other cetaceans, all of which are facing major threats. However, inside the Commission there are still many countries in favor of resuming commercial whaling, while others kill small cetaceans off their coasts. 6 Sonar (short for **So**und **Na**vigation and **R**anging) is a technique using sound propagation (usually under water) to navigate, communicate with or detect underwater objects. 7 UNCLOS (the **U**nited **N**ations **C**onvention on the **L**aw **o**f the **S**ea) is an international agreement concluded in 1982 to establish 'a legal order for the seas and oceans which will facilitate international communication, and will promote the peaceful uses of the seas and oceans, the equitable and efficient utilization of their resources, the conservation of their living resources, and the study, protection and preservation of the marine environment.' 8 Whale Sanctuaries have been created by the international community and certain countries in order to provide shelter and asylum for whales: the Indian Ocean (1979), the Southern Ocean (1994), the Ligurian Sea in the Mediterranean (2001) and the Exclusive Economic Zones of Mexico (2002) and Chile (2008). 9 An **E**xclusive **E**conomic **Z**one (EEZ) is a sea zone prescribed by the Law of the Sea over which a state has special rights to explore and use marine resources, including energy production from water and wind. It stretches 200 nautical miles from the country's coast. 10 According to Robert Hunter, *The Greenpeace Chronicle*, Picador 1980. 11 According to the International Union for Conservation of Nature Red List of Threatened Whales in 2011.

> 'Most ignorance is vincible ignorance. We don't know because we don't want to know'
>
> Aldous Huxley

4 Poison and hope

This chapter is dedicated to the memory of Crizel

Introducing Crizel
Toxic-free Asia tour (1999-2000) Bhopal • Shipbreaking • River and sea pollution • Incineration
• Landfills • A clean future
Crizel's story
Hope

Introducing Crizel

This chapter had its origin in a picture-composition that occupied most of the bulkhead of the *Rainbow Warrior*'s small office. The heart of the composition was a large children's drawing showing the ship on the open sea with its large blue sails. The ship was surrounded by the sun, a rainbow, clouds, birds, three boys and a girl with her name written underneath. The date was also included: 1 February 2000. At the bottom of the drawing appeared the name of the campaign: 'Toxic Free Asia Tour 1999-2000'. The drawing was bordered on the right by six photographs from the Tour. The top one showed a completely bald girl driving a Greenpeace inflatable (see page 81). The girl driving is the same as the one in the drawing. Her name was Crizel and she was also the creator of this little masterpiece. 'Steering' that boat was the last thing that this small Filipino artist did in her life.

A group of visitors to the *Rainbow Warrior* in the ship's office – they are facing the wall where Crizel's painting hung. The author is pictured just above center, with auburn hair.

69

Crizel, pictured just before her death in 2000.

Crizel's story became part of a series of stories rescued from oblivion by the various mementos found on the *Rainbow Warrior*. Anyone standing in front of Crizel's drawing (whether people from Greenpeace or external visitors) were moved by the memory of what had happened and tears were often shed. Crizel's story is a sad one... We would often leave the office with a heavy heart but a smile on our faces. The smiles that appeared in the drawing were contagious. In her creation, Crizel had put a smile on anything that could have one: on the sun, on the faces of the boys and the girl and on the balloons they were holding. The last days of Crizel's life were filled with a light and strength given by hope. The hope that everything would get better for her, and for all the other sick children, was carried by the sea and aboard a boat with large blue sails.

This chapter is dedicated to Crizel because she represents the rest of human beings without exception. All of us – and all life on Earth – are, to a greater or lesser extent, victims of toxic contamination of one sort or another. Human-made toxic chemicals are present in both the North and the South, in both rich and poor countries, in cities and in the countryside. They have infiltrated us all, those who live surrounded by mini-Bhopals and those living thousands of miles away. Persistent toxic substances have even reached the remotest uninhabited places. The toxic pollution black spots in Asia where the *Rainbow Warrior* worked during this tour illustrate the big picture very well. Reading this introduction, you may think I am exaggerating. But you may not have the same opinion after you have read this chapter.

Toxic-free Asia Tour (1999-2000)

In the late 1970s and early 1980s, several large chemical companies in industrialized countries were forced to close down because their technologies and production processes were extremely destructive to the local environment. Whether their activities were directly prohibited, or mandatory Western safety measures became too demanding, these companies sought new territories and markets in which to continue production without hindrance. Asia was one of the continents where these chemical companies found unregulated 'paradise'.

Ironically, these foreign 'investments' were sold to the Asian general public as something extremely positive: creating jobs and contributing to progress. However, the huge economic growth that parts of Asia experienced in a short period carried with it environmental degradation, and health problems inevitably skyrocketed.

In the late 1990s, after several serious accidents and toxic pollution disasters, the overall picture was bleak. The alarm needed to be raised and alternatives and solutions had to be found. The best way for Greenpeace to do this was to organize a long tour, during which the *Rainbow Warrior* would visit several countries, starting in India and then going on to Thailand, the Philippines, Hong Kong and Japan. This tour encompassed a large

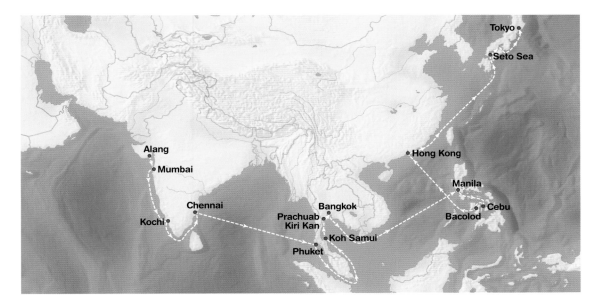

area of the planet that was rich in cultural diversity. Hotspots in need of urgent attention were chosen (a difficult choice in some cases) and it was confirmed that these countries were involved in some of the worst polluting activities in the world (incineration, pesticide factories, shipbreaking yards...).

As with all long campaigns that the Greenpeace ships engaged in, aside from the formally planned activities there were also surprises, unforgettable experiences, moments of tension and laughter, and both exhausting and relaxing situations. However, as I said earlier, on this occasion, a chapter was to be written in the history of the *Rainbow Warrior*

that would have been impossible to predict or even imagine in advance. For death, when it comes, always catches one by surprise. Crizel put a name and a face to the victims of the poisoning that was occurring with lawlessness and impunity in that part of the world. The hotspots highlighted in this chapter were Greenpeace's main areas of concern.

In the final days of the ship's visit to India, a newspaper wrote: 'A small boat, a great organization and some little people fighting big challenges.'

One of many actions that Greenpeace activists have staged to remind the world that the victims of the Bhopal chemical disaster are still suffering (see overleaf). This one took place on the 20th anniversary of the disaster, in 2004. Activists erected a memorial sculpture of a woman and two children near the Dow Chemical factory in Rheinmuenster, Germany. The banner reads: 'Bhopal is dying – Dow is silent'.

Bhopal

Around midnight on 2 December 1984, a pesticide plant owned by the Union Carbide corporation released about 40 tons of deadly methyl isocyanate gas[1] and other unspecified chemicals into the atmosphere. The gas cloud spread at ground level covering most of Bhopal, a town in Madhya Pradesh, midway between Mumbai and Delhi. Its inhabitants awoke coughing, with eye and throat irritations and severe vomiting. It is estimated that over 500,000 people breathed in the deadly gas. Many did not get to see the sunrise. A 'simple' gas leak left a city littered with corpses and diseased for life. The tragedy was of such magnitude that it is known as 'the Hiroshima of the chemical industry'.

In the early 1980s, Union Carbide had decided to cease production but had left large quantities of hazardous chemicals stored on site. In response to small accidents and leaks that had been occurring, as well as 61 safety and maintenance deficiencies officially detected in 1982, the company fired four of the six employees of this department.

Consequently, that fateful night none of the six safety systems to contain leaks was functioning. As the warning siren never sounded, the toxic cloud fell upon the unsuspecting inhabitants of a city asleep. The exact death toll during that dreadful night will never be known because trucks took away thousands of bodies that were immediately burned in massive pits or buried in mass graves.[2] Those who survived after breathing the gas suffered lifelong damage: to the eyes, lungs, kidneys, liver, intestines, muscles, brain and immune and reproductive systems. Deaths as a result of the accident continue to this day.

With incredible cynicism, the company tried to cover up the scandal of its extreme negligence by reporting that the accident was due to sabotage by an angry worker.

Fifteen years later, the *Rainbow Warrior* arrived at the overwhelming super-city of Mumbai, one of the most populated cities on the planet, where extreme poverty and immense wealth exist side by side. The first Greenpeace toxics tour in Asia started in 'Bollywood' (home to the largest film industry in the world) and was marked by

Remember Bhopal 2003 – an action in Mumbai, India. To this day, the Dow Chemical Company (which took over Union Carbide in 2001) is being pressurized to declare the exact composition of the lethal gas that escaped from the Bhopal plant, to clean the site properly, to ensure the long-term medical treatment and rehabilitation of the victims and to provide clean drinking water for the contaminated communities.

commemorating the anniversary of the mass poisoning of Bhopal, an episode more scary than in any horror movie.

Aboard the ship, the worldwide release of a major report took place: *The Legacy of Bhopal*. For the first time ever, results of water and soil analysis of the area surrounding the plant were published, revealing the presence of several highly toxic chemicals, including heavy metals. Fifteen years after the accident, the factory was still silently poisoning thousands of people on a daily basis. At the same time as the report was released, a mass demonstration demanding justice took place in New Delhi, where supporters of Greenpeace India left a four-meter reproduction of the Union Carbide factory in front of the national Parliament.

Sunil Kumar, who lost his entire family on that tragic night, aptly described the powerlessness of the situation: 'Carbide never showed any interest in the condition of the victims... Now they seem to know that their factory is poisoning a new generation – and they do nothing to stop it. People are sick in the communities. The kids are sick... It's

SHAILENDRA YASHWANT / GREENPEACE

The path of impunity

• In 1989, the Indian government came to an agreement with Union Carbide on the total sum of compensation: $470 million. To justify this ridiculous amount, the government stated that 93% of victims suffered temporary damage. The company itself had officially recognized that the harm caused by methyl isocyanate is permanent.

• Union Carbide never made public its own reports revealing the high level of contamination of soil and water inside the facility. In 2002, official analyses revealed that the water drunk by surrounding communities contained high doses of mercury, trichloroethane, trichlorobenzene, dichloromethane, chloroform, naphthalene, Sevin, copper, nickel, lead and the pesticide HCH.

• On the 27th anniversary of the accident, about 2,000 victims were arrested while peacefully demonstrating to demand fair compensation. They were later charged with offenses punishable with life imprisonment. Neither Union Carbide nor Dow Chemical Company (now the parent corporation) have ever been taken to court.

• Figures up to 2011: more than 25,000 people have died and over 120,000 have suffered serious consequences from the Bhopal disaster. Another 30,000 people have been made sick by drinking contaminated water.

• Dow Chemical Company was one of the sponsors of the London 2012 Olympic Games.

as if they really hate us... What kind of people are doing this?'

From Mumbai, the ship travelled around India and finished in multicultural Chennai (formerly Madras), another of the most densely populated cities in the world and the fourth largest in India. During the tour, a photo exhibition of the Bhopal victims accompanied the ship in all ports. In Chennai, as the finale of the Indian visit, a massive concert to raise funds for the cause was held. Two *Rainbow Warrior* crew members joined various groups performing with a small contribution: Satish with the didgeridoo and Paula on guitar and vocals.

It has now been almost 30 years since the accident and the Bhopal case is still open. We must not forget that the nightmare is still not over for many of its victims.

Shipbreaking

Under the guise of recycling, many old ships were brought to Asian countries (among them India, Pakistan, Bangladesh, China and the Philippines) to be dismantled, as protection levels and conditions for workers there were well below Western minimum standards. This supposed recycling resulted in a *de facto* and uncontrolled release of dangerous waste substances, not only from what the ships carried but also from the toxic components of the vessels themselves (for example PCBs, asbestos[3], biocides[4] and several heavy metals).

While the *Rainbow Warrior* was in India, members of the so-called Basel Convention, which regulates

SHAILENDRA YASHWANT / GREENPEACE

Shipbreaking in Alang, in the Indian state of Gujarat: about half of the world's ships are scrapped here.

the cross-border movement of hazardous wastes and their disposal were holding their fourth meeting in Switzerland.[5] The way in which ship-breaking was carried out in Asia was a flagrant violation of this Convention. Greenpeace seized the opportunity to take its ship to Alang – in the state of Gujarat, on the Pakistan border – a place whose once-idyllic endless beaches now hold the largest shipbreaking yard in the world. While the international meeting was happening, the *Rainbow Warrior* orchestrated various activities to denounce the highly toxic contamination that originated from shipbreaking. This time, those attending the Basel Convention finally listened, and the meeting ended with a commitment to take effective action to end this illegality.

The issue of shipbreaking was highlighted a second time during the tour on the *Rainbow Warrior*'s visit to Cebu, the second-largest city

in the Philippines. There, the ships for scrapping come mainly from Japan and the pollution problem is exacerbated by waste incinerated inside the shipyard. In this case, the workers had a right to know the health risks involved both in their work and in incineration: the ashes had been found to contain high levels of several heavy metals as well as benzene, a known carcinogen.

POPs

• Persistent Organic Pollutants (POPs) are highly toxic chemicals that do not degrade for decades. They are incorporated into food chains and accumulate in the fatty tissues of living organisms. Furthermore, they 'biomagnify', progressively increasing in concentration. The higher up the food chain, the higher are the concentrations.

• A mother transfers POPs accumulated in her body to her baby during the formation of the fetus and through her breastmilk.

• The specific effects of POPs include: cancer, asthma, allergies and hypersensitivity, damage to the nervous system and serious reproductive disorders. They disrupt the endocrine and immune systems.

• The Stockholm Convention, a global agreement for their total elimination, established 12 priority substances in 2004 (including PCBs, dioxins and furans, DDT and HCB) and added nine more substances in 2009 (including lindane and hexaclorocyclohexane). Around 400 POPs are known to exist.

• The number of fatalities (human and animal) caused by POPs is impossible to count. POPs have been found in the bodies of falcons, polar bears and whales.

• The use of DDT is still permitted in some countries, for the purpose of killing the mosquito that causes malaria.

• Dioxins are among the most toxic chemicals synthesized by humans. Currently they are massively produced in incinerators and also by companies using chlorine. They have a lifespan of hundreds of years.

River and sea pollution

For years, the World Bank financed the construction of so-called Common Effluent Treatment Plants (CETPs), which were sold to developing countries as a means of cleaning up all types of waste, including industrial waste. Time has proved, however, that these expensive treatment plants are unable to remove the most toxic and hazardous substances. These substances need special treatment (which in turn generates new waste).

The inadequacy of CETPs to the task has been proved and reported in several countries. For example, the parts of rivers that pass close to these kinds of treatment plants in the state of Gujarat in India are contaminated with PCBs, HCBS and several very dangerous heavy metals. Millions of people drink, bathe in and irrigate their fields with these waters. The Pasig River, which passes through Manila, the Philippine capital, was at the time of the Tour being contaminated with heavy metals from two factories that had their own effluent treatment plants.

The production of waste and toxic substances has also occurred in rich countries, Japan being a prime example. There has been, for example, multiple toxic pollution in the Seto interior sea, a meeting point between the three main southern islands and one of the most industrialized parts of the country. The most pressing pollution problems that were addressed by the *Rainbow Warrior* there included leaks in landfills on the islands of Teshima and Kamikuro (the latter within a National Park) as well as the discharge of dioxins by several PVC plastic factories.

The 'heavy metals'

• Heavy metals are chemical elements that can pose serious health and environmental risks because of their high toxicity. They are not chemically or biologically degradable and their concentration increases in living tissues through the food chain.

• Among the most dangerous are lead, cadmium, chromium, mercury and copper. Most cause kidney and liver damage and some are carcinogenic. They also cause neurological and psychological disorders, infertility and sexual impotence, osteoporosis, spontaneous abortions and fetal damage, dermatitis, damage to nerve tissue and to the circulatory system.

• Their use is varied, and includes the manufacture of batteries, pipes, paints, dental material, and alloys.

• It is estimated that a single drop of mercury can poison tens of thousands of liters of water and that about 18 million children suffer permanent neurological damage due to lead poisoning.

The man who takes care of a river

He is called VJ Jose. Greenpeace named him 'Periyar River Keeper' in 2002. He had by then already been fighting for 21 years against the pollution of the river where he had bathed as a child, enjoying its clear water. Today these waters burn the skin.

The Periyar River crosses most of the Indian state of Kerala, running through Eloor, the state's largest industrial belt, which is considered the 35th most toxic place on the planet. The crew of the *Rainbow Warrior* travelled as far as this inland city to join the locals in a peaceful rally, organized by Jose, among others, at the gates of Hindustan Insecticides Ltd, a factory that has been pouring POPs such as DDT and hexacloro-cyclohexane into the river for years.

In addition to periodic water sampling and analysis, Jose has launched an awareness campaign that has already reached 350,000 students. He funded this with the money he earned in mainly night-time jobs.

Incineration

It is generally accepted that matter is not created or destroyed, only transformed. If we think we can get rid of the big problem of the quantity and variety of waste produced by our societies just by burning it, we are ignoring the fact that we are merely changing its form: from solids to solids (ultra-toxic ash and slag), to liquids (by water pollution) and to gases (toxic fumes). Even worse, in many cases, these new residues are just as or more dangerous than in their previous form because they have been converted into heavy metals, dioxins and furans. Thus, in trying to solve one problem, we are creating an even bigger one.

For every three tons of waste burned in incinerators, about 1 ton of highly toxic ash is generated, representing both a health and an environmental hazard.

The problems caused by incineration were observed at many different points during the Tour. The ship and her crew sought to alert and inform the public about the scale and seriousness of the incineration problem through press conferences, open days, concerts and protest actions.

After India, the ship went to Thailand, where it visited two touristic paradise islands with beautiful sandy beaches strewn with palm trees, with coral

When the *Rainbow Warrior* visited Bangkok in February 2000, a drawing competition was held on the dock next to the ship. This colorful Thai landscape was painted there and adorned the ship's mess for years. Messages in Thai written on the black patch under the tree say: 'Continue fighting', 'From our hearts', 'Do not give up', 'For a beautiful world', 'We are the children who love nature', and 'We will always be on your side.'

THIJS NOTENBOOM

reefs teeming with marine life and with dense rainforests. Tourists are rarely aware of how their presence contributes to waste generation and to the involuntary slow poisoning of the natural havens they visit. On the beautiful island of Phuket, in the Andaman Sea, 70 per cent of which is covered by rainforest, toxic ash from its incinerator is piled in open pools and dispersed freely by the wind. In the depths of the rainforest of Samui, in the Gulf of Thailand, a toxic beast with a capacity far in excess of the waste production on the island had just been put into operation. The risk that this paradise would become a garbage destination for the rest of Thailand and even for other countries was very high.

Not even those who live in places with high levels of technological and economic development are guaranteed to be free of the toxins produced by incinerators. For this reason the ship stopped in the Chinese city of Hong Kong – until 1997 a British

---

A time bomb
• We live with more than 140,000 substances that factories have generated over the last hundred years. Although the health and environmental effects of the vast majority of these substances are unknown, we continue to create new monsters.
• Many of these chemicals are found in products we have at home – for example, computers and their accessories, toys, perfumes, soaps, creams, food containers, furniture, clothes and cleaning products.
• Diseases associated with exposure to toxic substances have skyrocketed: hormonal changes (cancer, diabetes, thyroid problems), reproductive problems (infertility, malformations), immunological diseases (dermatitis, allergies) and neurological problems (autism, hyperactivity, learning disabities, Alzheimer's, Parkinson's).
• According to the World Health Organization, about 65% of childhood illness stems from environmental degradation and pollution and more than five million children die each year from toxic pollution.

ALAN HINDLE / GREENPEACE

The *Rainbow Warrior* in an action protesting against Hong Kong's waste-management policy and the dioxins it generates, in 2000.

colony – which has one of the highest per-capita incomes in the world. There, vast quantities of urban waste end up in incinerators, which is the only waste-management option offered by the government. Meanwhile, Japan not only has the same policy as Hong Kong but also exports incineration technology to other countries – the incinerator on the island of Samui being just one example. In the year 2000, Japan had over 2,000 incinerators. A banner proclaiming it as the World Capital of Dioxins was unfurled on the planet's highest incineration tower, which is located in Tokyo. The Japanese government's response involved police officers storming the *Rainbow Warrior* and the Greenpeace office, confiscating vast amounts of campaign material and detaining the climbers without charge for 11 days.

Landfills

The first 'solution' generally adopted to manage the vast amounts of rubbish being generated is simply to pile it all up in one place. With the passage of time, it became clear that this was not such a good idea since, apart from anything else, highly toxic elements such as heavy metals began to seep into the soil and to contaminate the groundwater.

It was in the Philippines – in Quezon, a city

It is estimated that in the last 50 years we have produced more garbage than was generated by humans from prehistory right through to 1960.

near the capital, Manila – that the issue of the toxic contamination produced by landfills was addressed. In a huge open-air dump there, scores of men, women and children rummaged through the waste for anything that was edible, useable or sellable. The scale of the human misery that lay behind the work of those rag-pickers on that great mountain of garbage left the Greenpeace activists profoundly moved. Not only does the landfill method of waste disposal cause huge environmental problems, it also creates these mountains of human misery in and around major cities all over the planet.

A clean future

On a couple of occasions during this tour, the *Rainbow Warrior* supported communities that were struggling to prevent the construction of coal power plants. In Prachuab Khiri Khan, south of Bangkok, the ship was greeted by about 40 small fishing boats and the crew then assisted in

JOSE ENRIQUE SORIANO / GREENPEACE

'Solar Generation Youth' – a group of young Greenpeace volunteers – hold paper windmills as the *Rainbow Warrior* sails into the Philippine port of Bacolod in 2005.

the planting of 200 trees in the planned location of a huge power plant. In the city of Bacolod, on an island in the southern Philippines, the ship supported a plan submitted by a coalition of local organizations. Their goal was for the total energy production in their province, Negros Occidental, to come from renewable sources.

Five years later, the Greenpeace ship again visited both these places during a tour advocating the development of clean energy. The planned central power station projects have been stalled and, in both cases, its inhabitants have created the legend that due to visits from the *Rainbow Warrior*, the projects will never be carried out. The confidence in the power of the *Rainbow Warrior* may be somewhat misplaced but so far, at least, the developments have been resisted.

Crizel's story

Her full name was Jane Crizel Valencia. Born in the Philippines, she was to end her life on 25 February 2000, at the age of just six. Crizel found a very special place to die. She closed her eyes to rest on a bunk in the *Rainbow Warrior* and never opened them again. However, she had just enjoyed a wonderful experience: she had finally seen her childhood dream come true. In that sense, Crizel was very lucky. She had had a terrible life but at least had had a happy ending. How many millions of children die without ever experiencing joy?

The *Rainbow Warrior* had come to Manila three days before. It was the first time the ship had visited the country and news of the ship's arrival had aroused much expectation, especially in the various communities of the victims of toxic pollution to whom the ship would provide direct

The *Rainbow Warrior* went back to India in 2003 to highlight three unresolved cases of serious toxic contamination: shipbreaking in Gujarat, the Bhopal case and the DDT factory on the Periyar River. The Indian government – under pressure from the corporate lobby – raised many obstacles and forced the ship to leave the country immediately after its first action at a shipbreaking yard.

This small carved statue of the Hindu elephant god, Ganesh – also known as Ganapati, the remover of obstacles – was given to the *Rainbow Warrior* by Shailendra Yashwant, then campaigns director of Greenpeace India, and found its place in the wheelhouse of the ship.

support. The ship entered the harbor under sail and with an escort of three traditional dragon boats. There was a grand welcoming ceremony at the dock that included a traditional dance group accompanied by loud percussion. At the same time, a US Navy ship that had just docked at the next wharf was also performing a ceremony. This time, the music coming from the peace boat drowned the neighboring military band – a small symbolic victory for peace over arms.

Arriving in February, as it did, the ship found the country immersed in celebrations commemorating the peaceful popular revolution that toppled the dictator Ferdinand Marcos in 1986 and returned full sovereignty to the Philippines as an independent state.

In June 1991, just five years after the revolution, an event occurred that was directly to affect Crizel's fate. The whole country was literally shaken by the eruption of Mount Pinatubo, which left 700 dead and 200,000 homeless. The volcano also seriously damaged the Clark Air Base, which was then evacuated. Soon after, the Philippine government refused to extend the lease contracts for this base and the Subic Naval Base (the two US military bases in the country).

So it was that the foreign soldiers left the country. The authorities used the abandoned facilities to give a temporary home to thousands of refugees from the volcano while a definite place to live was being set up for them. The Clark base (next to Angeles City, north of Manila) was perfect. It covered an area of 37 square kilometers and had been the largest US military base on foreign soil, housing 15,000 people.

The military had gone, but they had left behind a terrible toxic legacy. Neither the government nor the Filipino temporary inhabitants knew how badly contaminated the drinking water and soil was – though the US military were certainly aware of the situation. There had even been a proposal before US forces' departure to remove the PCBs, asbestos and other hazardous wastes accumulated over the years, which would have cost about $8.4 million. The clean-up project was 'parked' in a drawer and then finally abandoned after the failure to renew the lease agreement.

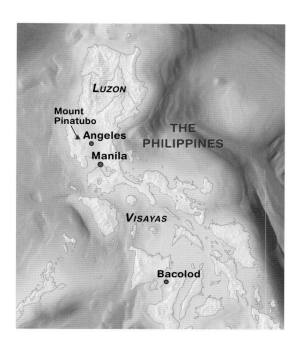

The Pinatubo volcano was active for about a decade, leaving thousands of families homeless. In May 1994, the village where Crizel's family lived was literally swallowed by mud and the survivors were taken to the Clark base. Crizel was just one year old when she arrived in her makeshift home and, shortly after, her family was relocated to a nearby settlement. They had just escaped death, but little did they know that their stay at the base would leave them a cruel legacy.

Within a few years, there was an alarming increase in the number of children and adults diagnosed with serious diseases who had passed through the refugee centers at the former military bases. When she was five, little Crizel was diagnosed with leukemia. She fought against the terrible disease for a year, undergoing chemotherapy and multiple blood transfusions.

When the *Rainbow Warrior* arrived in Manila, Crizel was receiving a blood transfusion every two days and it had been decided that she needed a bone marrow transplant. Two weeks earlier, while in hospital, Crizel and her mother had been interviewed by the local media. Crizel's mother said: 'The water we got from the wells smelled so bad and it was like that everywhere.' Despite being very weak, Crizel told reporters: 'The Americans, they ought to clean... They did this.' Along with them, there were another 20 people in the hospital, mostly children, who were also victims of contaminated water.

Despite her young age, Crizel was very feisty. And besides this, she was an artist. While spending long hours in the hospital she painted colorful butterflies, birds, flowers, hearts and happy children; drawings that were then transformed into cards whose sales paid not only her own medical bills but also those of other victims. The travelling exhibition mounted by the *Rainbow Warrior* on the toxic legacy of US bases contained these drawings and they even went all the way to the US.

On that sunny afternoon, the ship's third in the Philippines, the *Rainbow Warrior* received a visit from a group of about 20 children who had grown up inside or in the vicinity of the former military installations. Getting kids on board always involves, on the one hand, a bigger logistical effort and more crew involvement, because of the greater responsibility. On the other hand, there is greater enjoyment in planting a seed of awareness of the need to care for the planet, our common home. That group of children was also very special because all of them were seriously ill. Crizel was among them.

As soon as the young visitors came on board, the ship's doctor, Lawrence 'Butch' Turk, was called up to the bridge to examine a girl who was very ill. He found Crizel in a semi-lethargic state, with a trickle of blood flowing from her gums. Butch and Crizel's mother decided to take her to hospital immediately. To make the trip to the boat, she had skipped a blood transfusion and on the road (an hour and a half's drive) she had vomited blood. When they were at the wharf, Crizel gathered her remaining strength and began to turn in her mother's arms, crying and hitting her shoulder. It was obvious that she did not want to be taken away.

Of course she did not want to go. She had been waiting for that day for a long time. Her doctor had prescribed having her wishes fulfilled as the best possible medicine for Crizel and visiting the *Rainbow Warrior* was undoubtedly the greatest

Crizel's painting of the *Rainbow Warrior*.

dream that she had in those critical moments of her life. Weeks before, she had been told that a sailing boat with a rainbow drawn on her hull would come to help her and all the other children suffering from terrible diseases. She was also told that it was called the *Rainbow Warrior* and that it was from an organization called Greenpeace. Knowing that she could visit the ship had been a source of great excitement for Crizel. Showing off her artist's heart, she reflected it in the large drawing mentioned at the beginning of this chapter and reproduced above, a work of art which was eventually to become the Greenpeace poster for the Philippine leg of the 'Toxic Free Asia Tour'.

Given the child's reaction, it was decided to bring her back on board. There she also had the invaluable help of Nerissa Augustine, a nurse who had been in charge of caring for the sick children in the bases and who had known Crizel for a

Water analysis of the Clark base in 2002 showed that it contained PCBs, asbestos, solvents, nitrates, benzenes, various heavy metals (with a high presence of mercury) and pesticides, among others.

Diseases resulting from this contamination include cancer, nervous system and kidney disorders, babies with genetic defects, abortions, liver tuberculosis, skin diseases, and respiratory and heart problems.

long time. Nerissa was an active member of the Philippine organization The People's Task Force for Bases Clean-up, which had been supporting the victims of this toxic pollution since 1994.[6]

Amongst other activities, a small tour of the harbor in one of the *Rainbow Warrior*'s inflatables was organized for the children. It was outrageous to hear during the tour that the US warship *Fort McHenry*, which was anchored close by, radioed port security to say that the Greenpeace boat carrying children was getting too close and that they would be shot at if they continued to approach (it was unclear whether the threat involved steel bullets or a water cannon).

Obviously Crizel did not want to miss the experience of a short ride in the inflatable. When it was her turn, she sat on Butch's lap, holding the wheel, assisted by Captain Pete Willcox. A smiling Crizel felt the movement of small waves on the hull and the sea breeze caressing her face while having the small boat 'under her command'.

Back on the ship, the girl was exhausted but happy. She was taken to the hospital-cabin to rest after so much excitement. Crizel laid back, closed her eyes and never opened them again. She surely

went to sleep thinking about the last two hours she had just lived. They may well have been the happiest two hours of her life.

The death on board the *Rainbow Warrior* of this little environmental warrior greatly helped her cause. The news of her death shocked not only the crew and the others present, but spread across the country and beyond its borders. The horror that had been left behind by the US military in the Philippines had been highlighted all over the world, including in the country that had caused the tragedy.

Working on Greenpeace ships allows you to have an overall sense of the level of destruction suffered by the planet, not just from what you read in the press, or watch on TV. You see it with your own eyes, you feel it under your feet or your nose smells it. You witness all kinds of terrible assaults on the planet and the beings who dwell here. As a direct witness to these assaults, you can be overwhelmed by a mixture of emotions – anger, outrage and impotence among them. However, I believe that very few of those on board had ever experienced the feeling of desolation that descended upon them when Crizel died. Incredibly, it was Crizel's mother

One fine last ride: Crizel steering the Greenpeace inflatable, the *Avon*.

SHAILENDRA YASHWANT / GREENPEACE

The actual number of victims of the 'drinking water supply' pollution in the two former US bases is unknown because the only available data is on children with serious illnesses and disorders. Crizel was victim number 81. In the case of poor families, adults prefer to die at home rather than go to a hospital and become a burden on their families.

who consoled the afflicted crew, grateful for her daughter's happiness at her moment of death. That night, a special silence reigned on board the ship.

But it was not just grief or sadness that was felt on the *Rainbow Warrior*, there was also a huge sense of rage at this gross injustice. The following day, the crew returned to work even harder than before. Sometimes it was necessary to hold back the tears. But giving up would have meant betraying Crizel.

On the 10th anniversary of Crizel's death, the *Rainbow Warrior* returned to the Philippines, this time on a tour advocating the development of clean energy. A simple ceremony was held in her memory on the bridge. There were many people present who had lived through Crizel's death.

Each anniversary of her death should serve as a reminder that there are many Crizels in the world. There is still much to do to eliminate all the chemicals that are causing so much harm to the living creatures that populate this planet. There will come a day when toxic substances will be a thing of the dark past.

Hope

A Spanish saying goes: '*La esperanza es lo último que se pierde*' – Hope is the last thing you lose. Hope is vital for survival. In the most terrible adversity, humans draw the strength to keep going by relying on the hope that the situation will eventually improve. If hope is lost, all is lost.

Greenpeace is physically present in many countries through its offices and also has an important role in international political lobbying in defense of the environment and peace. After 40 years, the organization is well known almost everywhere. For a small community that is facing a major ecological problem, the simple fact of having Greenpeace

On the morning of 3 March 2000, Greenpeace deposited a large container in front of the US Embassy in Manila. It contained two transformers with highly toxic elements (including PCBs) that had previously been removed from a residential area near the Clark base. The looting of the bases had been constant, contributing to the spread of the toxic-pollution problem and the creation of numerous uncontrolled dumps in new residential areas.

The US government merely stated that its troops maintained environmental standards when they were in the Philippines and that they bore no legal responsibility for the toxic-waste problem.

SHAILENDRA YASHWANT / GREENPEACE

The *Rainbow Warrior* in the North Pacific, on the Japanese leg of the Toxic-free Asia Tour.

support often means that their problem transcends the local and gains the notice of the national and sometimes international media. With this, hope that the problem will be resolved greatly increases.

However, Greenpeace amounts to much more than its offices. The organization's most distinct symbols are its ships. The Greenpeace ships sail the planet's oceans and, thanks to them, we can be witnesses to what happens in places that are only accessible by sea. This makes them a very useful campaign tool. Since they also attract intense media interest, the ships carry the hope of finally being heard to communities and environmental groups all over the world. In this particular case in Manila, when the *Rainbow Warrior* opened her doors to the victims of the toxic contamination at the Subic and Clark bases, she was bringing hope.

Certainly, the injustice suffered by the victims of the accidents, oversights or excesses of big business (whether civilian or military) would be much greater if they were also forgotten. Particularly in relation to the two cases of mass poisoning covered in this chapter, it is worth remembering the International Criminal Court's definition of Crimes Against Humanity: 'Any inhumane acts causing great suffering or harm to the physical or mental health of those who suffer it if such conducts are carried out as part of a widespread or systematic attack against any civilian population, with knowledge of the attack.'

However, it is also true that the hope of improving the situation is also part of the present. After awareness-raising campaigns about toxic damage, more and more large companies are shifting to alternative or clean technologies, as is the case of IKEA (for furniture and fabrics) and electronics giants such as HP, Samsung, Nokia and Sony. Thanks to the Greenpeace 'Detox' campaign, which began in 2011, sportswear giants such as Puma, Nike and Adidas and, later, Zara, Levi's, Mango,

C&A and Benetton have pledged to eliminate toxic substances from their supply chain and products.

Perhaps due to the increase in environmental problems, more and more people are becoming aware and are doing what they can to address matters in their own local areas. The combination of all these efforts has the effect of improving the global situation and thus the hope that we will create a healthier planet greatly increases. The more of us who act to protect the environment, the stronger will be the pressure, and the more we will achieve.

Twelve years after the tour

• India: The struggle of the Bhopal victims continues. In October 2009, the Indian government prevented the US ship *Platinum II* from stranding (being driven ashore) at Alang, as it was suspected it would circumvent the Basel Convention. Internationally, several agencies work together to regulate shipbreaking.

• Thailand: No more incinerators have been built. Mainly due to strong opposition from local communities, there is now more control over the emission of dioxins, and alternatives for waste management (including composting and recycling) have begun to be implemented. The central power plant in the province of Prachuab Khiri Khan has not been built and there is an energy plan in place that promotes renewable energy.

• Philippines: the government has set a timetable to close all landfills. It also promotes the principle of separating solid waste at source, and incineration and open burning have been banned. A coalition of 150 organizations (including Greenpeace) has achieved the banning of plastic bags and Styrofoam trays in over 30 municipalities. All factories that polluted the Pasig River have been moved to industrial parks with water treatment plants and the river is being cleaned. Today, water pollution in the former US bases remains unsolved but the construction of the first Asian non-combustion facility for destroying PCBs was completed with UN assistance in Bataan in 2012.

• Hong Kong: The territory still uses incineration as its only way of managing waste.

• Japan: Just months after the *Rainbow Warrior* left the country, the Japanese government announced a plan to rehabilitate the island of Teshima and to clean up contaminated land around the landfill.

• An example of progress in the control of chemicals is the REACH Regulation, which entered into force in the European Union on 1 June 2007. It regulates safe chemical use in each member country.[7]

1 Methyl isocyanate gas is more toxic than cyanide. 2 Depending on the source, numbers vary between 3,800 and 15,000 deaths. 3 Asbestos has been used in construction, steelmaking, and packaging due to its fire-resistant qualities. The two diseases associated with breathing in its fibers are asbestosis (a type of pulmonary fibrosis) and mesothelioma (lung, pleura and peritoneum cancer). Both have a long 'latency period' which can exceed 30 years so although asbestos has been banned in many countries there could still be thousands of deaths in the coming years. 4 Biocides are chemicals that destroy undesirable life forms as they are toxic to micro-organisms. There are three classes: insecticides, herbicides and fungicides. 5 The Basel Convention on the Control of Transboundary Movements of Hazardous Waste and their Disposal came into force in 1992 under the auspices of United Nations. It currently has 170 member countries. 6 The People's Task Force for Bases Clean-up and was born in 1994 as part of the 'Nuclear Free Philippines' coalition. The group has forced the government to undertake research into pollution at the former bases. It also offers the victims ' families legal assistance in taking the US to court to establish the country's responsibility for the illnesses produced and for cleaning up the contaminated areas. 7 *REACH* (Registration, Evaluation, Authorization and Restriction of Chemical substances) is a European Union regulation addressing the production and use of chemical substances. It primarily seeks to ensure a high level of protection for human health and the environment while promoting competitiveness and innovation in the industrial sector within EU member states. It calls for the replacement of the most dangerous chemicals with safer alternatives.

'What we are doing to the forests of the world is but a mirror reflection of what we are doing to ourselves and to one another'

Mohandas Gandhi

5 In defense of forests

This chapter is dedicated to the memory of Mar Olivar

Introduction
Save or delete? Bloodwood (Spain, 2002) • A question of *Honour* (Spain, 2003)
Paradise on Earth To the beat of drums (Papua New Guinea, 1997) • Riots in Papua (2006) • On the road to Bali (Indonesia, 2007)

FOR MILLIONS OF years, human existence and development has depended on the largest plants living on our planet. In addition to food and shelter, trees have provided us with medicine, fuel, building materials for our homes and boats as well as furniture and pulp to make paper. Above all else, they have provided us with the oxygen that keeps us alive. Without these planetary lungs, we would not be able to breathe.

'Even if I knew that tomorrow the world would go to pieces, I would still plant my apple tree,' said Martin Luther King Jr. Despite rampant deforestation, there will, according to the UN Food and Agriculture Organization (FAO), be an increase in global forest cover during the decade from 2011 to 2020 once new plantations are taken into account. However, plantations, although positive developments in themselves, can never substitute for the ancient forests that originally covered the Earth.

'Ancient Forests' is the name given to the large unbroken original forests that have remained intact and in which two-thirds of the Planet's biodiversity survives. There are only seven areas of ancient forest left, which cover just seven per cent of the Earth´s surface. They are located in the Amazon basin, in the Congo, in Southeast Asia, in eastern Siberia, in North America, in Patagonia and in parts of northern Europe.

Millions of plant and animal species, along with diverse indigenous human groups, make their home within the varied habitats of these

It has been calculated that during periods of normal extinction a species disappears every four years. Mainly due to the loss of forests, currently thousands of species become extinct every year – we are effectively talking about the sixth-largest mass extinction in the history of our planet. This time, the great biological crisis is not due to any single catastrophe but to the actions of a single species: humans.

85

forests. Progressively, in recent centuries, so-called 'development' by humans has brought with it the destruction of huge tracts of forest area on every continent and thus, the death and disappearance of those forest inhabitants.

In Western societies, most people do not ask where the wood from their table comes from or what trees have been felled so that they can use a tissue or a sheet of paper. Simply put, the environmental cost involved in many of the small actions that we perform on a daily basis is ignored. I feel a great sadness when I consider the millions of trees that have already gone and those that will be swept away in our toilets or discarded in our wastepaper bins.

In the world that we have created, trees are worth more dead than alive. They are quantified either in terms of something inert (the long pole that will be transformed into something consumable) or in terms of the benefit created by their disappearance (with pastures cleared for cattle, minerals extracted or plantations established).

Deforestation now has many different drivers. For example, production of paper has been a major cause of deforestation in North America but in the Amazon the major destruction of forest areas

According to the FAO, between 2000 and 2010, 13 million hectares of forests – the equivalent of the surface area of Costa Rica – were lost or converted for other use every year. Ancient Forests used to account for 36% of the Earth's total landmass but in that 10 years they declined by more than 40 million hectares – an area the size of Germany and Denmark put together.

has been driven mainly by cattle ranching and soybean crops.

Greenpeace has spent many years working on different fronts to stop the destruction of the last great forests. We work with the authorities as well as local communities in the countries or regions where Ancient Forests still exist to develop sustainable forms of exploitation, to promote protective legislation and to create protected areas. In the countries which receive the raw material, Greenpeace carries out campaigns to generate awareness and also lobbies for change in legislation to prevent illegal importation.

Finally, we also work to protect forests by using the organization's ships since, in many cases, they are the perfect tools for direct action in this field.

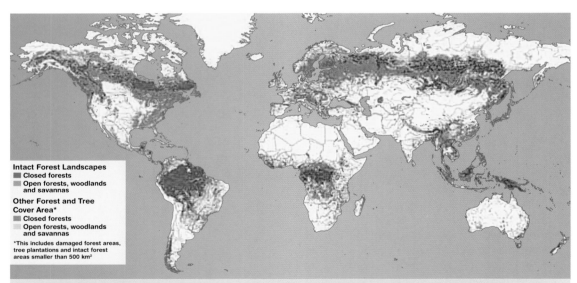

Intact Forest Landscapes
■ Closed forests
■ Open forests, woodlands
   and savannas

Other Forest and Tree
Cover Area*
■ Closed forests
□ Open forests, woodlands
   and savannas

*This includes damaged forest areas,
tree plantations and intact forest
areas smaller than 500 km²

As of 8,000 years ago, ancient forests covered over half of the Earth's surface. Around 80% of these original forests have been destroyed or altered – and those remaining are under threat.

Amazon rainforest in all its density. Life on Earth depends on forests, which are among the principal carbon sinks and thus vital to climate stability. In addition, a fifth of all greenhouse gases derive from deforestation and the changes in land use associated with it.

Save or delete?

For two consecutive years, 2002 and 2003, the *Rainbow Warrior* toured the Mediterranean visiting European countries that were importing illegal timber from tropical forests. This was how the ship contributed to the great efforts that the organization was making worldwide to try to save the last ancient forests before they were completely and irrevocably destroyed – a campaign that had as its slogan the words 'Save or delete?'.

The European Union is one of the world's largest importers of wood and the main objective of this campaign was to establish a legislative policy guaranteeing that timber imports would not come from illegal logging.

In the two stories below, the ships that were intercepted were carrying logs from African forests, the largest remaining tract of tropical forest after the Amazon. These forests are home to the great apes as well as to 400 other species of mammals, over 1,000 species of birds and at least 10,000 plant species.

Bloodwood (Spain, 2002)

Josevi Alamar finally finished positioning the little banner in the right place so as to serve as a windbreaker for the night. Up on the mast's little platform, the wind was chilly that March morning in 2002. Tucked into his sack, he reviewed what had happened on that tiring day. That same morning, he and Juan Antonio Valle (Juanito) had been picked up at the port of Sagunto, near Valencia, Spain, and been taken to the *Rainbow Warrior*. Both had been very excited: it was their first action on a ship. After dinner, with adrenaline coursing through their bodies, an inflatable speedboat had transported them to their target: the *Meltemi*, a ship loaded with illegal timber from Liberia. Although it had been easy to board the ship, once up on deck they had encountered resistance from some sailors – one

DANIEL BELTRÁ / GREENPEACE

(Far left) A Greenpeace Spain poster opposing forest destruction. It translates as: 'Don't destroy my home to build yours.'

[Left] The Spanish activist and biologist Josevi, photographed on his platform on the mast of the *Meltemi*, where he spent two nights. In the background are the logs the ship had transported from the forests of Liberia. The banner translates as 'Save the primary forests'.

of them had even rushed at Josevi and snatched a small banner. Keeping calm, each one climbed up a mast to replace the two activists who had been occupying those positions for over 15 hours. All curled up, Josevi recalled how stringing the large banner between the two masts had proved to be a nightmarish task lasting several hours – partly because of their inexperience but also because Juanito was such a perfectionist. Exhausted by his endeavors, and rocked by the gentle waves of the Mediterranean Sea, Josevi fell asleep.

The sun had already risen by the time the activists descended to inspect the huge logs, many more than two meters in diameter. With them, they discovered spiders, many different insects and even one small reptile. Josevi, a biologist, was doubly outraged: in addition to being illegal timber, this would mean tropical wildlife entering the continent unnoticed. Unexpectedly, the past came back to him. As a child he had lived near the port of Valencia, and had spent many hours climbing and running around logs exactly like these, some of them so huge that his young mind could not imagine they were trees. He also recalled seeing unusual animals in between the logs. However, walking among these large logs and discovering exotic animals was no longer a

game. Now he was part of the desperate struggle to prevent the remaining tropical trees from being converted into dead wood and to ensure the survival of its sheltering wildlife.

That is when the Greenpeace activists made another discovery that gave the situation an entirely unexpected twist. They saw a group of African men taking it in turns to poke their faces through the small barred windows of a locked room under the bridge. The ship was carrying stowaways! Juanito had just communicated this by radio to the *Rainbow Warrior* when the captain of the *Meltemi* invited him to his cabin for a chat.

While Juanito swallowed the bitter and earthy Turkish coffee as best he could, the captain told him how, after each of the stowaways had appeared, they had been fed and housed in that room. They had sneaked on board in Monrovia, the Liberian capital. Despite having communicated this to the authorities wherever the ship had docked, so far no country had accepted these refugees. The captain, a Greek man in his sixties, seemed to Juanito both to be sympathetic to the refugees and to understand their plight.

It was afternoon when Juanito, back at his post, saw him. A very tall and extremely thin man, barely managing to crawl up the log pile. His black skin was covered in a white powder. As fast as he could, Juanito descended from the mast and ran to take the exhausted body in his arms. His face had the pallor of a corpse and his gaze was unfocused. He had been hiding for three weeks. The crew moved into action straight away: they covered him and brought him water and a hot soup which Juanito fed him in small sips. Finally, he was moved to a cabin.

A while later, Juanito was again in the captain's cabin struggling with another bitter and thick coffee. In a state of semi-shock, he learned that it is common practice on fishing boats and cargo ships to throw live stowaways overboard. If there's no person, there's no problem. How many people die annually, murdered in this manner? The captain had a horrifying story to tell from Monrovia. While still in port, three stowaways had been discovered and the police called. While the third one was being dealt with, the other two, who were already handcuffed, had jumped overboard. They had preferred suicide than to live through what awaited them: torture or death amid the horrors of the Second Liberian Civil War.[1] Enveloped by the starry sky, each in his own little platform, it took Juanito and Josevi a long time to fall asleep that night – despite the delicious warm soup 'courtesy of the house' and despite their tiredness. They were simply too disturbed by all that they had learned.

Next morning, Juanito went to the *Rainbow Warrior* to discuss the new situation that had presented itself, carrying with him a note from the stowaways: 'Help, help, help! We need your help and the help of United Nations. We are seven Liberians we fled the war. War. We seek refuge, our whole life is in danger in Liberia.'[2] The stowaways had also asked him to call the police. 'Don't worry, the police will come,' Juanito had said to them.

The fate of Liberia, a country founded in the mid-19th century by freed US slaves, was for several years tragically bound to its neighbor: Sierra Leone. Mined diamonds (whose trade was banned internationally in 2001) were exchanged for weapons from Liberia which in turn had been bought with money obtained from the illegal trade in tropical timber. Both countries were engaged in bloody civil wars with different factions vying for control of their natural resources.

The *Meltemi* was not only carrying logs stained with blood. Direct victims of the conflict were also on board. Legitimately fleeing from poverty, hunger, violence and death, they had to be helped to escape this horror. As a spontaneous reaction, the crew from the *Rainbow Warrior* sent them food. On land, Greenpeace Spain was already contacting several organizations (Amnesty International and SOS Racism, amongst others) requesting refugee status for them.

After the meeting, Juanito returned to the *Meltemi*. Taking advantage of calm seas and light breezes, the *Rainbow Warrior* decided to try out the towering sail-banner – 'Save the Last Ancient Forests' – that had been made for the campaign. It had been planned that, later on, one of the ship's inflatable boats, the *Avon*, would be sent to the port to pick up some journalists, along with a group of activists dressed as 'The Magnificent Seven' (seven animals chosen as symbols of the ancient forests at risk). The plan was to hoist the 'forest sails' to receive them. But none of these things took place...

At this point Josevi reluctantly had to leave, and his departure coincided with the arrival of the guests. The *Avon* was nearing the entrance to the port when a Guardia Civil patrol boat came out to meet it – the Guardia Civil being a Spanish national security force, separate from the police and military in nature.

Rainbow Warrior II displaying the banner sails for the Ancient Forests campaign.

DANIEL BELTRÁ / GREENPEACE

'Hold on tight', shouted the driver as he turned the wheel of the *Avon* 180 degrees and began to fly over the waves. On board the *Rainbow Warrior*, the captain, Pete Willcox, had just sounded the general alarm after detecting on the radar several points moving out of the port at great speed.

The news caught everyone by surprise: the previous day, the Guardia Civil had amicably told the Greenpeace people that they could relax as 'tomorrow is Sunday and in Spain nobody works on Sundays'. Having believed this, the activists were less than prepared and now had to scramble to put their boats into the water. They had to try to stop the pilot from boarding the *Meltemi* and directing the ship into port.

Back on the *Meltemi* itself, Juanito was at that point having yet another coffee with the captain in his cabin when an officer burst in with the news. The captain immediately said to Juanito: 'Quickly! Take your position – the police are coming!'

From the platforms of their respective masts, Juanito and the activist who had replaced Josevi then watched the dramatic arrests of their companions below. A light aircraft which had been rented to take pictures of the ships appeared on the scene and also witnessed the arrests. Despite the repeated calls from the airport control tower ordering the pilot to leave the air corridor immediately, he managed to make a couple of loops, responding that he had problems with the radio and did not hear them well. He did not want to miss the spectacle taking place below.

Guardia Civil officers, dressed all in black, jumped from their boats on to those belonging to Greenpeace and the activists in their orange overalls tried to dodge them as well as they could. Some activists who had already been arrested jumped into the water or on to other boats in an attempt to escape.

In little more than half an hour, however, all the activists had been arrested and the *Rainbow Warrior* had 'surrendered'. As the Greenpeace inflatables arrived in port, driven by the Guardia Civil officers, Greenpeace supporters mistakenly applauded, not realizing what had just happened. A little while later, the *Meltemi* was finally tied to the dock and those arrested were released, along with their boats.

It was not until the next morning that the police finally managed to evict the two climbers from their positions on the masts of the cargo ship. Subsequently, the ship unloaded its illegal timber.

But what happened to the other 'illegal' cargo on board? Sadly, hypocrisy triumphed. Despite pressure from Greenpeace and the other organizations involved, no lawyer was permitted to talk to the eight stowaways. The Red Cross was given permission to give them a medical examination, on the basis of

Spiderman at large. It took the Spanish firefighters more than two hours to capture this activist once they had boarded the *Meltemi*. Every time they reached for him, he would escape by climbing up and down the greasy cables of the ship's cranes.

PEDRO ARMESTRE / GREENPEACE

which the Spanish authorities allowed one of the refugees to stay in the country, as he was a minor.

So the illegal timber was unloaded on to Spanish soil without further problems, but the people whose lives were on the line failed to be accepted as refugees. Aboard the *Meltemi*, they continued their journey of uncertain destination, in search of shelter in any European country that would take them in.

The international community eventually responded in the face of the great environmental and human rights tragedy unfolding in Liberia. On 7 May 2003, the UN Security Council established a worldwide embargo on wood from Liberia.

A question of *Honour* (Spain, 2003)

Barely a year after its dealing with the *Meltemi*, the *Rainbow Warrior* found herself again at the port of Valencia. She was anchored there for days, waiting for the *Honour* to appear on the horizon – another cargo ship laden with illegal wood, this time from the tropical forests of Cameroon in Central Africa.

At about one in the morning of 6 June, the silence of the bridge was interrupted by a radio call: the captain of the *Honour* was requesting a pilot to guide them into port. Nacho Garnacho – a Spanish volunteer who had just stepped on board the *Rainbow Warrior* for the first time – felt his heart jump. At last the ship had arrived! The absolute stillness on the *Rainbow Warrior* swiftly changed into a great bustle of preparation for the action.

The first phase of the protest was conducted with great success. Greenpeace's small boats managed to prevent the pilot from climbing on board the *Honour* and, in the face of that, its captain decided to drop anchor. It was another Spaniard, Gonzalo Montón, who first climbed up the anchor chain and attached the small board that would serve as a seat. With the activist in place, the cargo ship could not move in any direction. It was about four in the morning and in that position – not exactly comfortable – Gonzalo remained for eight hours in relative solitude despite *Honour* crew members showering him three times with freezing water.

The new Forest Tour in the Mediterranean had begun in Spain on 29 May with the arrival of the *Rainbow Warrior* in Barcelona and the presentation of a report that exposed the reality of illegal timber imports to Spain. Prior to this night in Valencia, the ship's crew, together with Spanish volunteers, had already conducted a couple of actions in Catalunya[3] denouncing the situation and calling for obligatory certificates of sustainability for all imported wood (in the form of logs, paper and furniture) as a way of halting the ravaging of ancient forests.[4]

This demonstration in Barcelona carries its slogan in both Catalan and Spanish: 'No more illegal timber.' According to Greenpeace Spain's report, illegal wood made up 10.5% of the total timber imported in 2001 – an overwhelming 860,000 cubic meters. This compared with imports of just 4,000 cubic meters of sustainable forest wood.

DANIEL BELTRA / GREENPEACE

Gonzalo was not relieved until noon. On arriving back on the *Rainbow Warrior,* the activist launched himself onto his bunk to stretch his body and finally sleep. Meanwhile, Nacho and other volunteers were in the hold getting ready to climb the masts of the *Honour.* The unexpected appearance of the Guardia Civil changed everybody's plans. Gonzalo was awoken from his short slumber and a little later he was back on the *Honour,* this time perched on the pilot's ladder with the job of blocking it.

The Guardia Civil's boats were divided into two groups. The first of them focused on attacking the *Rainbow Warrior.* Two military patrol boats chased the Greenpeace ship and their greater speed soon had them positioned on each side, at which point officers began to board. Several Greenpeace crew members physically tried to prevent the officers accessing the deck, but it was useless – there were more than 30 of them! While some officers headed to the upper deck, others penetrated the interior of the ship. Tapio Pekkanen, the Chief Engineer, could not hide his astonishment when various officers descended *en masse* to the engine room – the lowest point of the boat – and asked for the wheelhouse.

Meanwhile, outside, the wheelhouse was being attacked. An officer grabbed a metal bar used to secure the sail ropes and started to pound one of the wheelhouse windows. All those inside at that point decided to give in and open the doors. Having taken control of the ship, the Guardia Civil headed for the port.

While this was going on, several military inflatables headed to the *Honour.* Seeing them coming, Gonzalo climbed aboard and up a high ladder from which he was later removed by yanking and a few wallops, especially on one leg. Given this rough treatment, the activist was subsequently surprised by the cordial treatment he received at the police station. There, an agent showed him his screensaver, a photo of himself as a civilian visiting the *Rainbow Warrior.* He opened up to Gonzalo and said: 'We follow you. After the Greenpeace protests, many legal activities are considered crimes and then we act to pursue these new offenses.' This remark may have had some truth in it but it did not excuse the bruises on

Invasion under way: officers of the Guardia Civil in the process of boarding the *Rainbow Warrior* on 6 June 2003.

DANIEL BELTRA / GREENPEACE

this pacifist's leg. Once in his cell, an exhausted Gonzalo was finally able to sleep.

The next morning, as the six detainees were released after paying a fine of 630 euros, the *Honour* began to unload its illegal logs with impunity. The big surprise was that the Spanish government decided to impose a bond of 300,000 euros for the release of the *Rainbow Warrior.* This disproportionate figure was the highest bond ever requested for the release of a ship in Spain, even higher than that asked for the *Prestige* (see Chapter 7). Ship's captain Joel Stewart made the Greenpeace view clear: 'The Spanish government should be pursuing the criminals who destroy the forests of the planet rather than challenging the democratic right of peaceful protest.' In defense of that important civil right and to avoid a dangerous precedent, Greenpeace decided not to pay the bond and began to fight inside and outside of the courts while the *Rainbow Warrior* was detained at the port in Valencia. The days passed by and the protests calling for her release continued.

A week after the action, the news that the parliament in Catalunya had approved a law promoting the purchase of certified wood was received with euphoria. Despite this, the ship remained under arrest. By the end of the second week, more than 30,000 email messages had arrived calling for its release. As the days went by, the situation became more outrageous and support for Greenpeace grew. It was anecdotally reported that a diver, who regularly collected mussels in the port, gifted several bags to the *Rainbow Warrior*. Once he had left, the mussels were thrown overboard, returned to the polluted waters from which they had come.

Bikes on the 'Peace Path'

Several crew members joined the monthly Critical Mass bike ride.[5] A few days later, Critical Mass Valencia organized a bicycle protest in support of the *Rainbow Warrior*, which the authorities did not allow to reach the ship.

On the morning of 2 July (the 19th day of the ship's detention), Gonzalo and other Greenpeace Spain activists unfurled a large banner at an iconic building in Valencia denouncing the destruction of our ancient forests and asking for the release of the *Rainbow Warrior*. The activists still managed to get to the ship in time for lunch, however, where they met Chrissie Hynde and her band, The Pretenders. That night, the rock group gave a gala concert and the large banner that had been used that morning was now displayed as the backdrop to the stage. While the *Rainbow Warrior* remained under arrest, timber extracted illegally from the last ancient forests of the world continued to enter unhindered into different ports in Spain and the rest of Europe.

Two days later, there was a flood of protests in front of Spanish embassies on all five continents. On Day 21, news arrived that the Spanish government had lowered the bond from 300,000 to 6,000 euros. The organization agreed to pay that amount. In a final surprise, however, it was also forced to pay the expensive mooring costs for each day it had spent in port! But finally the Greenpeace flagship was free to sail to other Mediterranean countries to continue her campaigning work.

After 10 years of campaigning, the European Parliament banned the trade in illegally harvested forest products in July 2010.

Rainbow Warrior captain Joel Stewart with rock musician Chrissie Hynde of The Pretenders, who said: 'The Spanish government is more interested in persecuting the protesters than the companies importing illegally logged wood.'

Gagged. The country's main ecologist organizations, trades unions and many Spanish celebrities united in proclaiming that the arrest of the ship was a violation of civil liberties.

Paradise on Earth

The so-called 'Paradise Forests' are a big blanket of green covering Indonesia, Malaysia, West Papua, Papua New Guinea and the Solomon Islands. They include both mangrove and swamp forests as well as rainforest. They form the world's third-largest tropical forest and the incredible biodiversity they shelter includes over 500 species of mammals and more than 1,600 species of birds, as well as 30,000 species of higher plants.

In the 1990s, these ancient forests came to the attention of some transnational logging companies, mainly based in Malaysia, which quickly secured rights to clear huge areas. In this part of the world, illegal logging and corruption within the forestry industry is particularly savage – it is estimated that, if 70 per cent of logging in Indonesia is illegal, in the case of Papua New Guinea the figure reaches 90 per cent.

In recent years, the intensive cultivation of palm oil has been identified as the main cause of forest destruction in Indonesia and Malaysia.

The visit to the Maisin indigenous people of Papua New Guinea in 1997 marked the beginning of a campaign for the protection of the Paradise Forests in which the *Rainbow Warrior* was to show her support on many different occasions over the years. In 2004, the ship visited Indonesia for the first time and in the Solomon Islands gave her support to an ecotimber project run by the Lobi Community. The establishment of Forest Rescue

> **Indonesia has the highest rate of deforestation in the world. In just 50 years, an area of ancient forest equivalent to twice the size of Germany has been logged, burned or degraded.**

Stations and Forest Defenders Camps involving local communities and organizations has been instrumental in halting *in situ* the destruction of these forests. The *Rainbow Warrior* was present at the launch of the station in Lake Murray in Papua New Guinea (in 2006), as well as the camp established in Riau, in the heart of Sumatra (in 2007).

To the beat of drums
(Papua New Guinea, 1997)

In the early 1990s, the different Maisin clans had joined together to fight for the preservation of their ancient rainforest, refusing to let any portion of its more than 200,000 hectares disappear under the chainsaw. Success in the struggle lay in the sustainable development of the entire community through marketing their unique tapa cloths, made from the bark of a tree on which each clan prints its own design.

'If heaven exists, it is located somewhere around the corner from Collingwood Bay,' thought Stephanie Mills, marvelling at the landscape that could be seen from the port side of the *Rainbow Warrior*: intact tropical forest spreading from the fringe of palm trees on the coastline all the way

Stopping points on *Rainbow Warrior*'s tours of the Asia-Pacific region between 1997 and 2007.

LUIS VASQUEZ

Boats of the Maisin indigenous people paddle out to meet and greet the *Rainbow Warrior* in northeast Papua New Guinea in 1997.

'Logging and mining is destruction, not development. We come from the land and are part of the land. We want to be the initiators and implementers of sustainable development, not observers or to be dictated to by people outside.' These words, uttered by Sylvester Moi – president of the local organization that manages the production and distribution of tapa cloths – epitomizes the spirit of the Maisin people.

up to the distant mountains, a vast palette of green hues that extended beyond sight. The ship had reached the territory of the Maisin people, located in the northeast of Papua New Guinea.

Deckhand Kingsford Rarama was especially excited when the ship finally anchored in front of the villages of Uiaku and Gangiga because he actually came from the latter. Two large canoes welcomed the ship with the rite, widespread in the South Pacific, of 'challenging' the outsiders in a dance in which men make threatening gestures. When the crew reached land they were surrounded by hundreds of people dancing for them, dressed in beautifully decorated tapa-cloth skirts and wearing many precious ornaments (feather headdresses, necklaces of shells and flowers). The women bore magnificent facial tattoos with designs similar in pattern to the tapa cloths. The white coral sand under their feet resonated to the beat of the drums.

There was cause for celebration. Greenpeace Pacific had been working with the Maisin people for three years to develop a market for the export of their tapas (with the support of other organizations in host countries) and they had achieved very good results. The arrival of the *Rainbow Warrior* was an event of such magnitude that the 30 clans had joined together in the preparations, something which had not occurred for more than 100 years. The Maisin were grateful for the help and could finally show their various collaborators how they produced their 'treasure'. The other cause for celebration was that the *Rainbow Warrior* carried some solar panels in her hold which would operate the territory's first telephone.

The next day, after the telephone's inauguration ceremony and Sylvester Moi's speech, there was a great feast. To the sound of drums, the hosts took the crew to huts so as to dress them in tapa cloth and adorn them with ornaments. Although local women had their breasts exposed, they covered those of their guests following the mores of the evangelical church. For some of the guests, wearing the heavy feather headdresses was an unforgettable experience, as some of the feathers were like thorns.

Song dedicated to Greenpeace and sung by the children during the Maisin telephone's inauguration ceremony.

Peace, give us peace, Greenpeace
We are about to face a war
Maisin warriors against developers
Of our resourceful land

Rainbow and Maisin warriors
Together we stand to fight the war
Preserve for us our Melanesian way
In protecting our land

We stand out proud today
We have protected our land
Against developers of our resources
Through our wisdom

Peace, give us peace Greenpeace
Conserve Melanesian ways
Extend your rays of love, O Rainbow Warriors
And give us Peace

The crew would never forget the huge full moon that rose to the rhythm of the drums, a rhythm that they were completely unable to follow. Sitting on the beach, the weary visitors watched in amazement at how these people could not stop dancing while the drums continued to sound. And they sounded late into the night.

It seemed that the whole community wanted to see the *Rainbow Warrior* and so her inflatables ferried adults and children to and from it throughout the whole of the next day. During their breaks, crew members were able to accompany the women, the traditional manufacturers of tapa cloth, and discover the long, laborious and delicate process by which it was made. While the men spent days away from home hunting, these women worked as mothers, artists, cooks and farmers.

As it was the last night that they had with their guests, the rhythm of the drums filled the air until dawn. The ship's visit had brought about the union of all the clans, and therefore a revival of Maisin culture in which almost-buried old stories and half-forgotten songs returned to life. This greatly strengthened the identity of the community and its commitment to stop the destruction of its forests.

LUIS VASQUEZ

A Maisin woman showing off her decorative tattooing

PAPUA NEW GUINEA

PROTECT OUR ENVIROMENT

When *Rainbow Warrior II* visited the Maisin community in 1997, the crew received many tapa cloths as mementos. This tapa was made specifically for the ship and decorated the bulkhead of the hospital cabin until the ship's decommissioning.

THIJS NOTENBOOM

It was just noon when the *Rainbow Warrior* weighed anchor. It seemed it was difficult for the ship itself to leave and the reason was not because of the extra weight from the many tapas and other gifts that it was now carrying. The biggest ballast on board was the memory of every moment lived with the Maisin people, so much had the crew members learned about a way of living so different from their own. For Greenpeace Pacific, the visit had also been very important in terms of confirming on the ground the effective forest protection the Maisin had achieved in their territory.

In 1999, a small group of Maisin living in Papua New Guinea's capital, Port Moresby, betrayed their tribe by registering their ancestral lands in the name of a company that leased them to a Malaysian transnational logging company. Thirty-four Maisin elders went to court and managed to halt all logging activity. Finally, in May 2002, they obtained a ruling that recognized them as the legitimate landowners. The production of tapas had played an important role in linking the Maisin to their forests during the trial.

It took years for crew members Belén Momeñe and Joel Stewart to solve the mystery of 'the rhythmless' beat of the Maisin drums. A documentary on television was showing a male bird of paradise performing an incredible courtship dance to impress a female. When the bird began to beat its wings loudly, both jumped at once, 'That's it, that's the pace!' The Maisin are so close to their forest that they dance to the flapping rhythm of a bird in courtship.

Riots in Papua (2006)

It was a Friday morning in 2006. Two cars were speeding through the back streets of Jayapura, the capital of Papua. The two vehicles were avoiding major traffic routes, as these were being patrolled by armed police on motorbikes. Their occupants were Greenpeace people heading to the airport to drop off Emily Johnston and Bustar Maitar, who had to fly to Jakarta to continue co-ordinating the logistics of the *Rainbow Warrior* tour in defense of the Paradise Forests.

Bob Marley's album 'Exodus' was playing in one of the cars. The music was the perfect complement to the moment. The tension in the air could be cut with a knife. The day before, in student protests against the giant Freeport mine, the largest gold mine in the world, several police officers and civilians had been killed. These protests high-lighted the local antagonism against Indonesian rule in the western half of New Guinea, which is the second-largest island on the planet.

New Guinea owes its name to the Spanish that 'discovered' it in the 16th century. Subsequently, it was divided in two by its colonizers along the meridian line of longitude 141°, with Papua New Guinea – initially divided between the British, Germans and Australians but since 1975 an independent state – to the east. The western half, Papua, was part of the Dutch East Indies but has been subject to Indonesian rule since it was annexed in 1962.

For hundreds of years the inhabitants of New Guinea have suffered the consequences of these and other imaginary lines drawn on the territory by people alien to it. The lines follow obvious economic interests: a colony, a gold mine, wood for paper or land for palm oil. When these lines are drawn, the rightful owners of the land, the people who have lived there since ancient times, continue to be ignored. The decisions about their future are taken in offices far, far away.

'Exodus, movement of Jah people...' was heard over the speakers of the car. The *Rainbow Warrior* had already put out to sea and Emily and Bustar were the only two Greenpeace people that had not yet left Papua. Despite the fact that they were departing as scheduled, they had the terrible feeling of being on the run. They were also leaving with a heavy heart, knowing that a lot of

This is the *Rainbow Warrior* in the imagination of a six-year-old girl called Galuh, who knew her father would be away for many days as he was going to save the beautiful forests of the land of Papua – Hapsoro was responsible for the forest campaign in Indonesia and was on board throughout the whole of the 2006 Tour. Galuh drew this picture just days before her father finally came to Jakarta with the *Rainbow Warrior*, to show how proud she was of him, the ship and Greenpeace.

The colorful painting formed part of the ship's mess on the second *Rainbow Warrior*; on the third boat it found a place in the lounge. This painting is a fitting tribute to one of the most tenacious defenders of tropical forests: Hapsoro died in 2012.

the people they had met were at risk. High-level corruption as well as voracious economic interests inhabited the dark side of paradise. But they knew they would come back as soon as the political situation allowed. Bringing the *Rainbow Warrior* had only signalled the beginning of the work there.

The ship had just been in neighboring Papua New Guinea to support the launch of the 'Forest Rescue Station' in Lake Murray. Now it was time to focus efforts on Papua, since it housed the largest intact forest in the Asia-Pacific region, home to 16,000 species of plants, many birds and mammals, including marsupials, and the largest lizards and butterflies in the world.

When the ship arrived in Jayapura, the Kayopulau people gave it a colorful welcome with traditional dances. For a couple of days it was possible to follow the planned program: the ship opened to the public and, more importantly, a forum was held dedicated to sustainable forest use based on community management – the first such gathering of this kind. The forum was attended

In 2006, after discovering a large number of new species in the Foja mountains (about 3,000 square kilometers of almost intact tropical forest), scientists compared it to the 'Garden of Eden'.

OKA BUDHI / GREENPEACE

The arrival of the *Rainbow Warrior* in Jayapura, the capital of Papua, was marked by colorful traditional dancing by the local Kayopulau people.

by influential politicians, representatives of other NGOs and leaders from more than 15 indigenous groups. Everything was working well despite the social tensions. In this sense, the political instability of Indonesia's easternmost province was taken as read and the biggest concerns on board ship revolved around one theme: to unite locals so as to stop the dizzying destruction of these unique forests.

On the third day, several crew members had the morning off. The ship was due to set sail the day after and the temptation to exchange the cold metal of the deck for the warm sand and the masts of the ship for the trunks of palm trees was too much. So, early that morning, this little group went off to enjoy a beach break in this tropical paradise.

At that very moment, in the university area of the city, students began a protest calling for the closing of the big Freeport gold mine.[6] Like wildfire, word spread that violence had broken out and, with it, fears that civil war was beginning. The alarm went off on the ship – on the very day that part of the crew had gone to the beach! A rescue mission had to be hastily organized to bring them back to the ship. There was such a sense of peace in their little corner of paradise that it was hard for them to imagine what was happening just a few kilometers away.

A farewell ceremony had been scheduled for that evening, and many people had confirmed their attendance. What should be done? There were concerns as to whether the physical integrity of the *Rainbow Warrior* and the safety of her occupants could be maintained. After numerous consultations, it was decided to go ahead. The ceremony was performed and the guests were able to return safely to their homes. However, by the time the musicians and caterers finished tidying up, the police had blocked the roads. It was now too dangerous for those remaining to return to their homes. The *Rainbow Warrior* ended up giving shelter for the night to a few unexpected guests.

Leaving Jayapura and its tumultuous protests behind, the *Rainbow Warrior* continued on her westward journey to enter the waters of the newly created Indonesian province of West Papua (still part of the territory annexed in 1962) patrolling

At the *Rainbow Warrior*'s welcoming ceremony in Port Moresby – the capital of Papua New Guinea – in February 2006, this ceremonial paddle was presented to the ship. It had been carved at Lake Murray, near where Greenpeace had just settled a Forest Rescue Station. The ceremonial paddle was placed in the mess of *Rainbow Warrior II* and is currently in the lounge of *Rainbow Warrior III*.

and searching for forest crimes to report. During the ship's stay in Manokwari, the provincial capital, another successful forum on sustainable forest management involving different social sectors was held.

Finally, before leaving West Papua, the *Rainbow Warrior* carried out a nonviolent direct action in Sorong against the *MV Ardhianto*, which was carrying 9,000 cubic meters of illegal timber converted into cheap plywood. This inert cargo was destined for Japan, Korea and the US and consisted of more than 4,500 trees stolen from the rainforest of Papua.[7]

Greenpeace currently runs a small office in Papua.

On the road to Bali (Indonesia, 2007)

Sumatra is a large Indonesian island located southwest of the Malaysian peninsula. The Strait of Malacca is a shipping corridor, notorious to sailors as the haunt of pirates, which extends longitudinally between both of these territories. The island is particularly famous for two of its large mammals: the tiger and the orangutan. Both species (along with many others) are now critically endangered due to habitat loss. It is estimated that in less than 40 years, 50 per cent of Sumatra's forests have disappeared, to be converted into palm-oil plantations.

The protest against the *MV Ardhianto*, which was carrying a consignment of plywood derived from illegal timber destined for Japan, Korea and the US. An estimated 24% of Papua's forests and 46% of those in Papua New Guinea have been sold as concessions to logging companies.

STOP ANCIENT FOREST DESTRUCTION

DEAN SEWELL / GREENPEACE

In December 2007, a major global meeting was held on the island of Bali: COP13.[8] There, representatives of governments, institutions and organizations met for the 13th time to discuss climate change. Throughout the year, Greenpeace had been conducting numerous activities around the globe in a campaign called 'On the road to Bali', highlighting the urgent need to take serious steps to curb climate change. Taking the *Rainbow Warrior* to the meeting place was the final step in the campaign strategy.

Last-minute preparations for the ship and crew happened in Singapore. Brad Edge, the Action Co-ordinator, was one of the last on board. He had not set foot on the *Rainbow Warrior* since 2004 when he worked on the ship for the first time in Australia and his life changed forever: in that campaign he met his future wife and the mother of his children. The delight in returning to the ship soon turned to anguish when he discovered that the folder containing all the campaign documents (some of them essential) had been deleted from his laptop. Not even the super-efficient radio operator Hans Monker managed to find it. It took some time to get the documents back and Brad swore to himself that it was the last time he would use Windows as his operating system.

The first port of call was Dumai in the central Sumatran province of Riau. The transit from Singapore was short but quite risky and shifts were organized to watch out for pirates. As the ship neared its destination, crew members were amazed at the size of the existing palm-oil processing facilities in Dumai, from where more palm oil is exported than anywhere else in Indonesia. The atmosphere that surrounded them grew more dense, sometimes even becoming a stifling haze that caused the first coughs and chest irritations. Breathing in Dumai was so difficult that the use of a gas mask was required if one was to be outside for a while.

The first mission of the *Rainbow Warrior* aimed to block the exit of a ship carrying palm oil – the *Westama*. The ship anchored and preparations were made on deck. It was Brad who had solved the big problem of how to keep the ship near the tanker so as to prevent it moving, without being affected by the strong ocean current. The Australian proposed employing a common maneuver for small boats: using a double anchor to stop the ship turning around the anchor when the wind or current changed direction. It would be the first time that the environmentalist ship had used this technique and it was unclear as to whether it would be able to endure the pressure of a current that changed direction every six hours.

Captain Mike Fincken brought the *Rainbow Warrior* up to the *Westama*, passing within 50 meters of the big ship. When the ship reached the middle, Edward Patrick, the bosun, dropped the first anchor, thus beginning a maneuver that ended with the ship running parallel to the tanker, securely restrained by one anchor at the bow and another at the stern. The vessel was then in position and the *Westama* and its cargo of palm oil were blocked.

This high-caliber piece of direct action by the *Rainbow Warrior* and her crew met with huge media coverage in Indonesia – and succeeded in

An aerial shot of a palm-oil plantation bordering the forest in Riau, on the Indonesian island of Sumatra in 2007.

Despite the great strain the stern anchor was suffering – ships' hulls are designed to have the anchor at the bow – the *Rainbow Warrior* coped well. It was the third day of the action before the Indonesian authorities decided to intervene. The *Westama* was taken out 'by force' with the help of a large tug boat that pushed mercilessly at the rear of the *Rainbow Warrior* in order to open the way for the large tanker. The *Westama* and the 33,000 tonnes of palm oil that it was carrying were therefore soon lost on the horizon. Not, however, without one last attempt to halt its departure: the tanker's propeller had snagged the line attached to the buoy marking the *Warrior*'s stern anchor position and the ship had to stop once again to rid itself of the tangle.

finally opening a serious debate on deforestation at national level. Much of the public supported Greenpeace. With just two weeks to go before the opening of COP13, senior Indonesian politicians started to become nervous. The country's president convened an emergency meeting to discuss our request for a complete moratorium on forest destruction and the forest minister himself agreed to meet with Greenpeace.

It was not only the Indonesian authorities who did not sleep very well while the action lasted. If something had failed and the *Westama* had

The *Rainbow Warrior* is forced to give way to the *MT Westama*, which was carrying palm oil. This is exported for use in cosmetics and food as well as for conversion into biofuel. Greenhouse-gas emissions from the destruction of its forests makes Indonesia the world's third-biggest contributor to global warming.

Some other key victories in recent years
Brazilian Amazon Through presidential decrees, 8.4 million hectares have been protected. In 2006, McDonald's agrees not to be supplied by companies feeding their chickens with soybeans from newly deforested areas.

Canada In 2009, the agreement to protect the Great Bear Forest comes into force. That same year, the paper giant Kimberly-Clark (maker of brands such as Kleenex and Scott) incorporates recycled fibers and Forest Stewardship Council certification (FSC) in its supply chain. In 2010, Greenpeace and eight other NGOs agree to a truce with the logging industry.

Finland In 2010, the government excludes industrial logging in 80,000 hectares of intact forest in Lapland (preserving the way of life of the Sami people).

Indonesia In 2008, the giant corporation Unilever (maker of brands such as Dove and Sunsilk) supports the moratorium on the clearing of rainforests and peatlands for oil palm cultivation. After a global campaign against the brand KitKat in 2010, Nestlé commits to not buying oil from suppliers that destroy rainforests. A year later, the toy giant Mattel establishes a policy on packaging that excludes companies linked to deforestation. In 2013, after four years of campaigning, the large Indonesian company Asian Pulp & Paper announces that it will not use wood from tropical forests to make paper.

---

been damaged, Mike and Brad could have faced extremely harsh penalties.

The toughness of the legal system was not the only cause for concern in Indonesia. Work on the ground had become dangerous as it involved attacking the corrupt and powerful timber and oil sectors. After numerous threats, private security guards had to be contracted to ensure the safety of the camp volunteers in the forest as well as of the crew and the ship during their stay in Bali.

Working in defense of forests in Indonesia was, and still is, a highly risky business.

More than 10,000 people participated in the Climate Change Conference in Bali. Governments committed themselves to working towards a global climate deal at COP15, which is covered in Chapter 10.

Greenpeace International (along with many other organizations) is still on track to win a global moratorium on the destruction of ancient forests.

A few months before the arrival of the ship, a Forest Defenders Camp was set up in the heart of Riau. On 29 October, about 30 volunteers from the camp had, together with local communities, begun the construction of five dams to stop the drainage of some recently destroyed peatland forests.[9] These wetlands are drained for planting palm oil and the carbon stored for millions of years in the peat decomposes, releasing huge amounts of CO_2 into the atmosphere.

The peat soils in Riau have the highest concentration of stored carbon per hectare in the world.

DMITRI SHAROMOV

I landed in Bali the day before the *Rainbow Warrior* left the island. As I arrived, my companions were loading into the hold a very special vehicle: a solar taxi with its trailer of solar panels. The Swiss Louis Palmer and his German assistant Thomas were going around the world with the taxi, promoting the sun as an energy source.
Having met up with people from Greenpeace at COP13, they had managed to obtain a free ticket to New Zealand/ Aotearoa, the *Rainbow Warrior*'s next destination.

1 Liberia suffered two periods of civil war: 1989-96 and 1999-2003. **2** The note was written in English. **3** Catalunya is an autonomous region situated in the northeast of Spain. **4** Increasingly, there are more and more sustainable management forest systems that are certified by independent bodies such as the Forest Stewardship Council (FSC). **5** Critical Mass is an event which usually takes place once a month, in which groups of cyclists meet in cities around the globe. While the groups cycle together, they call attention to cyclists' rights and also promote a model for sustainable cities. **6** The mine is operated by a subsidiary of the US-based mining transnational Freeport McMoRan. **7** Japan is the main importer of Indonesian plywood, accounting for over 60% of Indonesia's exports in 2005, followed by the US (14%), the EU (13%) and China (9%). **8** The so-called COP13 was the 13th session of the Conference of the Parties on Climate Change organized by United Nations. It took place in Bali and brought together more than 10,000 participants, including representatives of over 180 countries, together with observers from intergovernmental and non-governmental organizations as well as the media. **9** Peat is a combustible fossil fuel formed from organic residues accumulated in wetlands. When set alight, it produces a dense smoke.

> 'Life is what happens while you are busy making other plans'
>
> John Lennon

6 Expect the unexpected

Introduction
Of stowaways and castaways Running away from Cuba (Caribbean Sea, 1992) •
The Djibouti boys (Middle East, 2001) • Mayday in the middle of the night
(Western Mediterranean, 2006)
Emergencies on board A hole in the hull (South Pacific, 2005) • Maite alarm
(Cyprus, 2006)
Humanitarian missions The Great Tsunami (Indonesia, 2005) • Beirut under bombs
(Eastern Mediterranean, 2006) • The story of Chile Willy (Chile, 1996)

'EXPECT THE UNEXPECTED' read a large sign posted on the door of Cabin 3, one of the five cabins located under the main deck. I don't think any of those working on the *Rainbow Warrior* ever expected to have a penguin as a travel mate, or to be carrying humanitarian aid in an emergency instead of the maintenance or whale watching that had been planned.

It is true that unexpected events occur in everybody's private life from time to time. However, when you work on Greenpeace ships (and indeed throughout the organization), such situations are so varied and frequent that there is a word that springs to everyone's lips: *flexibility*.

Of the many stories I could have told, I have gathered just a handful of anecdotes – though they are each very different from the other, as you will see.

Of stowaways and castaways

Running away from Cuba
(Caribbean Sea, 1992)

The *Rainbow Warrior* was sailing along the north coast of Cuba and those on board were harboring a forlorn hope that they might be able to visit the capital, Havana. The opportunity for a Greenpeace ship to visit that country for the first time had just turned up unexpectedly.

Bridgetown, the capital of Barbados, had been the schooner's last port of call. The first Global Conference on the Sustainable Development of

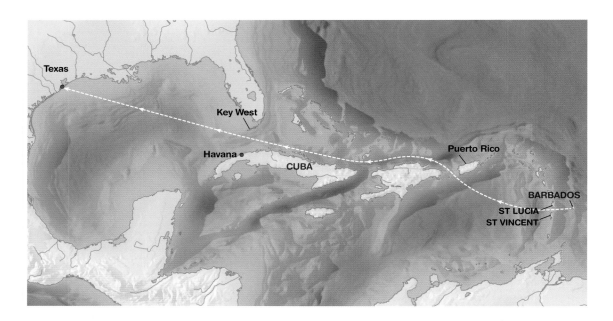

Small Island States, mandated by United Nations, had just been held there, following on from decisions taken two years earlier in the so-called 'Earth Summit' in Rio de Janeiro.[1]

Only two leaders accepted the invitation to visit the *Rainbow Warrior*, those from French Guiana and Cuba. Fidel Castro stayed on board for about two hours and invited the crew to visit Havana. He even proposed donating a building that could be used as a Greenpeace office, but his offer was immediately rejected: 'You see, Mr President, Greenpeace does not accept any donation from governments. Thanks for your kind offer but we cannot accept it.' The invitation to go to Cuba was passed on to the Greenpeace International office and, after long discussions, the *Rainbow Warrior* was told that it had better not go at that time. Given the US embargo on Cuba (see box), a visit might well have had a negative effect on the planned campaign in the United States that was to follow, possibly changing its focus entirely.

The Summit ended and the *Rainbow Warrior* started sailing towards Texas. Havana was certainly on her way and, despite the official 'no' received from head office in Amsterdam, the crew still held out some hope that this might turn into a 'yes' at the last moment.

When the ship was passing north of Cuba, still many nautical miles from the capital, Joel Stewart, the captain, saw a strong reflection shining intermittently in the distance. He grabbed the binoculars to see what it was but he could not quite make it out. Joel went to the helm and changed the ship's course to investigate.

It turned out that the reflections were actually signals that the passengers of a small fiberglass

---

The 'rafter crisis'

In 1959, the leftwing revolutionary movement led by Fidel Castro and Ernesto 'Che' Guevara overthrew the dictator Fulgencio Batista and seized power in Cuba. Since 1962, the US has maintained a total embargo on trade with the country, which aligned itself with the Soviet Union during the Cold War.

Following the collapse of the Soviet Union, which caused great economic hardship in Cuba, in 1994 there was a massive wave of emigration in small boats to the US, which welcomed them with federal assistance. It is estimated that about one and a half million Cubans have left the country since the revolution.

---

11 September 2001

In early September 2001, the *Rainbow Warrior* headed to New York where she was to moor at a pier close to the World Trade Center, a complex of several office buildings – including the famous Twin Towers – in Manhattan. The ship was to arrive on 11 September in order to load provisions and change crew before crossing the Atlantic.

The *Rainbow Warrior* was approaching the city when the Port Authority ordered her to divert to another port, without any further explanation. Soon after, they learned why: the Twin Towers had just been hit by two planes. The new crew members who were on their way had to make a bizarre return journey home and wait to embark in Cadiz, Spain. The next place where the *Rainbow Warrior* would campaign was Doha (Qatar); a brief stop in Djibouti had also been planned.

rowboat had sent using a mirror. They were three young Cuban men who wanted to reach the nearby US coast of Florida. Their boat had a crack in it that they had attempted to fix with candlewax, and some old tubes had been lashed all over it to keep it afloat. A little black plastic tarpaulin kept the sun out but the young men were completely out of water and food. As if this situation were not critical enough, they were drifting towards a dangerous area of shallow reefs excluded from shipping routes.

'Where are you going?' the refugees asked as soon as they came on board and had drunk some water.

'Well, Fidel Castro has invited us to go to Havana and we don't know yet if we are going.'

'Ah, if you are going to Cuba, then please give us some food and water and put us back on the ocean.' This sealed it: it was clear that, having picked up the Cuban youngsters, it was now impossible for the ship to visit Havana.

Two days later, a US Coastguard vessel came and took the three Cubans and their boat to Key West, the southernmost US city, and the *Rainbow Warrior* continued on her voyage to Texas.

The Djibouti boys (Middle East, 2001)

The scent coming from the barbecue was irresistible. It was Sunday, the sea was calm. There was a big moon in the sky and a beautiful dusk light. The ship had left Djibouti a few days before and was finally out of Somali pirate waters. The crew of the *Rainbow Warrior* were having a relaxed dinner in front of the bridge. Daniel Rizzotti was in command of the ship and, like a typical Argentinean, also in charge of the barbecue. He was in the wheelhouse when, out of the corner of his eye, he saw something like a shadow moving near the mizzen mast. He came on deck, putting his fingers to his lips, and beckoned to a few other guys to follow him.

And that is how they discovered Yabem, a boy who had stowed away while the ship had been in Djibouti. They then decided to inspect every corner of the ship. Shortly afterwards, the bridge phone rang: they had found another boy in the engine room. Samud, noticeably younger than Yabem, climbed the steep stairs up to the bridge deck full of pride, his chest popped out and his chin up in the air.

The unexpected discovery of the two boys had instantly put an end to the relaxing Sunday afternoon. An already tricky situation had just become even more complicated. After the recent attack on the Twin Towers (see box), there was some fear and a lot of uncertainty in international affairs. The *Rainbow Warrior* was going to Doha (capital of Qatar) to be present at a meeting of the controversial World Trade Organization (WTO). Qatar, an Arab country that was difficult to access, had been chosen after the massive demonstrations against the previous meeting (in the US city of Seattle, in 1999). Carrying two stowaways on board not only posed a serious humanitarian problem but also threatened the ship's own mission: challenging the WTO to take social and environmental concerns into consideration before pushing to expand 'free trade'.

Everybody but the captain, who was busy communicating the latest development to Greenpeace International key staff, was back on the bridge deck, clustered around both the barbecue and the two unexpected guests. Finally they understood

KAREN ROBINSON / GREENPEACE

Making themselves at home: stowaways Yabem and Samud chatting to the crew on board the *Rainbow Warrior*.

the strange little incidents of the last few days, some of which had been exasperating: food disappearing and remnants left all over the place, oil stains on the floor along the alleyway and, worst of all, the presence of dark fingerprints on the cheese. The kids used to come out of hiding in search of food at night, as soon as the deckhand on watch finished their hourly round.

It was impossible to tell their ages although Yabem, the older one, seemed to be coming out of adolescence while Samud had not even entered puberty. They had not met until they encountered each other while looking for a hiding place in the engine room. Samud was from Ethiopia and Yabem from Eritrea – neighboring countries that had until recently been at war.

In a few days, the *Rainbow Warrior* was due to arrive in Dubai, the capital of the United Arab Emirates (UAE), to embark both campaigners and campaign materials. From the Greenpeace Political Unit, Rémi Parmentier contacted the United Nations High Commissioner for Refugees (UNHCR) seeking refugee status for the two boys. The alternative of returning the stowaways to Djibouti was totally dismissed on the grounds that they would be abused there and then deported to their home countries.

The UAE authorities gave the *Rainbow Warrior*

Eritrea and Ethiopia

The recent two-year border conflict (1998 to 2000) between the two countries had caused an estimated 70,000 deaths and involved trench warfare. Despite both being among the poorest countries in the world, their governments had spent millions of dollars on weapons and had forcibly recruited thousands of teenagers. At the point when the boys stowed away, one year after the ceasefire, the situation remained tense.

permission to come into port on condition that the presence of Yabem and Samud was not made public and that they remained in their cabin the whole time. Eventually the Qatar authorities allowed the ship to dock there under the same stipulation: that the crew maintained silence about the presence of the stowaways. The two boys were interviewed by a UNHCR representative in Doha. The crew was very worried because it seemed that Yabem was much less likely to obtain refugee status than Samud.

So the African children remained hidden while their situation was being quietly resolved and the *Rainbow Warrior* was doing her job. The ship was opened to the public as well as to many government representatives attending the Doha

The World Trade Organization (WTO)

According to its own account, the WTO is the international agency that deals with the global rules of trade between nations and where the 169 member governments try to sort out their trade problems. Its declared purpose is to help trade flow as freely as possible – so long as there are no undesirable side-effects – because this is important for economic development and wellbeing.

For Greenpeace, the social and environmental impact of WTO policies on communities across the planet is devastating. In essence, the WTO is a tool of the rich countries – notably the US, EU, Japan and Canada – and their powerful corporate lobbies that tend to work against the interests of poor countries.

The Doha Round is a phase of negotiations about world trade that began at the meeting in the Qatar capital that *Rainbow Warrior* visited in 2001. The WTO seeks to advance its free-trade agenda through these talks, which cover agriculture, services and intellectual property issues, among others. Developing countries and Non-Governmental Organizations have consistently challenged the WTO line that a trade deal will work to the

Official delegation: members of the WTO organizing committee in Doha visiting the ship.

benefit of the poor, pointing out, for example, that the US and EU maintain agricultural subsidies to their own farmers that effectively serve as trade barriers for the rest of the world. The WTO has not been able to escape the charge that it serves the interests of the richest nations and transnational corporations and the Doha Round therefore shows no sign of coming to an end.

meeting and she also hosted a radio station via the internet, named 'No New Round Radio', to broadcast independent media coverage of the WTO meeting to the world through interviews, analysis, seminars and press conferences in English, Arabic, French and Spanish.

Days passed before the long-awaited news finally arrived: UNHCR had granted refugee status to the two boys. This began a new phase of 'diplomacy' to find a country that would accept them, Jo Dufay now being the person in charge. When the Doha meeting concluded, the *Rainbow Warrior* sailed towards the Mediterranean, carrying Yabem and Samud on board.

Despite little relish for Western food, Yabem and Samud started gaining weight and their physical appearance began to change significantly. Both became deckhands in a 'limited' way, sometimes helping out on deck, other times helping in the galley, and also enjoying more leisure time. The deckhand Meredith Adams became specially responsible for their care and she and Lesley Simkiss started to teach them English. Meredith suggested that she talked about life and culture in her country, Canada, and that they in return should tell her about life and culture in Ethiopia and Eritrea. Yabem had had some very bad experiences with family members on both sides of

Alternative perspectives on the WTO

'The "new tool" allows the US to intervene profoundly in the internal affairs of other countries, compelling them to change their laws and practices. Crucially, the WTO will make sure that other countries are "following through on their committments to allow foreigners to invest" without restriction in central areas of other countries' economies.'
Noam Chomsky[2]

'The WTO TRIPs[3] agreement sets enforceable global rules on patents, copyrights and trademarks which extend to living resources so that genes, cells, seeds, plants and animals can now be patented and "owned" as intellectual property,' says **Vandana Shiva**.[4] For her, patents on living material are an ethical perversion, criminalize saving and sharing seeds and encourage biopiracy.

'In the WTO, all countries can vote on equal terms, but they never vote. Majority voting is possible but it has never been used... The WTO's decisions are taken by consensus behind closed doors... Thus, the WTO secretly, with impunity, sacrifices hundreds of millions of small farmers around the world, on the free trade altar.' **Eduardo Galeano**[5]

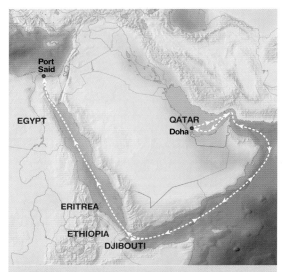

The boys stowed away in Djibouti, on the African coast, stayed on board in Dubai and Doha before finally being set ashore in the Egyptian city of Port Said.

the new border, and Samud had been set on a train by his mother so that he could have a better future than war. Every evening, the *Rainbow Warrior* was filled with the sound of *djembes*, African drums newly acquired in Djibouti, so that Samud's talent for music was discovered.

The kids became rather like mascots on board but they also had to deal with 16 people acting as their parents, telling them what they should or shouldn't do. 'Please do not call me *mama*. Just call me *Lesley*', the nurse-deckhand from New Zealand/Aotearoa told Yabem, who had probably begun to call her that because she was the oldest woman on board. To her despair, the boy then started calling her 'Mama Lesley', a nickname that she has never since been able to shake off.

Yabem and Samud finally left the *Rainbow Warrior* in Port Said, Egypt. The whole crew came out on deck to see them off and many of them were visibly touched while watching as the boat containing their five-week companions headed off. Yabem and Samud did not look back or wave goodbye but instead firmly looked forward to what the future would bring. The refrain of a popular song from those days by Nelly Furtado remained in the air. Despite Samud not really understanding its words, he used to sing it all day long: 'I'm like a

What came next

Yabem and Samud were handed over to the care of UNHCR in Egypt and were fostered by a family while a country for them to live in was being sought. They were eventually accepted by Canada but not before many obstacles had to be overcome – some of them by Greenpeace staff or volunteers (including arranging foster care and a school for them, organizing a group of individuals to provide financial sponsorship for them, and getting them papers). It was almost a year before Yabem and Samud arrived in Canada, where they finally started a new chapter in their lives.

bird, I'll only fly away, I don't know where my soul is, I don't know where my home is.'

Mayday in the middle of the night (Western Mediterranean, 2006)

'Mayday Mayday Mayday.'[6] Suddenly the emergency call broke into the night calm that had hitherto ruled on the *Rainbow Warrior* bridge. Russian second mate Dima Sharomov, and Turkish medic-deckhand Bahadir Riza, both on duty, were startled by a female voice calling for help. The ship had just been working with Médecins Sans Frontières (MSF) taking humanitarian aid to Lebanon.

'Mayday Mayday Mayday. We are sinking! Help! Help!' A French coastguard immediately answered the call. The *Rainbow Warrior* had just left the island of Corsica behind on her way to Marseilles, France, and also responded. It was just past two o'clock. When the scared woman at the other end of the radio gave her boat's position, it was clear that the *Rainbow Warrior* was relatively close. Dima picked up the phone and called the captain.[7]

Mike Fincken was jolted awake when the phone rang. His cabin was pitch black and, his placid dreams suddenly interrupted, he was not totally sure where he was. Where the hell was the phone? He hastily scrambled out of bed and almost fell from his bunk. Where the hell was the light? Mike had embarked just that morning and this was his first day as the *Rainbow Warrior* captain. He did not know his own cabin very well yet but he soon reached the bridge.

There was no time to waste. The *Rainbow Warrior* altered course immediately but it would take almost four hours to reach the sinking vessel. The rescue boat had to be immediately prepared and Bahadir went to wake up the bosun, Sarah Watson, and the outboard mechanic, Phil Dunn.

Hooked up to the radio, Mike was trying to calm down the woman in the distressed boat while getting some more information from her: they were three Portuguese women, their sailing boat had run aground on a rock and they were in a bay near the coast of Corsica. When the captain asked them to repeat their co-ordinates, he realized that the first position they had given was wrong and

Lookouts in the dark

'You know, Maite?' Jon Castle said to me. It was a dark night and we were sailing on the *Esperanza* in the North Atlantic. 'The lookout sailor's job on the night-watch (that being my case) is very important. You can't imagine the number of castaways who have reported their despair at watching ships passing by very close to them. Nobody seeing them, not even after they have launched flares or other distress signals.' As the captain spoke to me, he was looking at the black horizon surrounding us. 'Yes, your job can save lives. It's important not to forget that.'

Safety and success. The *Avon* inflatable arrives back at the *Rainbow Warrior* having rescued the three Portuguese women.

111

that the *Rainbow Warrior* was much closer to them than had initially been thought.

The *Avon* was launched and Phil, Dima and Bahadir went to the rescue of the three women in distress. Within minutes, a blinking light could be made out from the inflatable. They had found them! As they came closer, they saw that it was a 10-meter-long racing boat. It was aground on a rock that Dima remembered having seen marked on the nautical chart. The three scared women were waiting for them on deck with their lifejackets on.

Finally relaxed, and with a hot drink in their hands, the castaways struck up a conversation with the few crew members awake on board the *Rainbow Warrior*. They had just taken part in a competition that had been organized in the Mediterranean to demand an end to the war between Israel and Lebanon. The woman in charge, who was some years older than her two shipmates, had a lot of experience in navigation, having even crossed the Atlantic several times.

A couple of hours later, a French coastguard was alongside the *Rainbow Warrior*, picking up the rescued women. Finally the Greenpeace flagship could again take up her course towards Marseilles, where another surprise was awaiting her (see Chapter 10).

Emergencies on board

A hole in the hull (South Pacific, 2005)

'Good morning Cat. There is a beautiful sunrise and we are sinking.' Caterina Nitto will never forget the words captain Pete Willcox addressed to her when she arrived at the bridge that morning.

The *Rainbow Warrior* had just been working on a whale campaign in South Korea. After a long journey, the ship was now quite near her next destination, New Zealand/Aotearoa, though running late. At the first light of dawn, a sharp sound had broken the silence ruling in the wheelhouse. It was the bilge alarm of the lower lower forecastle (LLF), the foremost compartment of the ship beneath the water. The captain sent the deckhand on watch to check what was happening. Shortly after, he returned with the news that

actually there was some water on the LLF's floor. 'Wake up Flavio' was the order that followed.

There was a furious knocking on the bosun's cabin door.

'Flavio, Flavio! The captain wants you immediately. We have a leak!'

'What? Are you kidding?'

'No, I'm not. Hurry up!' The Brazilian hurriedly started dressing, remembering, as he did so, a brief conversation with Amanda Bjuhr, the cook, the previous evening. The ship had already by then been motoring into the wind for hours, slamming into waves a meter and a half high. Every time her bow received the blow of a wave, the whole vessel shuddered and, at one of these blows, the cook exclaimed: 'So good we are almost there!'

'Look, Amanda, if the boat continues doing this, we will not make it!' Flavio Nakazono had said it as a joke. But at six in the morning, his words were looking prophetic.

Cat and another deckhand were woken up shortly after Flavio. To find the place where water was coming in, it was first necessary to clear the LLF, full as it was of all kinds of stuff accumulated over the years. While the deck crew started emptying the compartment – the only access to which was an almost vertical ladder from a small hatch – Dave Caister, the electrician, began to operate the big firefighting pump as well as two smaller pumps.

The spot was finally found. On the starboard side, an area of approximately the size of a hand had rusted and water was seeping in every time the ship's bow entered the waves. The damaged area looked to be in pretty bad shape. The captain altered course to minimize the impact of the waves. After discussing different options, it was eventually decided to try to plug the leak by bracing a plywood plate of about 50 square centimeters against the ceiling with a piece of wood. The plate had its side to the hull lined with neoprene but at one of the hits to the wedge that locked it, a rusty piece of the hull yielded and gave way to a hole about six centimeters in diameter. Now, every time the ship's bow submerged, a stream of water reached the ceiling as if it were a fountain.

By then, the entire crew was at the bow giving

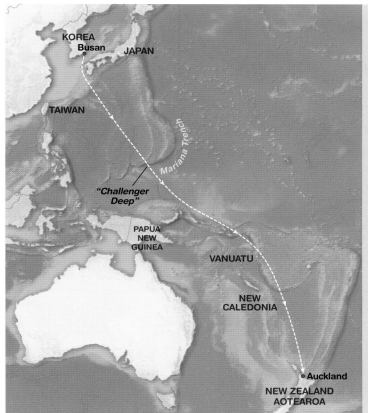

A special swim stop
It was a quiet beautiful night and the sea was completely calm. The *Rainbow Warrior* was approximately halfway on her transit from South Korea to New Zealand/Aotearoa. Around 10.30pm, Pete Willcox stopped the ship's engines and called the crew. 'Does anyone fancy a swim?', the captain suggested. They were sailing across the Mariana Trench, the deepest place in the ocean, the greatest abyss in the Earth's crust.[8]

More than half of the crew happily accepted the offer without hesitation. But then, when time for getting into the water arrived, things became a little impressive: What kind of beings would be living in those dark depths? In order to prevent any possible temptation the abyssal creatures might have, each swimmer took a little gift to the gods, a coin or alike. A few minutes later, the *Rainbow Warrior*'s engines roared again and the boat continued on its journey.

a hand. Some were preparing a maneuver that involved wrapping a sail around the hull (it had been a good decision to keep the old sails on board!), while others were in the forecastle. In the LLF, stress had produced an unusual situation. Flavio (Brazilian), Cat (Italian) and chief mate Óscar Macián (Spanish) were down there getting the space empty of gear and water. Each one had started speaking in their own language but they were understanding each other perfectly (as Greenpeace ships carry people from all over the world, the *lingua franca* on board is English). They only realized what they were doing when an English speaker asked them, with great curiosity: 'What language are you speaking? Is it Esperanto?'[9]

The firefighting pump was working frantically, sucking water out to be thrown back into the sea from the main deck, two decks above. The level of water had been lowered substantially when

the pump filter got stuck and suddenly stopped working. To the crew's consternation, water began to rise again very quickly. If they were not able to start this pump, there would be no option but to seal the whole forecastle (the upper as well as the lower) and let it flood. That would not have meant the sinking of the ship but it would have entailed the loss of valuable material. After a few minutes of great tension, the engine spluttered back into life. The big pump was running again!

Once placed and well secured on deck, the large blue sail fulfilled its 'shield' function pretty well, considerably reducing the water flow coming through the hole, and the crew could breathe again. Then an idea that had been initially suggested was brought back: covering the damaged area with concrete.

The plate lined with neoprene was put back in place over the hole and then a wooden box put on top of it into which concrete was poured. For good luck, someone put a coin into the mountain of cement, which kept growing until the bosun had used all they had. Since water was still leaking in, there was a risk that the concrete would not harden and a third alternative was prepared just in case.

It was already dark by the time Flavio could finally relax as it was evident that the concrete was going to hold. The next day, he and Amanda were chatting on the main deck when Pete went down to inspect the LLF. As he came back, he stopped for a moment and patted the bosun's shoulder, saying: 'Look, Flavio, I am very impressed with the work you did yesterday. Thank you!' The captain went on his way to the bridge, leaving Flavio behind, speechless. He recalls that as the best compliment he ever received in his career as a sailor.

A few days later, the *Rainbow Warrior* arrived in Auckland – delayed, and with a broken hull, but she had made it safely.

Maite alarm (Cyprus, 2006)

At the end of the meeting about tuna in Dubrovnik in 2006 (see Chapters 8 and 9), the *Rainbow Warrior* returned to Cyprus, this time to the port of Limassol. In the days that followed, a big crew change was due to take place. As a goodbye treat,

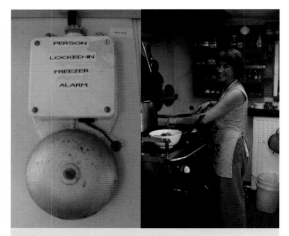

Left: The 'person locked in freezer alarm' was moved to the main deck after the incident described and renamed the 'Maite alarm'.
Right: The author cooking the farewell paella.

I offered to cook a 'paella' – a Spanish rice dish – for the last Saturday dinner we would spend together. The day came and, right after lunch, all my companions disappeared in their cabins to have a good nap. The previous day had turned out to be Pablo Korman's 35th birthday and we had ended up partying into the early hours in honor of our beloved volunteer deckhand.

'Well, I'll leave all the ingredients ready and get some sleep too,' I thought. I went down the stairs to the dry stores and fetched the rice. Then, wearing a short-sleeved T-shirt and shorts, I entered and went through the fridge and into the freezer, closing both doors to the cold stores. Hurriedly, I put everything I needed in the crate and made to leave but... the freezer door was locked! I started pushing it. It didn't move at all. I took a run-up and threw myself against it. Nothing – it didn't budge an inch. I rang the emergency bell. Its sound, though highly attenuated, came to my ears. Then a thought crossed my mind like lightning: 'If I can hear the bell down here, surely they won't hear it up in their cabins.' And they could not.

I threw myself against the door, kicked it and rang the bell again and again. It was impossible to say how much time had passed but I was starting to get really cold and the tips of my fingers were beginning to hurt a lot. Chilly air was being fed in through a grille next to the ceiling. I wondered what I could do. 'What if I break the pipes?' (Thank goodness I did not do this, as the gas that escaped would then have killed me!) 'What if I built a kind of igloo with some crates and shelves? What if I blocked the cold air inlet?' Thoughts were racing in my mind, one after another, as I kept desperately ringing the bell and charging at the door.

After a while, I stopped in an attempt to calm down: I could feel my heart racing and did not want to panic. Things were getting pretty serious. I imagined the headline news: '*Rainbow Warrior* deckhand dies after getting locked in freezer.' The situation was so surreal that I could hardly believe it was happening.

Full of anger, I mustered all my strength and gave the door a violent kick – and it opened! It narrowly missed hitting Naomi Petersen, the chief mate, who had gone to the pantry to make some tea and had heard some weird sounds coming from the lower deck.

First thing on Monday, the ship's electrician moved the freezer alarm from its original place, by the stairs leading down to the stores, into the accommodation alleyway, where it would be more easily heard. Beside it, Martin Steffens placed a label reading 'Maite alarm'. The farewell paella, the last hurrah of our trip in and out of war zones, turned into a celebration of my still being alive.

Humanitarian missions

The Great Tsunami (Indonesia, 2005)

The solid outermost shell of the Earth – the lithosphere – is broken up into large pieces called tectonic plates, which are in constant motion, pressing against each other.

On Sunday 26 December 2004, the ancient friction between two plates beneath the Indian Ocean triggered a 1,000-kilometer-long rupture of the crust, as one plate slid on top of the other. The seafloor was displaced just a few meters, causing the third-largest earthquake ever recorded, with a magnitude of 9.1 and an epicenter about 30 kilometers deep. The earthquake then triggered the worst tsunami ever known. The killer waves travelled in all directions across the Indian Ocean at the speed of a jet airliner. Within a few hours, it had slammed into the coastlines of 14 countries, even killing people in Africa, 4,800 kilometers away from the epicenter.

The *Rainbow Warrior* was spending the Christmas holiday in Singapore, doing maintenance work. The news of the disaster arriving at every moment was increasingly hair-raising. Two days after the tragedy, with most of the crew gathered in the ship's mess, Dima Sharomov, the second mate, said: 'Listen. We are here and have a boat. We should go and help!' Everybody supported the

Utter devastation – the aftermath of the Great Tsunami in Aceh, Indonesia.

CHRISTIAN ÅSLUND / GREENPEACE

idea and a proposal was sent to the Greenpeace International office. In fact, in Amsterdam, Meike Heulseman, Gina Sanchez and Elaine Lawrence had already started discussions with Médecins Sans Frontières (MSF) the day after the tsunami and Rob Taylor, the person who was to co-ordinate the whole operation on board, had been put on standby. Shortly after the news of this new mission arrived, the *Rainbow Warrior* set sail for Aceh on the Indonesian island of Sumatra, the west coast of which was the land closest to the epicenter, only about 160 kilometers away.

At dawn on 7 January 2005, 12 days after the tragedy, the *Rainbow Warrior* arrived in Krueng Raya, a port about an hour's drive from Banda Aceh, the capital of the region. Only one of its three piers had survived the onslaught of a 10-meter-high wave and, to reach this, the ship had to dodge sunken fishing boats, the masts of which sprouted

The Great Tsunami

The Tsunami destroyed entire towns and caused more than 230,000 deaths in 14 countries, with Indonesia, Sri Lanka, India and Thailand bearing the brunt of the impact.

Its environmental impact was also enormous, causing the destruction of mangroves, coral reefs, dunes, forests and diverse vegetation. Innumerable wells and aquifers, as well as large portions of arable land, were invaded by salt water, meaning they would be lost for decades.

over the water. The harbormaster, who had lost his wife, went to greet them in flip-flops, worn trousers and a dirty shirt. In Krueng Raya, almost everybody had lost at least one family member but life went on and people were still going about their business with admirable resilience.

Humanitarian aid was arriving there both by sea (ferry and navy ships) and land (trucks from the capital, which was connected to the rest of the island by an inner road). After filling up the hold with several tons of MSF materials, the ship sailed without delay for the town of Meulaboh.

After about 15 hours sailing with her engines set to full speed (as the *Rainbow Warrior* did the whole time it was in the area), they reached their destination and met with shocking devastation. One-third of the 120,000 Meulaboh population, along with thousands of homes, had been swallowed up by the waves. The Indonesian army was in charge and 12 navy vessels of various nationalities were unloading food and helping to clear debris. People there were still searching for their missing family members. Helicopters were constantly hovering above to capture images of the tragedy that would be beamed all over the world.

The transported material was unloaded with the help of small fishing boats, which lined up alongside the *Rainbow Warrior*. It was destined for the hospital (one of the buildings that had survived) and the makeshift refugee camp. As soon as unloading was finished, the ship headed back to Krueng Raya at full throttle. Three days

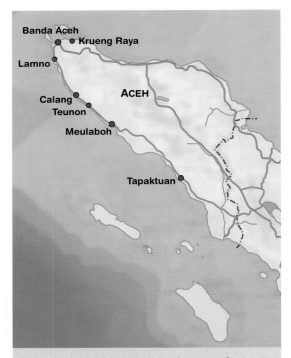

Most parts of the road along the coast from Meulaboh to Banda Aceh had been swallowed by the Tsunami. Aid could only reach the devasted villages by sea.

Mercy mission. Unloading aid from the *Rainbow Warrior* on to small boats in the port of Meulaboh. The bulk of the shipments carried for MSF was medical and surgical equipment but the ship also transported food, tools and mosquito nets.

later, 10 more tons of material were unloaded at the same place.

The next two trips transporting MSF stuff were to Lamno, placed on a river bank five kilometers inland, in order to supply the refugee camp there with materials mainly related to water and sanitation. Entire villages had disappeared in the river valleys as much as 10 kilometers inland, as anything not on a hill had been wiped out. The tsunami had altered the coastline so drastically that only with the help of local fisherfolk could the mouth of the river be found. The unloading again took place in the open sea.

The small amount of aid that had arrived in this area may have been explained by the fact that the government regarded it as a stronghold of the Free Aceh Movement (GAM), despite the ceasefire declared by GAM in the wake of the devastation.[10]

After five trips working for MSF, the ship put herself at the service of the organization Action Against Hunger, which had requested help transporting food. Past midnight on the day of their latest return to Krueng Raya, the *Rainbow Warrior* crew – together with 10 locals – finished loading the first 70 tons of rice. The exhausted sailors then took their rest rocked by the waves on the way to Lamno. Within hours, they were back on deck forming human chains and passing boxes to each other until the hold was empty.

The ship made two more trips to Lamno and then went to Teunon, a town between Lamno and Meulaboh, a couple of times. At Teunon, time seemed to have stopped: fully a month after the tragedy, everything remained virtually unchanged. The limited aid that had arrived had been dropped by helicopters. This was the only place the ship visited where people did not smile – all of them looked as if they were still in shock.

As the days passed, the changes became more noticeable thanks both to international co-operation

DMITRI SHAROMOV

Once there was a town. The waves were over 30 meters high when they crashed into Meulaboh.

Collateral healing

In August 2005, a peace agreement between GAM and the Indonesian government ended a conflict that had caused some 15,000 deaths.

and local mobilization. The massive amounts of aid mobilized by states and organizations made co-ordination tremendously complicated. In Krueng Raya it was common to see mountains of clothes and boxes of food next to the wharf. People came on foot, by bicycle or motorbike, and took whatever they needed. Sometimes the clothes in the pile were huge in size (two or three Indonesians could easily fit into some of the underpants) or even useless (as with the hundreds of pairs of socks that would never be used in that corner of the planet).

If at first what made the greatest impression on those on board the *Rainbow Warrior* was the destruction that unfolded before their eyes, it was the response of the survivors to the catastrophe that affected them most deeply in the long term. People who were recovering from the pain of having lost everything just a few days before, who were living in devastated places where the smell of death was not a metaphor, showed incredible resilience. Not a single complaint was heard from their lips, and they even remained capable of humor and laughter amid these

desperate circumstances. The whole crew threw themselves wholeheartedly into helping to alleviate the tragedy, resting and sleeping only when the ship was between destinations. They usually worked at tropical temperatures of about 35º Celsius, amid high humidity, and sometimes in the rain. Only Agus Suwesnawa, the sole crew member from Indonesia, took any time off at all, and that was because a terrible toothache forced him to go to Banda Aceh in search of a dentist. In the end, despite the great pressure on the ship's engines and crane, there was not a single technical problem – a real miracle!

Before the ship left Krueng Raya for her last mission on 3 February, the harbormaster came to

In one month, the *Rainbow Warrior* made a total of 10 trips from Krueng Raya – including one trip for **UNICEF** and another for **WALHI**, the largest and oldest Indonesian environmental NGO – distributing around 400 tons of miscellaneous supplies.

On 25 January, a media report announced that 12,000 US soldiers had distributed 8,000 tons of material (corresponding to less than one ton per person). The 20 people on board the *Rainbow Warrior* had moved more than 200 tons by that point (over 10 tons per person).

DMITRI SHAROMOV

Manna from below. The food supplies that the *Rainbow Warrior* carried for Action Against Hunger included rice, biscuits and, being unloaded here, noodles.

say goodbye. He was now wearing a uniform and had a mobile phone and a marine band VHF radio, essential equipment for someone in his role. In the city, much of the debris had been removed and some of the fishing boats had managed to restart work.

The *Rainbow Warrior* crew members left Aceh behind with the feeling that they had been doing 'something real' – something so vital and meaningful that it made them forget about their own exhaustion. It was an experience that was impossible to forget.

The story of an orphanage

After helping in Aceh, the *Rainbow Warrior* returned to Singapore and Russian second mate Dima Sharomov disembarked there. Instead of heading home, however, he returned to Aceh to work with NGOs aiding local fisherfolk. In Banda Aceh he learned of Fajar Hidayah, a school just founded there to take in children orphaned by the Tsunami. Dima made friends with a local called Abdullah, and together they travelled across Aceh by motorcycle, picking up children from refugee camps and villages, and taking them to the school.

With the financial support of friends in Alaska, Dima opened bank accounts to cover all the children's needs. Later on, some of his friends and acquaintances in his adopted country of New Zealand/Aotearoa sponsored 24 children, half of whom are still under age and therefore receiving some support as of 2014.

The photo shows Dima with a group from the Fajar Hidayah orphanage in Jakarta, who visit each time Greenpeace ships are in town. School founder Draga Rangkuti is on the far right.

DMITRI SHAROMOV

119

Beirut under bombs
(Eastern Mediterranean, 2006)

The calls from different Israeli navy ships were constant, the questions being always the same. Dima Sharomov, the second mate, patiently responded to all of them. What is the flag of the ship? Port of origin and next port of call? How many people on board and their nationalities? What is the ship's cargo? A big dose of patience was needed to answer them in a polite way again and again.

The *Rainbow Warrior* was heading to Beirut, the capital of Lebanon. Just three weeks before, the south of the country had been raided by its neighbor Israel, in response to attacks from Hizbullah (see Chapter 8). The ship had been planning, as its last campaign in the summer of 2006, to study the eastern Mediterranean cetacean populations, and had already sailed from Istanbul to Mersin, in southeastern Turkey, when war broke out. The change of plans was immediate: Greenpeace had offered Médecins Sans Frontières (MSF) the use of the *Rainbow Warrior* to transport urgent supplies to Lebanon, since the only way to access the country was by sea, and permission to enter the besieged waters had finally been granted.

When the ship arrived in Beirut, they found a ghost town: there was no-one at the harbor or in the streets, and no cars were moving through the city. Everybody on board felt very strange because,

Greenpeace crew arrive in Beirut to deliver the third load of emergency supplies brought by the *Rainbow Warrior* – flying the flag of Médecins Sans Frontières – from Larnaca, Cyprus.

> The first time the *Rainbow Warrior* was used by MSF to carry humanitarian aid in an emergency situation was in 1998, when Hurricane Mitch devastated much of Central America. The ship then carried clothes, food and medicines from San Francisco to Nicaragua.

although it seemed they were the only humans around, it felt like they were being observed by many eyes. Once the cargo was unloaded, the *Rainbow Warrior* set sail again and, 16 hours later, the ship was back in Larnaca, Cyprus, to stock up with more supplies.

Loading the ship was much more complicated and took much longer than emptying it. Phil Dunn, the outboard mechanic, did an excellent job welding steel bars to the deck in order to optimize the space available in the hold and on the main deck.

The ship completed the journey from Cyprus to Lebanon three times, always planning to reach Beirut and start unloading in the early morning, keeping within the strict time period insisted upon by Israel. Thus, Dima and deckhand-medic Bahadir Riza (who were on duty between midnight and 4am) were always the ones facing the exhaustive and repetitive questioning from the Israeli blockade. To Dima, who, as we have just seen, had been with the *Rainbow Warrior* in Banda Aceh after the Great Tsunami the year before, this was a humanitarian mission with a sad difference. The previous year, the tragedy had arisen due to natural causes. Now humans were killing other humans.

Over 75 tons of supplies (basic hygiene items, medicines, blankets, cooking utensils, milk powder, and so on) were transported in the operation. The *Rainbow Warrior* had just left Beirut for the third time and was only two or three nautical miles away when Israel broke the truce and bombs began to fall on the city. The breathless crew witnessed the attack and could hear the explosions clearly as their peace ship moved away from the war zone. The schooner was to return to Lebanon a month later in order to evaluate the environmental damage caused by this brief but devastating conflict (see Chapter 8).

The story of Chile Willy (Chile, 1996)

As the finishing touch in a campaign in Chile on the issue of overfishing, the *Rainbow Warrior* reached port in San Antonio, a city with a marine species recovery center. The center was treating mainly pelicans and penguins that had been injured in a variety of ways. To everyone's surprise, a young Magellan penguin was discovered among these. This animal was totally disorientated, since his species inhabits the much colder waters to the south. Once he became free of the viscous oil, it had to be immediately taken to its home.

Some volunteers of Greenpeace Chile – who were helping to take care of the animals at the center – had a fantastic idea. The *Rainbow Warrior* was soon to set off for the Strait of Magellan to cross over from the Pacific to the Atlantic. Why shouldn't the ship take the penguin and leave him with others of his kind on this journey to the

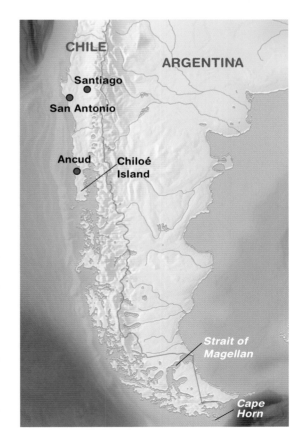

Chile Willy's story in pictures: making friends with crew member Emily Johnston; looking through the pilot door; and being released from the inflatable.

south? Although the proposal was very unusual, it seemed a very good idea to most people on board and in the local office. This new mission, 'saving the penguin', was thus enthusiastically accepted.

Shortly before the ship's departure, the penguin arrived inside a box and the crew was given brief instructions on how to feed him. Once at sea, they opened the box and the animal was 'free' to roam the main deck. The entrance to the forecastle became his home and the *Rainbow Warrior* crew ended up being his family, everyone worried about his wellbeing. He was baptized as Chile Willy not just because of the location but also in honor of a funny cartoon (*Chilly Willy*) that was very popular during the last decades of the 20th century. In addition, the blockbuster US film *Free Willy* – in which a child liberates an orca from captivity – had been recently released. This naturally led to jokes, since there they were, Greenpeace people on boats, saving whales, saving penguins, and saving whatever else needed to be saved!

The Magellan penguin lives mainly on the coasts of southern Chile and Argentina and the Falkland/Malvinas Islands. It measures around 75 centimeters and weighs up to six-and-a-half kilos. Today it is considered a 'threatened species', with the main threats being oil spills, overfishing reducing its food supply, and migration of fish (due to climate change).

It took Chile Willy a little time to become everybody's friend – not least the deckhands who constantly had to wash the deck in order to remove the animal's waste. Despite the penguin's terribly strong odor, very few were reluctant to approach and caress him, even those who publicly complained about him. As soon as anybody stepped on deck, the bird used to run behind them – with the sole exception of the chief engineer, a German called Micky, of whom Chile Willy was greatly afraid. This was not due to Micky's fearsome personality but was because the engineer was convinced that the penguin needed to be kept wet all the time. Whenever he had the chance, he would start chasing Chile Willy to throw buckets of sea water over him. The desperate 'prey' would try to escape by slipping between the inflatables, surely thinking: 'Oh, no! Here comes that bucket maniac again!'

The ship had already travelled a little more than 450 nautical miles south when the crew had to stop and anchor in the bay of Ancud, a city on the north of Chiloé island. The weather forecast had announced storms further south and they had to wait. Besides, they were not in a particular hurry, since the campaign in Chile had been shorter than planned and there was a bit of time before the start of the next scheduled campaign.

As they were already in a region inhabited by Magellan penguins, they decided to leave the starboard pilot door open in the hope that Chile Willy would launch himself into the water in search of his own fellows. However, the animal seemed to feel very much at home on board. Why leave a place where he was being spoiled (except by the bucket maniac) and fed so well? The penguin seemed content to stay where he was and to look out on the sea.

So, a change of tactic was decided upon. Chile Willy was placed in an inflatable, taken a little distance from the ship and then put in the water. But scarcely 10 minutes after they had said goodbye to their peculiar travelling companion in this way, the crew members were on a nearby beach when the little penguin emerged from the waters and approached them, looking very upset. 'Hey mates, how could you do this to me?' he seemed to be implying. 'You have abandoned me!' Chile Willy was accepted again with laughter. Although all were aware of how important it was for the penguin to make his own way, they could not deny that they were pleased to see him again.

With one thing and another, days passed while the ship was anchored in the beautiful bay of Ancud. So it happened that the crew met and became friends with a famous Chilean photographer, Nicolas Piwonka, who lived there. He explained that the best way to 'Free Chile Willy' was to take him to the other side of the island where there was a Magellan penguin colony. He was thus placed in an inflatable again and taken there. This time, everybody – humans and penguin – disembarked together and walked along the beach. A large colony of penguins could be clearly distinguished in the distance. About an hour later, Chile Willy waddled into the water and left, never to return. The special mission had finally been accomplished.

MAITE MOMPÓ

As is the case with all ships, many and varied bird species use the *Rainbow Warrior* as the place to stay for hours, sometimes days, while the ship is under way. This heron was one such unexpected guest. It came on board at some point in the China Sea, during the transit from Taiwan to South Korea in May 2011. At first it was a little shy but very soon it became accustomed to sharing the main deck with us and started to come near us.

Unlike Chile Willy, as soon as it saw the slightest chance, it left us by jumping on to a tug-boat that had come to help us in our docking maneuver in Incheon. To the astonishment of that crew, the bird then began to move on deck as if it were at home and only decided to take off once the boat approached land.

IVAN CATANEIRA

BLOOM COUNTY
by Berke Breathed

This comic strip was on the bulkhead opposite Crizel's composition in the little office. It was published in March 1985 as part of a collection called *Penguin Dreams and Stranger Things*, which, in turn, was part of *Bloom County*. This US comic by Berkeley Breathed addressed socio-political aspects through the eyes of very exaggerated animal characters and won the Pulitzer Prize for editorial cartooning in 1987.

In this strip, Opus the penguin wants to go to Antarctica to find his mother and embarks on the *Rainbow Warrior* after mistaking her for a luxury cruise liner and not realizing that the Greenpeace ship is intent upon confronting the Russian whaling fleet. Thus, the multifarious adventures awaiting the penguin on his long quest began.

So, while Opus was a fictional penguin who embarked on the first *Rainbow Warrior*, Chile Willy was the real penguin that lived for almost a month on the second ship.

1 The Earth Summit is covered in Chapter 11. **2** Noam Chomsky, 'The passion for free markets', *Z Magazine*, May 1997, nin.tl/1f6SHOJ **3** The Agreement on Trade Related Aspects of Intellectual Property Rights. **4** Vandana Shiva, 'Free trade agriculture rules threaten the world's farmers', International Forum on Globalization and Center for Food Safety, nin.tl/1dvWJLK **5** Eduardo Galeano, 'La monarquia universal', analitica.com/bitblioteca/egaleano/monarquia. asp **6** 'Mayday' is the word internationally used as a call for help in a case of imminent danger (for example, involving the risk of death). It is used not just by ships but by aircraft, police forces and firefighters. The word derives from the French *'m'aidez'* (help me). **7** Some of the ship's decks are connected by telephone (the cabins of the captain and officers together with the engine room, the office, the mess, the radio room etc). **8** The Mariana Trench is about 2,550 kilometers long but has an average width of only 69 kilometers. Its maximum detected depth at present is just under 11 kilometers. **9** Esperanto was an artificial language created by Lázaro Zamenhof in 1887 in the hope that it might become an auxiliary international language. The bulk of its vocabulary was drawn from Latin, though it also drew on Germanic and Slavic languages, as well as ancient Greek and Hebrew. **10** Despite its abundance of natural resources, the province of Aceh is one of Indonesia's poorest, with the benefits of exploitation commandeered by big corporations and central government. This situation has given rise to a number of rebel movements, of which GAM is the biggest.

> 'Prestige: Widespread respect and admiration felt for someone or something on the basis of a perception of their achievements or quality.'
>
> Oxford English Dictionary

7 **Prestige**

Introduction
The great escape (*Rainbow Warrior I*, 1980)
Rise to glory (*Sirius*, 1982)
The oil-tanker disaster (*Rainbow Warrior II*, 2002)
An assault (*Esperanza*, 2004)
The winds that blow these days (*Rainbow Warrior II* and *Arctic Sunrise*)

THE END of 2002 saw a great environmental disaster triggered by a ship inaptly named *Prestige*. The single-hull oil tanker split and sank, polluting with its toxic cargo the northern coast of Portugal and the entire northwestern Spanish coast. The oil spill even found its way to France.

Prestige is hard to attain but easy to lose. Given that part of the work carried out by Greenpeace involves reporting *in situ* the environmental damage caused by certain human activities, rather frequently we find ourselves in situations in which the public at large, a given group, or even governments have gone from being our most enthusiastic supporters to criticizing us fiercely, or, alternatively, changed from hating us to asking us for help. In the end, it all depends on the issue in question.

A good example of what I am referring to here is the relationship between Greenpeace and Spain's most northwestern region. Galicia is the European Continental area where the Atlantic Ocean meets the Bay of Biscay, a land renowned for its fisherfolk and shellfish gatherers. Over more than 30 years, at least six of the organization's ships have visited the Galician ports and waters under different circumstances and, on each occasion, they were received with either hostility or praise, the two faces of the prestige coin.

It was off the Atlantic coast of Galicia, only 140 nautical miles from the mainland, that the *Prestige* sunk. On this occasion, Greenpeace decided to send the second *Rainbow Warrior* to ascertain the magnitude of the disaster the people of Galicia were facing. The ship was heartily welcomed, but – as we are about to find out – that had certainly not been the case for her predecessor, the first *Rainbow Warrior*.

The great escape
(*Rainbow Warrior I*, 1980)

It was the second time the *Rainbow Warrior* had visited the coast of Galicia. Two years before, in 1978, the newly relaunched flagship had sent out her inflatables to stop the last Spanish whaling company from carrying out its deadly operations. The company was property of the Massó family; it used to sell most of its catch to Japan, and had two factories and five whaling ships. The Galician whaling ships needed only to sail 40-60 nautical miles into the sea to find the great cetaceans that travelled those waters in the early summer.

On 18 June 1980, a Spanish naval vessel arrested the *Rainbow Warrior* for blocking the whaling ship *Ibsa III* for several hours. Coincidentally, not long before the arrival of the Greenpeace ship, the *Ibsa I* and *Ibsa II* had been sunk within the harbor in an act of sabotage. Although several groups, including Sea Shepherd, claimed responsibility, it is still a mystery as to who really carried out this operation.

The *Rainbow Warrior* was tugged to the nearby Ferrol naval base. As the ships approached land, they heard the sound of Galician pipes welcoming them from the hills. Crew member Noah Morris brought out his Celtic pipe and started to respond. Once on the wharf, the military offered a rather different welcome, proceeding to take out several parts essential to the working of the engine, and imposing a 10-million-peseta fine.[1] Greenpeace refused to pay the exorbitant fine and the ship remained impounded while everybody waited for a ruling on the case. Days began to go by, then weeks, and finally months...

As time went by the media lost interest in the *Rainbow Warrior* and so the Spanish public simply

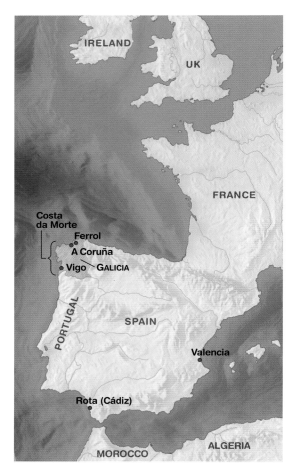

Whale army. There was widespread popular support for the *Rainbow Warrior* during its five-month detention in Spain in 1980.

PIERRE GLEIZES / GREENPEACE

forgot about the ship, except for a few supporters and the people of Ferrol. In that city, which had a long military tradition, an interesting change of attitude was beginning to take place. If at first crew members were seen as eccentric hippies inimical to the town's interests, little by little, distrust was overcome. Greenpeace members were regulars in the stores and bars of the city and eventually they made friends everywhere. Not only did they convince the locals that saving the lives of whales was the right thing to do but they even received the support of the police officers guarding the ship and of numerous navy personnel. They all recognized the absurdity of a situation that was dragging on for far too long. The people of Ferrol went from seeing the rainbow warriors as enemies to actively supporting their cause.

PIERRE GLEIZES / GREENPEACE

The *Rainbow Warrior* crew arrive in Jersey following their escape from Spain. Left to right: Pierre Gleizes, Tony Marriner, Athel von Koettlitz, David McTaggart, Jon Castle, Tim Mark and Chris Robinson.

While the first *Rainbow Warrior* was held in port, the Galician whaling ships carried on their activities, killing an estimated 500 whales.

The ship's crew was reduced to six or seven and, since the situation continued for so long, the environmentalists began to devise an escape plan. The first things they needed were the confiscated engine parts. The ship's captain, Jon Castle, explains how the problem was solved: 'We obtained the original plans and ordered the parts from London.' The total weight of the different engine parts was approximately 100 kilos and they were gradually smuggled on board by crew members in a laundry basket. Even so, the time window for making an escape was narrow due to the lack of fuel. The time spent in Ferrol had been too long and, one by one, the fuel tanks were being emptied just to provide the minimum electricity needed for day-to-day activities.

On the new-moon night of 8 November, the engine of the *Rainbow Warrior* came to life and, after being cast off, the ship silently left the dock

and sailed off to liberty. As it was the weekend, the activities around the military installation were much more relaxed. The *Rainbow Warrior* quietly made its way through the mouth of the Galician fjord[2] while the police monitoring the ship informed the maritime authorities of the escape. It is worth mentioning that the reaction from the Spanish authorities was terribly slow. The Navy took too long in setting out after a ship well on its way into international waters and the two patrol boats that were sent searched in vain.

Two days later, the *Rainbow Warrior* arrived triumphantly in Jersey, a British island in the English Channel, with only seven tons of fuel but with a great deal of euphoria.

The escape of the Greenpeace flagship was a surprise to everyone, including the volunteers of local environmental organizations who had been supporting the ship during her stay in Ferrol. It had been so long since the impounding that many believed the ship had been set free months before. The dramatic escape gained international media coverage and scandalized Spanish public opinion. It was really through this incident that Greenpeace became well known in the country – the Admiral of the Armada was forced to resign. Thanks to the arrest of the *Rainbow Warrior*, and especially to her audacious escape, whaling opposition grew immensely in Spain, particularly in Galicia.

Spain finally abided by the international commercial whaling moratorium in 1986.

In 1999, Jon Castle came back to Galicia, visiting the port city of A Coruña as captain of the *MV Greenpeace*. It was dawn when he, several crew members, and various Spanish activists left the ship to perform an action demanding the closure of a large incineration plant, which led to his being arrested – and beaten while the arrest was taking place. However, once at the police station, one of the high-ranking officers recognized him and, making no attempt to hide his amusement, started to point at Jon, saying: 'It's him! It is the captain who took away the *Rainbow* and fooled us all! It's him!' From that moment, everyone showed him a lot more respect.

Rise to glory (*Sirius*, 1982)

One image stands out in the history of Greenpeace. Who has not been captivated by watching two barrels of nuclear waste being thrown from a ship on to one of the organization's inflatables? The image was so powerful that it meant the push needed to stop the dangerous disposal of radioactive waste at sea.

The image dates back to 1982 and it shows inflatables from the Greenpeace ship *Sirius* on the second day of their attempts to stop the *Rijnborg* dumping its barrels at sea. The Dutch ship had 7,000 tons of nuclear waste stored in its hold.

From the very beginning, the generation of radioactive waste by nuclear plants created a serious problem with no clear solution: What should be done with it? For many years, several countries adopted an apparently easy solution – dump it into the deepest areas of the oceans. As the saying goes: 'Out of sight, out of mind.' So it was that the depths of our oceans – including many areas yet to be 'discovered' – became enormous atomic dumping grounds.

For years, the procedure – with all its unforeseen consequences – was carried out with impunity. It was not until the end of the 1970s that this terrible environmental threat was brought to light. Greenpeace and its ships played a major role, but the environmental organization was by no means alone. Help came from many different

Greenpeace activists opposing the dumping of nuclear waste have two barrels dropped on their inflatable. This image made worldwide news – and helped to put such dumping on the mainstream agenda.

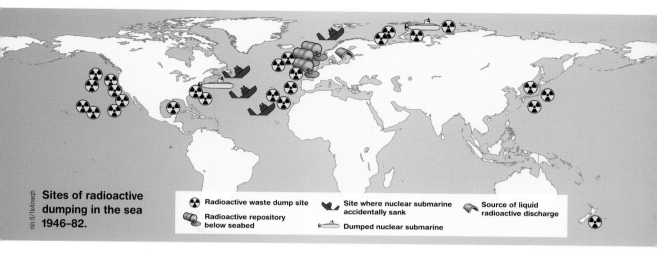

Sites of radioactive dumping in the sea 1946–82.

nin.tl/1k4nwqh

Legend:
- ☢ Radioactive waste dump site
- Radioactive repository below seabed
- Site where nuclear submarine accidentally sank
- Dumped nuclear submarine
- Source of liquid radioactive discharge

sides and the people of Galicia were among those providing it – for them, it was an issue really close to home.

The first time *Greenpeace* condemned the dumping of nuclear waste at sea was in 1978. Right after confronting Icelandic whalers, the *Rainbow Warrior* blocked the *Gem*, a British ship trying to dump 5,000 barrels of radioactive waste in the Atlantic Ocean.

Only 300 nautical miles northwest of the Galician coast lies the so-called Atlantic Trench, an area of approximately 2,500 square kilometers that is between 4,000 and 5,000 meters deep. No less than eight countries were using this ocean chasm as a radioactive dump.

In 1981, a small local political party in Galicia named Esquerda Galega called Greenpeace to propose a joint expedition to the Atlantic Trench. It was agreed that the environmental organization would send the *Sirius* – at that time moored in England – and that Esquerda Galega would charter a ship. Both were to meet at the location where the Dutch ships *Louise* and *Kristen* were in the process of dumping 6,800 tons of radioactive waste.

Ánxel Vila, captain and owner of a fishing boat named *Xurelo*, only a little over 20 meters long, presented himself and his ship for the cause. Not long after the Galician ship set sail, its captain and passengers – most of whom had never set foot on a boat before – were informed that, due to technical problems, the *Sirius* could not make the voyage. The crew of the small fishing boat was not intimidated by the news and decided to continue on its own. Not even the threat of sanctions nor the order to abort the trip received a few hours later from the maritime authorities made them turn back. The captain, crew and passengers – politicians, environmentalists, scholars and journalists – had no doubt about the need to denounce what was taking place so close to their coastline.

Despite the limited technology available to him – radar with a range of 12 miles and a few nautical charts with the Atlantic Trench co-ordinates – the Galician captain was able to find the ships he was looking for. They took images of hundreds of radioactive barrels being discarded while deploying protest banners. Before returning home, they sowed the sea with red flowers depicting an offering in a cemetery. The protest was simple but effective; it had huge repercussions in Galicia and the rest of Spain – and even elsewhere in Europe. Public awareness grew of an activity that was taking place covertly and with a total lack of control.

A year went by before a joint expedition to the Atlantic Trench was organized again. This time, two other Galician fishing boats accompanied the *Xurelo*, and the *Sirius* – fresh from a campaign to prevent the English ship *Gem* from dumping nuclear waste – joined them. The meeting point of

In those days, Spain was a country where environmental awareness was just dawning, yet Ánxel Vila, captain of the *Xurelo*, was already speaking of the need to leave our children and grandchildren a better world and to protect the sea for future generations.

this small fleet was the Dutch ship *Rijnborg*. Once there, the Galician protesters were impressed by Greenpeace's strategy, which involved more than mere protest: activists would place their lives in danger by maneuvering their small inflatables right up to the dumping site. On the first day, a pair of barrels fell so close to an inflatable that, in the abrupt motion of the waves that followed, the activist on board hit his head hard against the inflatable's engine. On the second day, the famous

Vigo, Spain, 1982. Huge crowds turned out to greet the *Sirius*, the *Xurelo* and the two fishing boats that had supported them in their anti-dumping actions.

PIERRE GLEIZES

incident captured on camera took place. When two barrels fell on to the bow of the inflatable, activist Willem Groenier went flying. What could have ended in tragedy ended up as just a huge scare, as Willem emerged with barely a scratch. But the images went out worldwide and the issue of nuclear waste was finally – and for good – at the forefront of people's minds.

If, the year before, only a few dozen people had come out to greet the *Xurelo* on its return, in 1982, thousands gathered at Vigo's port to cheer the *Sirius* and the three fishing boats home. Pierre Gleizes could not believe his eyes. Only two years previously, he had spent a night at Pontevedra's police station for sneaking into the whale factory at Cangas; later on, after the arrest of the *Rainbow Warrior*, he had been summoned by a military judge in Ferrol; and yet here he was being welcomed as a hero aboard the *Sirius*.

This euphoric welcome and support marked a milestone in the history of environmental protest in Spain. Shortly after docking, the crew of the *Sirius* were the guests at a special reception at the Town Hall. To this day, the *Sirius* is probably the Greenpeace ship that is most appreciated in Galicia.

There are 140,000 tons of nuclear waste deposited in the Atlantic Trench alone, which carries radioactivity of about one million curies. For comparison, during the Chernobyl accident of 1986, about 130,000 curies were released into the atmosphere.

For the record, this was the last time that nuclear waste was thrown from a ship into the sea. In 1983, the so-called London Convention, an international law that regulates all kind of discharges at sea, placed a moratorium on such dumping. A decade later, in 1993, the moratorium became a total ban. Yet to this day, believe it or not, monitoring on either the condition of the barrels resting on the seabed or on the level of radioactivity in the area has never been carried out. The great depths of our oceans have become the guardians of these large bombs, exposed to extremely high pressures and

Black days. Following the sinking of the oil tanker _Prestige_, thousands of volunteers worked for weeks to remove oil from the polluted Atlantic coast of Galicia, Spain.

the harshness of the marine environment. Today, the governments that placed them there continue to adopt 'ostrich tactics'.

The oil-tanker disaster
(*Rainbow Warrior II*, 2002)

The tar (popularly known in Spain as *chapapote*) was a black viscous mass which came on the back of weirdly smooth waves. There was no foam, the waves literally smashed by a mourning veil. Every time the tide carried the sea away, the tar remained, impregnating the portion of coast it had arrived at. It seeped in among the rocks and then formed little dark wells. When arriving at the golden beaches, it either came in large quantities and covered everything or, in other cases, it formed small croquettes of tar breaded with sand.

As the tide began to ebb, volunteers from all over Spain – and even from abroad – started to get ready for the cleaning. Soon the entire coast was filled with thousands of people armed with waterproof or disposable white overalls, rubber boots and gloves, and masks. It resembled an army of ants. While some of them were moving up and down with loaded rubber buckets, others were collecting tar, using either their hands or shovels, depending on the circumstances. The next tide would cover everything again with the slimy substance, or might pollute an area which had hitherto escaped. The clean-up task seemed never-ending and it was often not possible to hold back tears of sorrow and helplessness. Perhaps there was also a feeling of guilt: at the end of the day, we are all dependent on oil to a greater or lesser extent. From this perspective, every single bucket of tar removed could be considered as part of the price to be paid to Nature for all the harm caused by this dependency on the 'black gold'.

The story began on 13 November 2002. The *Prestige*, a single-hull tanker under a Bahamas flag loaded with 77,000 tons of fuel oil[3], sent an SOS from its position 28 nautical miles off Cape Finisterre – the place believed to be the very edge of the Earth in ancient times. A crack had opened in the ship's side. The Spanish authorities took the decision to move the ship off the coast. This was against the opinion not only of the captain himself (who asked to be towed and then anchored so as to transfer the oil to another vessel) but also of Greenpeace and most experts (who asked for the ship to be brought to port in order to control the spill). Six days later, as its captain had predicted, the *Prestige* broke in two and sank about 140 nautical miles off the coast of Galicia. It had covered 243 nautical miles in a storm, in an arduous pilgrimage that had already left behind an expanding trail of oil. Now, at 4,000 meters deep, the ship's opened guts continued releasing the dense dark poison.

Oil, the raw material that moves the most money on land, moves through the planet's seas mostly on boats with flags of convenience – in other words, on vessels registered in countries with minimal safety regulations that nevertheless offer economic advantages to the large companies that own the oil and the ships. In Galicia alone, four serious oil spills have taken place: the *Policomander*, the *Urquiola*, the *Aegean Sea* and the *Prestige*.

Greenpeace activists were strategically stationed as lookouts along the Costa da Morte.[4] Two days after that distress call, Mito Fernández-Obanza, one of the volunteers, gave the news that a large black spot was approaching. This was the first one, a mere foretaste of the disaster that was brewing. In less than a week, large amounts of fuel were riding the waves to arrive at the coast of Galicia. According to government representative Mariano Rajoy, later to become prime minister, the tar arriving was something similar to 'little threads of play dough'. Given the authorities' ineffectiveness, the local small-scale fishing fleet themselves protected some of the fjords, using their own boats and homemade anti-pollution barriers to build up a retaining wall. Given that neither the army nor any other national body was mobilized, thousands of volunteers began to arrive along the coast of Galicia. The only positive thing that this terrible tragedy brought about was this –

The sinking of the *Prestige* caused one of the worst environmental disasters in the history of navigation. The highly toxic oil spill affected 2,500 kilometers of coastline from northern Portugal to the south of France, with the biggest impact in Galicia.

The last moments of the *Prestige* on the surface before sinking to the seabed

ECOLOGISTAS EN ACCIÓN

the incredible social mobilization that it created, an authentic human flood of solidarity never seen before in an environmental crisis.

Although Greenpeace had been saying it from the outset, it was not until 15 days after the beginning of the spill that the presence of aromatic hydrocarbons (extremely toxic and potentially carcinogenic compounds) in the fuel was publicly recognized. Picking up tar involved high health risks! However, if in the early days – times of great confusion and despair – you could see people collecting tar in their shirtsleeves, later on there were no special controls, either. Many volunteers tried to protect themselves; for example, by using dust masks that were totally ineffective against these substances.

On 8 December, the *Rainbow Warrior* arrived on the coast of Galicia. A flotilla of 150 fishing and private boats went out to meet the ship as she approached A Coruña and about 2,000 people were waiting to greet it at the port. A few hours later, the ship was sailing towards the place where the *Prestige* had sunk in order to document what was happening there. The national government was claiming that the fuel had solidified and that there were no more leaks, while prohibiting aircraft from flying over the area so that no-one could check if this was true. The Greenpeace flagship arrived in the vicinity lacking the exact co-ordinates. She met the two tugs that had been with the *Prestige* but they gave false positions and consequently the ship could not achieve her target.

After the unsuccessful attempt to locate the wreck, the *Rainbow Warrior* went to the Cíes Islands. These islands are the 'jewel' of the recently created Atlantic Islands National Park[5] and are located at the entrance of the Vigo fjord. It was there that Greenpeace divers confirmed a terrible suspicion. Diving opposite an apparently intact sandy beach, they discovered that the fuel – compacted into cylindrical shapes – was creeping along the sea bed at the mercy of the currents and dragging many marine species into its deadly embrace.

The *Rainbow Warrior* docked in Vigo amid great expectancy and images of her arrival were widely distributed. The activists on board carried the evidence that the 'problem' was not just on the surface, as the authorities were still maintaining.

The *Rainbow Warrior*, with 150 other boats, arrives in A Coruña to document the pollution.

Before getting under way, a joint declaration by Greenpeace and 100 scientists was presented on board. It contained a number of measures to be taken that might prevent a tragedy such as the *Prestige* ever happening again.

90 per cent of the Atlantic Islands National Park was polluted, as not a single measure was taken to prevent the oil spill reaching it.

When the *Rainbow Warrior* departed from Galicia, thousands of miles of coast were in mourning. The Spanish government's strategy to combat the greatest environmental crisis the country had ever suffered basically consisted of constantly denying evidence, continually hindering the task of informing the public, and ostentatiously manipulating data. On 26 December, the Minister of Defense himself visited Galicia and publicly stated: 'There are no tar-stained beaches... The beaches were clean and magnificent.' That very same morning I had spent several hours removing the viscous fuel from Lariño beach, in the Costa da Morte. All the beaches in the area were in a similar state. It had already been 37 days since the sinking of the *Prestige* and the ship continued leaking fuel – yet the Spanish government was still lying about the reality.

The European Union banned single-hull ships carrying heavy fuel from entering its ports in 2003. However, despite the numerous accidents taking place, they still continue circulating freely within European waters and, indeed, all over the planet's seas.

On the 10th anniversary of the *Prestige* disaster, the trial considering accountability for the incident finally began. The captain is facing a 12-year prison sentence. Yet neither of the companies involved have been charged, nor any of those with positions of political responsibility at the time.

An assault (*Esperanza*, 2004)

'And where were you when the *Prestige* happened?' an angry fisher on the wharf asked Juantxo López de Uralde, who was on board the *Esperanza*. The then executive director of Greenpeace Spain calmly replied: 'Just here, at this very same dock!' In fact, the welcome the *Esperanza* was receiving in Vigo and the one that the organization's flagship had enjoyed in the same place two years before, were at opposite poles.

The *Esperanza* had arrived in town early in the morning. A press conference was supposed to be held on board at midday but it ended up taking place in the town square. The Port Authority had denied the 20 journalists attending the event entrance to the port. However, there were about 200 people on the dock at the point when Juantxo was rebuked by the fisher. They had entered the restricted area with no problem three hours later.

The organizers of this small demonstration against the *Esperanza*'s presence in town were the powerful owners of the industrial-trawler fleet in Vigo. The Greenpeace ship was coming from a hard month of campaigning in the Hatton Bank,

JIRI REZAC / GREENPEACE

Formerly a Russian navy firefighting ship, the *Esperanza* is the most recent addition to the Greenpeace fleet aside from *Rainbow Warrior III*. Following an extensive conversion, it began work for the organization in late 2001. It is the fastest and largest Greenpeace ship.

ROGER GRACE / GREENPEACE

KATE DAVISON / GREENPEACE

The biological treasure of seamounts

• There are between 30,000 and 100,000 seamounts and only about 200 have been studied. In fact, even today, more is known about the moon than about them.
• These extinct marine volcanoes rise at least 1,000 meters from the seabed and it is estimated that between 500,000 and 5 million undiscovered species live in them.
• Coral forests as old as 10,000 years have formed in many of them.
• The Hatton Bank is part of the longest mountain range on the planet, spreading from the Arctic Ocean to the Azores. In the bottom picture, *Esperanza* crew member Odin Sunquist holds a large spider crab killed by a bottom-trawler in the Hatton Bank.
• Only 11 countries, with approximately 250 vessels, carry out 95% of fishing by bottom-trawlers.

a fishing ground located between the northwest of Ireland and the south of Iceland. There we had carried out several protest actions against some bottom-trawlers that were fishing in the area. Bottom-trawlers drag fishing gear weighing several tons across the seabed, devastating life on underwater mountains. These unique seamounts are being destroyed before they can even be explored (see box above).

The group of people protesting on the wharf of Vigo were basically the ship-owners' families and their employees. All the ships we had met in the Hatton Bank had ended up being related to this city of Galicia and its crews had publicly accused Greenpeace of having been paid by rival fleets. They considered the *Esperanza*'s visit as an insult.

However, our main aim in going to Vigo was to explain our work in the Hatton Bank to locals. Our long-term goal was to bring about a planetwide moratorium on this type of fishing. As evidence that we do not care about the flag of the fishing

vessel operating, just a few months earlier, the *Rainbow Warrior* had itself been hampering bottom trawlers of diverse nationalities in the Tasman Sea (between Australia and New Zealand/Aotearoa). In addition, several international organizations (including more than 1,100 scientists) had called for emergency measures to protect these ecosystems. The UN General Assembly had also just asked for the provisional ban of bottom-trawling on seamounts.

Honestly, it is quite a curious experience to see a group of people demonstrating against you. In fact, it is good in the sense that everyone can exercise the right to demonstrate peacefully. The fishing workers' slogans and banners accused us of being paid by countries such as Canada, Norway and Japan. Some of them started to throw us coins. 'Girl, how much do they pay you?' someone shouted at me from the dock. 'Nothing: I volunteer,' I replied. The man was stunned. 'Nothing? They are cheating you!' he asserted.

Anger in Vigo.
A Spanish police
officer tries to stop
a trawler employee
from detaching the
mooring line of the
Esperanza during
protests against
the Greenpeace
ship in November
2004.

Approximately 50 per cent of the catch of a bottom-trawler is returned dead to the sea.

In the beginning, everything was relatively calm. Half an hour later, the atmosphere started to become tense. Dozens of chicken eggs and an occasional ostrich egg began to be launched at the *Esperanza* and its crew. The slogans chanted by the protesters changed into loud insults. A small group cut one of our mooring lines with a knife and lifted two more from the bollards to which they were secured. The *Esperanza*'s stern began to separate from the dock and the engines had to be started in an emergency situation. The police intervened and forced the demonstrators to put the lines back in place and then stayed to check that nobody touched them again.

At the same time, the first attempts to board the ship were taking place. The captain of the *Esperanza*, Jon Castle again, went down the gangway to try to calm the protesters down. Juantxo went with him. It was useless. They were determined to come up and continue their protest on board. Finally, it was decided to stop blocking their access to the ship, so about 30 protesters boarded *en masse* and then split into small groups.

I got to the wheelhouse with my tongue hanging out and my heart in my mouth. I had just gone from deck to deck blocking the accesses to our accommodation, running along the long alleyways and up the stairs two at a time. When I was about to go outside, a workmate stopped me and asked me if I was crazy. Meanwhile, Chris Hoare, the Australian radio operator, turned to me and desperately said, 'Maite, Maite. Tell them not to break anything, not to break anything!'

The invaders had already reached the highest point on the ship, the 'roof' of the wheelhouse – the place where most of the antennas and some rather expensive electronic equipment were located. Despite being very angry, the men there did not break anything but only put one of their banners up while irately addressing me.

At the stern, the situation had become much more tense. There, the invaders burned the ship's Dutch flag[6] and held it against an educational exhibition about the deep seas, thereby burning two of its panels and cracking several others. Then attention shifted to the middle of the ship, where a group of protesters were showering insults on Pablo Mascareñas, a Greenpeace Spain employee. A bunch of his female workmates were trying to form a shield to protect him while talking to the angry men. The demonstrators had confused Pablo with Sebastián Losada, one of the campaign leaders, who was also Galician. The most enraged wanted to see Sebas' head rolling and you could also hear things like: 'We're gonna bomb the ship' and 'We're gonna throw the ship's helicopter overboard.'

Among the protesters who assaulted us, there were two distinct types of people: those with a very aggressive attitude and those who, despite their anger, were still open to dialogue.

'You never interfere with the Japanese, do you?' one of them said to me in a high tone.

'Haven't you got a TV? Because we've been campaigning against Japanese whalers for many years...'

'Ummm, well, but you do *not* interfere with Canadian fishing, do you?' he replied.

Little by little, the ones open to dialogue calmed down the most aggressive guys and, after a while, our unexpected 'guests' decided to leave.

The *Esperanza* stayed in Vigo for four more days but finally had to leave two days before its planned departure date. The educational activities organized for several schools had to be cancelled and Greenpeace's request for dialogue had been knocked back. The bottom-trawlers' owners

organized a further demonstration in the streets and even asked the City Council to declare us 'undesirable people' – which thankfully never happened.

From the port of Vigo to the entrance of the fjord, the *Esperanza* was escorted by two Guardia Civil patrol boats together with several fishing boats whose crews did not lose the chance to hurl loud insults at the environmental organization.

In 2006, the UN General Assembly adopted a resolution calling for the protection of vulnerable seamount ecosystems and stating that countries must undertake environmental impact studies before authorizing bottom-trawling in these locations. To this day, however, this resolution is ignored with total impunity.

In December 2013, the European Parliament narrowly voted against a ban on bottom-trawling but has proposed a package of measures including closing areas to bottom-trawling where vulnerable deep-sea eco-systems are likely to exist. The EU fisheries ministers will consider this in 2014.

In the last action of the campaign, we spent the night on the deck of the bottom-trawler *Anuva*, sleeping on top of its nets. The ship's captain allowed the women to use the toilet next to the wheelhouse. It was impressive to see the ship's high technology. An array of screens depicted the seabed as if it were scanned by x-rays.

After the ship's activity had been blocked for 18 hours, the crew lost patience and decided to cast their nets, throwing two of the activists who were on top of them into the water.

KATE DAVISON

The winds that blow these days
(*Rainbow Warrior II* and *Arctic Sunrise*)

The *Rainbow Warrior* visited Galicia again in 2009, as part of the Tour commemorating the 25th anniversary of Greenpeace Spain. I was on board on this occasion. We were working on an issue related to climate change in the Arousa fjord when a group of fishers from Vigo gave us a call. They wanted our support to stop a luxury housing project (which included the construction of a marina) in what used to be the whaling factory in Cangas. We decided to go to their aid.

We were just entering the Vigo fjord when the fishers came out in their boats to welcome us. Right after anchoring, some of them came on to the *Rainbow Warrior* to provide us with more information about the issue. A little later, they and most of the crew went together on the inflatables to the abandoned factory site. As fate would have it, this was the very same factory whose workers had expelled two Greenpeace people, Rémi Parmentier and Pierre Gleizes, 31 years before – they had been trying to get information for the first *Rainbow Warrior* before she confronted the Galician whalers.

The first apologies for the assault and the whole behavior towards the *Esperanza* in 2004 came while we were on the inflatable. They were the first I heard but far from the last as the locals kept on saying sorry throughout the time we spent together. The oddest part of it was that they were apologizing for something done by others: by their 'sea colleagues', the ones fishing on bottom-trawlers.

Even if the housing project was finally abandoned for legal and financial reasons and not due to the our short visit, this ended up being very successful as it meant the beginning of a very good relationship with at least part of the Vigo fishing fleet.

In 2011, the *Arctic Sunrise* was the Greenpeace ship visiting Galicia and it was, once more, to talk about unsustainable fishing. The ship called at A Coruña in order to publish a report that exposed how deep-sea bottom-trawling receives large subsidies from the European Union – despite being the most destructive form of fishing for the marine environment and also overexploiting fish stocks.

In places such as Canada and Chile, biodiversity has decreased by 50% in areas with salmon farms. Amongst other reasons, this has been due to eutrophication[7], genetic pollution and the entry of antibiotics into the food chain.

A radically different reception. Small fishing boats turn out in force to welcome the *Rainbow Warrior* to Vigo in 2009.

Greenpeace members and fisherfolk from Vigo hold up a banner protesting against the Galician bank Caixa Nova. The *Rainbow Warrior* can be seen in the background.

ANA CARLA MARTINEZ

Then the ship headed south to enter Muros-Noia fjord. The small-scale fishing workers from there had asked Greenpeace for help as they were facing a serious problem: a proposed complex of salmon farms inside their fjord was set to have a huge impact on their fishing and shellfish-collecting grounds. That would jeopardize their livelihoods. A flotilla of small boats greeted the *Arctic Sunrise* and the fisherfolk invited the whole crew to have lunch in town. There was more than one ecologist who could not believe what they were experiencing as they shared a table with the fishing community in its home. Just a few years before, this would have been completely unthinkable.

In Galicia in 2004, Greenpeace was publicly accused of going against the fishing workers. However, the passage of time has shown that what actually drives the organization is the protection of the most valuable marine ecosystems and the promotion of sustainable fisheries.

As of early 2014, the 20 projected salmon farms have not yet been installed in Muros-Noia fjord. The local fishing communities, together with Greenpeace, continue fighting against them and for the closure of the two experimental farms that are already causing damage.

As years went by, small-scale fisherfolk – not only on the coasts of Galicia but from all around the planet – have realized that environmentalists are not enemies but rather allies. Ultimately, we are all in the same boat, joining forces and sailing together in order to ensure that the seas are filled with life now and forever.

1 The peseta was the official Spanish currency before the euro. One euro was the equivalent of 166 pesetas. 2 Galician fjords – called *rías* in Spanish – are like sea rivers that enter into the land, creating an indented shoreline. The largest are found on the western coast, facing the Atlantic Ocean. Some are ancient flooded river valleys, others are former tectonic plates and, finally, some are caused by erosion of the mainland which facilitated the sea's infiltration. 3 The fuel, also called fuel oil, is a liquid fuel derived from crude oil. 4 La Costa da Morte (literally 'the Coast of Death') is the northern part of the Atlantic coast of Galicia, extending from Malpica to Fisterra. It received its name due to the outstanding number of shipwrecks along its treacherous rocky shore. 5 The National Park of the Atlantic Islands of Galicia includes the islands Cies, Ons, Sálvora and Cortegada, positioned at the entrance of the great fjords located south of the Costa da Morte. 6 The three ships *Greenpeace International* owns nowadays (the *Arctic Sunrise*, the *Esperanza* and the *Rainbow Warrior*) are registered in the Netherlands and therefore have a Dutch flag. 7 Eutrophication is the response to the presence of fertilizers, such as nitrates and phosphates – naturally or by human action – in an aquatic ecosystem which may have fatal consequences. When organic matter grows excessively due to a nutrient discharge, bacteria, toxic algae and pathogenic microorganisms bloom, triggering the disappearance of vegetation and animal life.

'There is no path for peace. Peace *is* the path.'

Mohandas Gandhi

8 **Wars and walls**

Introduction
Action against the Iraq War (Spain, 2003)
The voyage of wars and walls (Eastern Mediterranean, 2006)
Lebanon and Israel (Lebanon) • Israel and Lebanon (Israel) • The divided island (Cyprus)• The strength of a wind (Croatia)

GREENPEACE IS KNOWN worldwide as an environmental organization that has ships and engages in actions that are often spectacular. The green-ecological side of the organization is much better known than the peace-pacifist side. Given that the actions we take form part of our identity, I think it is important to note that we engage in nonviolent direct action – in other words, when we denounce, hinder or paralyze the aggressive activities of the world, we do not resort to violence. Nonviolent (or pacific) resistance and nonviolent direct action are practically synonymous and directly relate to civil disobedience. Although nonviolent resistance is unquestionably most closely associated with Mohandas ('Mahatma') Gandhi's campaigns against British colonialism in India, there are countless other examples, ranging from the strike of the plebeians in the Rome of 494 BCE and the peaceful resistance of the Maori of New Zealand/Aotearoa in Parihaka at the end of the 19th century, through to the celebrated examples of more recent times, such as Martin Luther King Jr in the US and Aung San Suu Kyi in Burma.

Gandhi said that nonviolence is the most powerful force there is at the disposal of humanity. In the voyage that might be said to have started

The power of nonviolence in world societies

From 1966 to 1999 civil nonviolent resistance played a primary role in 50 of the 67 cases of transition from authoritarian to democratic regimes.

In 2010 the so-called Arab Spring began in Tunisia[1]; a wave of peaceful protests extended to the countries of the Maghreb and other parts of the Arab world, prompting the downfall of various authoritarian regimes – though, as in Syria and Libya, some of these turned to armed rebellion.

AMRIT BAKSHI

On the *Rainbow Warrior*'s upper bridge, known as 'the Monkey Island', was depicted the symbol of peace that is recognized worldwide. The symbol was designed in 1958 for Britain's Campaign for Nuclear Disarmament (CND) and combines the letters N and D in the semaphore alphabet (the communication system that uses the human body and flags). The photo shows the author sitting smack in the middle of the symbol.

Greenpeace, the only 'weapon' the crew of the *Phyllis Cormack* aimed to use to impede the nuclear test in Amchitka was to go to the place and bear witness. Later on, bearing witness to an 'ecological crime' started to be supplemented, in many cases, with nonviolent direct actions. These could involve activities as diverse as painting seal skins or placing zodiacs between the harpoon and the whale. The many actions that the organization has undertaken over the last four decades have required an enormous and constant exercise of imagination. Peaceful protest offers myriad possibilities and victory has often been won because of it.

From the outset, Greenpeace has argued for global disarmament through peaceful means and, amongst other things, has actively opposed the testing and proliferation of nuclear weapons. Furthermore, the organization has opposed all wars not least because, alongside the terrible loss of human life, war causes environmental contamination and degradation.

Greenpeace is pacifist not just in the means it uses but also in its very essence since, from its inception, it has campaigned specifically on the theme of war. In addition to our anti-nuclear campaign (see Chapter 2), we also work to achieve the prohibition of anti-personnel mines and cluster bombs, and for the creation of international norms to regulate the arms trade. We also positioned ourselves publicly against the two US-led wars in Iraq, amongst others.

To represent the many occasions on which we participated in campaigns related to war, this chapter focuses on the action taken by the second *Rainbow Warrior* against the second Iraq war at the Rota naval base in Spain in 2003. Also, war (recent or very recent) and walls (for protection or separation from the enemy) were the common denominators linking the four countries of the eastern Mediterranean that we visited during my first trip on the *Rainbow Warrior* in the autumn of 2006.

February 2003, and the war machine is gearing up for the invasion of Iraq. Greenpeace sets up a peace blockade in the Marchwood military port in Southampton, England, aiming to stop military hardware heading for the Persian Gulf.

Action against the Iraq War

(Spain, 2003)

There they were, a few committed eco-pacifists, spending all day scraping rust, making repairs and painting. While the *Arctic Sunrise* was in Amsterdam undergoing maintenance, the start of the invasion of Iraq seemed imminent and there were strong and widespread protests against the war all over the planet. Greenpeace was clear in its opposition to the war and many of its offices were working on this campaign, part of which involved the *Rainbow Warrior* touring many European countries in the cause of peace.

Those who were aboard the *Arctic Sunrise* found a way of adding their grain of sand to the campaign by organizing brainstorming sessions and sending the results to Greenpeace International. A few days later, three crew members happily agreed to be sent to Spain to board the flagship and participate in an action. This was precisely what they had been wanting to do! It was especially important for Lawrence 'Butch' Turk (medic-deckhand), from the US, and for Edward Patrick (deckhand), from the UK, since their countries, together with Spain, were the ones threatening to launch the invasion.

The *Rainbow Warrior* had arrived at the city of Cádiz, situated on the southeast Atlantic coast of Spain, on 10 March having, in the previous month,

conducted protests for peace in Southampton (England), Amberes (Belgium) and Rotterdam (The Netherlands).

It was 2003. Never before had Spain seen such massive demonstrations and, according to polls, the vast majority of the population was against the invasion of Iraq. Nevertheless, the Prime Minister at the time, José María Aznar, was insisting on involving the country in the war, which Greenpeace saw as being directly related to Iraq's oil reserves – the fifth-largest in the world.

On the morning of 12 March the ship left Cádiz for the nearby Rota naval base and anchored a few meters outside the military exclusion zone. From that moment, the ship was continually accompanied by two boats of the Guardia Civil[2] and two other military vessels. A few hours later, three inflatables containing activists, with Guardia Civil launches in close pursuit, crossed the prohibition line, arriving at the mouth of the military harbor to display on their banners Greenpeace's opposition to the war.

On the following day, a couple of our small inflatables with banners began to follow the 115-meter US Coastguard ship *Dallas* as it left the base bound for the Gulf.[3] A police helicopter joined the chase of the activists and came so close that its rotorblades whipped up the surrounding water. In those two days of 'light' protest, no-one was arrested or injured.

On the third day, however, the stakes were raised. With various boats in the water making maneuvers as a distraction, the *Rainbow Warrior* headed for the mouth of the military port and dropped two anchors in the water at a point where she could block the exit of an enormous US warship. The departure of the *Cape Horn* – almost 230 meters long – was imminent. Zigzagging to try to evade the military boats and the helicopter that were pursuing them, two boats managed to leave activists Butch Turk and Teresa Ambrós perched on two large floats which, like a string of giant sausages, closed the way into the military zone. The aim of Butch and Teresa was to chain themselves to the floats but the rapid intervention of police special forces prevented this and they were both detained immediately (and freed a little later).

The crew of one of the boats, Ed Patrick and Dima Sharomov, saw that the other had been detained and brought alongside a Guardia Civil patrol. They also noticed that the two Greenpeace crew members had not been handcuffed and immediately took the decision to attempt their rescue. Ed and Dima swiftly changed course and swept up beside the other inflatable so that their comrades could jump aboard and then made off at speed back to the *Rainbow Warrior*.

At the tripartite summit in the Azores (14 and 15 March), the heads of government of the US, UK and Spain sent an ultimatum to Iraqi leader Saddam Hussein to surrender the 'weapons of mass destruction' that he allegedly possessed. After the invasion, no weapons of this kind were found in Iraq.

At six in the evening, a Guardia Civil patrol delivered to the ship a judicial order to leave the place. This was probably the first and only time a judge had ordered Greenpeace to stop a protest in Spain – and reflected the wrath of the Spanish government. The crew replied that they needed time to take a decision and, anticipating an assault, sealed off the living quarters from the inside. A little later, the ship was boarded by some 20 agents. There ensued a long impasse lasting several hours, during which nothing happened apart from the besieged giving some food to the hungry agents walking around on the deck.

Around midnight a tugboat arrived and the Guardia Civil cut the anchor chains. The *Rainbow Warrior* was towed by the stern (something of a barbarity in marine terms) to the port of Cádiz. Once the ship had been moored to the dock, the security forces began an assault on her most

Blowback. A Spanish Guardia Civil helicopter hovers over Greenpeace inflatables so as to drench them in spray.

PEDRO ARMESTRE / GREENPEACE

vulnerable point, the bridge. Breaking the glass of the starboard door, the agents made a whirlwind entry. The crew from the bridge scampered down the interior staircase, hoping that the last one down would be able to close and block the hatch that isolated the bridge, but they were not in time. One crew member stayed behind to calm the agents and ask them not to break anything; this was Carlos Bravo, Greenpeace Spain's disarmament campaigner, who was immobilized almost immediately.

The Guardia Civil plunged down the narrow accommodation alleyway like bulls in a china shop. There was some shoving and several photographs on the bulkheads fell to the floor. Some of the crew tried to block the route to the captain's cabin since the agents were clearly aiming to arrest him. One of these, Ed, clung on to the handrails on either side as he watched the tangle of arms, heads and legs advancing in his direction. A Guardia Civil managed to reach Ed and began to hit him on the arms to force him to let go. Seeing that this would achieve nothing, the officer instead put his arms around the activist's neck and twisted it sharply. Ed heard a 'crack' and felt a sharp pain. A little later he would also feel blood streaming from his nose.

Daniel Rizzotti, the captain, was taken in handcuffs to the police station. An hour later the agents returned and arrested Carlos Bravo and the bosun Phil Lloyd.

The assault had taken place early on a Saturday morning. During that weekend, demonstrations against the war had been called in many cities in Spain and around the world, since at the same time a decisive meeting between George W Bush, Tony Blair and José María Aznar was taking place in the Azores. At the Saturday demonstration in Madrid, José Saramago – Nobel laureate for literature – in his speech asked for the Greenpeace activists to be freed. When they were finally released on the Sunday, they were met by a big crowd and a large media scrum. The *Rainbow Warrior* was delayed leaving Cádiz because the ship first had to be given back the two anchors left in the naval base.

On 23 March 2003 the United States and its allies began the invasion of Iraq. A year later, after

Under siege. Greenpeace activists and crew members on the bridge with Guardia Civil officers outside before they broke in. On the right are Captain Daniel Rizzotti (white shirt) and deckhand Timo Marshall.

Invading force. Deckhand Ed Patrick being dragged away.

a terrorist attack in Madrid left 191 dead and 1,500 injured, Aznar's party lost the general election. The new prime minister withdrew Spanish troops from Iraq immediately on taking power.

In 2005, the trial took place of five people who had participated in the Rota protests: Daniel Rizzoti, Carlos Bravo, Phil Lloyd, Butch Turk and Teresa Ambrós. The situation was serious: the prosecution was asking for a sentence amounting to a total of 12 years in jail. In the end, although the captain did receive a six-month sentence, none of the accused went to prison. And the focus on the trial led to the work of the Greenpeace national office being celebrated in the media and the organization gaining a large number of supporters.

The death toll in Iraq

According to influential medical journal *The Lancet*, the number of Iraqi civilians killed in the war reached 116,903, while Allied troops suffered 4,804 deaths. The number of Iraqi soldiers killed is unknown.

The voyage of wars and walls
(Eastern Mediterranean, 2006)

I had already sailed four times on Greenpeace International ships before I embarked in Barcelona at the start of September 2006. However, the emotion I felt on this occasion was different, and not just because, unlike the others, this one was a sailing ship (sailing is my great passion). My embarkation on the *Rainbow Warrior* fulfilled a childhood dream.

My own first trip on the *Rainbow Warrior* taught me a great deal about wars and walls – as well as marking the beginning of some great friendships. For those of us travelling on the Greenpeace ships, sharing the voyage with people from the many different countries that we visit is a great gift. The friendships you make give you a deeper understanding of what life is like in other parts of the world.

Once the ship had been provisioned we set out for the island of Cyprus, at the other end of the Mediterranean. We stopped off in Larnaca just long enough to prepare materials and embark the rest of the crew before heading for one of the most conflict-ridden places on the planet at the time. Just 34 days earlier, a ceasefire had been signed in the latest confrontation between Israel and Lebanon and we intended to visit both countries. The *Rainbow Warrior*'s mission was to document the environmental consequences of this war.

Lebanon and Israel (Lebanon)

Little by little, we began to make out Beirut. It was very early and I noted my heart shrinking in a cold that was absolutely unrelated to the atmospheric temperature. Scarcely a month before, bombs had

Blitzed. The remains of the bombed Jiyeh power station, 30 kilometers south of Beirut. Fuel from here burned for three weeks while 215,000 tons contaminated 150 kilometers of the coast.

DMITRI SHAROMOV

been falling on the Lebanese capital. Among the jumble of buildings of different heights, modern skyscrapers stood out. A great rounded form floated over them. Could we believe what we were seeing? Yes, indeed it was: a hot air balloon for tourists. From the sea, no trace of the war was visible.

That same day people from the Greenpeace office in Beirut took some of us crew, along with video cameras, to the bombed Jiyeh power station, 30 kilometers to the south. Looking out from the window of the van as we crossed the city, I felt as if I were in a film. Intact buildings alternated with those bearing infinite numbers of bulletholes..'That is not from this war, but from the one before, in 1982,' said one of the local Greenpeace staff.

With great precision, only the five fuel tanks had been bombed, leaving the rest of the power station intact. Looking south, the horizon was dominated by two colors: the blue of the sky and the black of the charred deposits. We walked right to the sea on earth and rock covered by the great black blanket of burned fuel that only ended at the point where the Mediterranean began.

When the media talk about wars they rarely mention the damage done to the environment. They talk a lot about human victims and the destruction of human works (airports, museums, historic or emblematic buildings), but they devote very few words to describing the impact that an attack has on the soil, the air or the water of a place – or on the other living beings that inhabit it.

We returned to Beirut in silence, passing over many bridges repaired in a makeshift way. We saw on the road many Hizbullah posters proclaiming 'Divine Victory' (in Arabic, French and English) and showing a variety of images of the war and its leaders. Hizbullah is a Shi'a Islamic group founded in Lebanon after the Israeli invasion in 1982. It has a political as well as a military wing. In the 2006 Lebanon War, the confrontation was between the Israeli army and Hizbullah military forces.

We remained in the southern part of the city to visit Dhajiyeh, the neighborhood most damaged by the bombs, where Hizbullah had its headquarters. Even the surroundings had semi-destroyed buildings. We left the van to enter 'Zone 0'. After 50 meters or so, an enormous expanse of land opened up before us, with large areas of rubble, twisted metal and craters. A part of the city of Beirut – about 250 buildings – had simply been wiped off the map. All that remained of a 10-story building was a giant crater where you

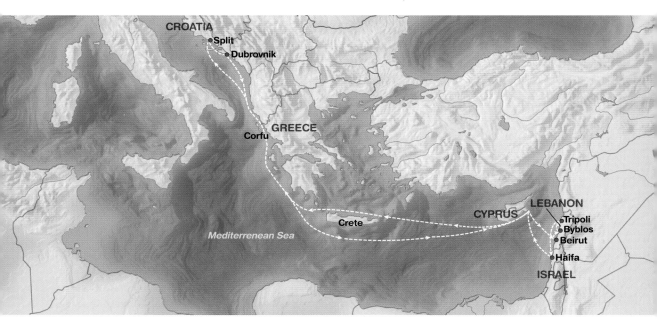

PIERRE GLEIZES

Farewell to the totem gangway sign
For a few years, this was the sign (made by Ed Patrick) that we used to put at the beginning of the gangway to say that the ship was closed to the public. One night in Beirut a group of French sailors who'd been having a good time in the city returned to their frigate, which was moored behind the *Rainbow Warrior*. When they reached the Greenpeace ship they began to abuse Pablo Korman, who was on watch duty. Making as if to come aboard, they approached the sign, untied it and promptly ran off with it. It may even now be on display as a trophy in the home of one of those sailors.

direction, chased by the police. Enveloped in the sound of sirens, they all disappeared into the city. 'Pachum, pachum, pachum...': life goes on in mistreated Beirut, once known as 'The Switzerland of the Middle East'. In the end, this was what life had been doing in that city for more than 5,000 years.

Because the Jiyeh power station was bombed at the start of the conflict, five weeks passed before it was possible to start the clean-up. By that time part of the burnt and seeping fuel oil had been transformed into tar which had coated the sea bed at many points on the coast. To start the work of researching and documenting this, the *Rainbow*

Underwater impact: Greenpeace divers survey the damage done by the Jiyeh power station oil spill.

MARCO CARE / GREENPEACE

could look down upon the second basement floor. Of the many printing presses and libraries that had once been there, all that remained were damaged books piled into little mountains. Excavators were removing rubble while small groups of curious people wandered past the place. There were also children playing in the ruins. Their laughter mixed with the range of noises produced by the work of the excavators.

In this extraordinary city, everything was possible. That same night, I was on port watch from eight to midnight. The wind carried the sound of a nearby disco: 'pachum, pachum, pachum...' From the bridge of the ship I saw cars passing at high speed and later heard the screech of tires: at the end of the port road there was a competition to make cars spin like tops. I then heard a siren and a few moments later saw cars driving in the opposite

Warrior anchored off the power station. Our divers made maps of the contaminated sea bed to be taken to the Italian authorities, who were in charge of cleaning this zone. On our way back to Beirut, we passed near one of the port's lighthouses. Someone from the local Greenpeace office commented that it was the ugliest lighthouse in the country and yet it was the only one where, instead of being blown up, as had happened to most of the others, they had simply shot the bulb. Could this have been an Israeli 'joke'?

Our next mission would be to gather oysters at several points on the coast to be studied by the American University of Beirut. Since they filter

Blackened: the oil-damaged coastline at Byblos, Lebanon, with the *Rainbow Warrior* at anchor offshore.

PIERRE GLEIZES / GREENPEACE

sea water to obtain their food, these mollusks are a good indicator of environmental contamination.

As we sailed, we could make out in the distance the white summits of Mount Lebanon and, on the rich land between, we could see woods and terraces created for agriculture. The shoreline seemed to be packed densely with housing. In the Palm islands nature reserve off Tripoli, one of the few remaining spawning grounds for the green turtle, we found swimming pools of oil among the rocks.

Heading south again, we stopped for some days in the mythical city of Byblos, a World Heritage Site and the place where the Phoenician alphabet, the source of our own alphabet, was created. The sea currents had deposited enormous quantities of fuel oil on its coast and sea bed. Volunteers from a Lebanese organization were cutting the sticky substance into cubes. A tragic chapter had been added to the history of what is one of the oldest cities in the world, inhabited without interruption since the Bronze Age.

While the *Rainbow Warrior* headed to the north of Beirut, the camera crew went south by land, beyond the River Litane. The territory between that river and the border had suffered the severest attacks by the Israeli army and they wanted to document the destruction. As well as all the

Innocuous-looking but deadly. Cluster bombs are released in their hundreds and float down like parachutes and burst into tiny metal fragments upon detonation. Many fail to go off on landing but continue to pose a grave threat.

Some 90 per cent of the cluster bombs in the south of Lebanon were dropped by the Israelis in the 72 hours before the 2006 ceasefire.

bridges, the petrol stations had been blown to bits and the roads were full of holes. Hundreds of houses were in ruins or partially destroyed. In some villages no more than two homes were left standing. Those people who, despite everything, had not left or had already returned, wanted to show us up close a particular legacy of the war. However, all you had to do was leave the road and you came across plenty of evidence of this: everywhere was littered with unexploded cluster bombs.

The camera crew came back on board in Tripoli. Everyone met up in the ship's mess and we saw the images of devastation and the faces of those who had lost everything (including members of their families) – and those images provided our lasting, moving memory of Lebanon.

Israel and Lebanon (Israel)

We watched the coast slip below the horizon as we secured the mooring lines on the bitts on deck. There was no need to stow them in the hold because this was to be a very short journey. As soon as we left the territorial waters of Lebanon we set all the sails and cut the engine, leaving the *Rainbow Warrior* to proceed at a leisurely four knots. Feeling the gentle breeze on your face with your eyes closed seemed to lift the weight of everything seen in the land of the great cedars.

We entered the port of Haifa accompanied by a

military frigate. A soldier aimed a cannon on its bow directly at us. Was this his own idea, or had he been ordered to do so? I asked myself. Israel too had just been through a war and we had come from the enemy country. No sooner had we moored the ship than immigration officers came aboard, though this is entirely normal when arriving in a country by sea. Once the paperwork for the ship

---

Balance sheet of the war in Lebanon

• About 200,000 people were left homeless and about a million displaced. Practically the entire infrastructure of the country was damaged (amongst other things, 149 bridges were bombed).

• The destruction of many factories and petrol stations caused the contamination of the air with PCBs and other very dangerous toxins.

• About a million unexploded cluster bombs (among other types of munition) remained scattered, mostly south of the Litane River.

• Many farm animals died for lack of feed, thousands of trees were burned and most of the harvests were lost. Oil spills also gravely damaged the fishing and tourist sectors.

• 1,191 people were killed (mostly civilians, hundreds of children among them) and more than 4,400 were injured.

---

and for each of the crew had been completed, the volunteers and workers from the Israel office were finally able to enter the *Rainbow Warrior*.

Looking towards the city, our attention was drawn to enormous gardens with zigzag stairways climbing the hill on which Haifa sits. This is the second most important sacred place in the Baha'i religion, hosting the tomb of its founder. A few kilometers away, near Acre, is the most venerated place of all: the tomb of its prophet. The Baha'i faith, which began in the middle of the 19th century, is now reputedly the second most extensive religion in the world (judged by the number of countries and ethnic groups represented within it). Its followers advocate for the unity of humanity and religions, and for world peace. It surprised me to discover this new religion with such positive intentions – and it surprised me even more that its two most sacred places were in Israel, in a land where there have been so many bloodbaths in the name of God.

Two days after our arrival, some members of the crew – together with people from the local Greenpeace office – were taken in a van to the north of the country, and the border with Lebanon, to assess the effects of Hizbullah attacks on Israeli territory. First we went to Mount Meron, the highest mountain in the country, with its largest nature reserve. With the objective of hitting some of the military domes and satellite dishes

Menaced by rockets. Israeli installations at Mount Meron, near the Lebanese border, face the constant threat of attack by Hizbullah's Katyushas.

MAITE MOMPÓ

that dominate the top of the mountain, or perhaps installations half-hidden in the tree cover, the Katyusha rockets of Hizbullah had left their mark on the woods and started several fires. According to what we were told, the area of trees burned in the park covered 12 square kilometers.

Then we went northeast to Kiryat Shimona, the most-bombed city during the war. From some points on our route we could see into Lebanese territory, strewn with black patches. We passed through the Hullah Valley, a wide expanse brimming with water and fertility, its eastern border – in the form of a great mountainous wall – the famous Golan Heights, Syrian territory occupied by Israel since the 'Six Day War' of 1967.

At one point on our route we stopped to see a toothpaste factory that was being rebuilt. We could see that the road had been repaired at many points. It became obvious that the effects of many Katyushas launched onto that part of Israeli territory were scarcely visible due to very effective reconstruction.

In Kiryat Shimona, a woman agreed to take us to an air-raid shelter in the building where she lived. In that city each building had a shelter. Sat on bunks in a small rectangular room, we listened to the Israeli woman – surrounded by her three small children – recalling how they had spent every night of the conflict there. From inside that austere place they had heard rockets fall and felt the ground shake. It was a great relief to go out from such an oppressive space and to breathe fresh air again, and you could not but be conscious that these people had had to use the shelter on and off throughout their lives. But at least they were fortunate enough to have survived the attacks – and they had a house to return to as well as land to cultivate. If only that could be the last time they had to use the air-raid shelter.

We made one last stop. Next to the road a small shrine had been erected. Here a vehicle containing 12 soldiers had been blown up: all of them died. Several people were paying their respects to the victims, and we were conscious again of something shared by people on both sides of every armed conflict all over the world – the pain caused by the loss of a son or daughter, brother or sister, a friend.

Regular refuge: an Israeli air-raid shelter for citizens living near the border with Lebanon.

A few days later the *Rainbow Warrior* was full to overflowing – as many as 70 people crowded the inside and the deck! On board were four members of the Israeli parliament, the Knesset, people from other organizations and many journalists. We headed for the north of the great bay of Haifa, staying as close as possible to the coast, intending to verify the agglomeration of industries there. During the war there had been real concern about the possibility that rockets might reach some of these vulnerable spots and cause great environmental contamination. Many of the guests asked us for our impressions of the effects of the conflict in Lebanon. Their own media had carried no images of the destruction in the neighboring country.

On my day off I took the chance to visit Jerusalem. Going towards the south, I began to discern the great grey wall stretching on my left, internationally known as the 'wall of shame' – the wall of separation that Israel has constructed across the West Bank. Jerusalem, holy city of the three great monotheistic Western religions, also presents the visitor with a great old rampart that surrounds it, the oldest parts of which date from the 16th century. It is sad to see how, centuries later, new walls are being built to segregate the neighborhoods of the legendary city.

In this mad world, Lebanon was left with great destruction and hundreds of human victims but the country was full of posters proclaiming victory. In Israel, meanwhile, which had suffered little material damage and much smaller numbers of victims, the population felt the sorrow of having suffered a defeat. The reality is that both sides had been defeated and hatred, fear and pain were the only winners.

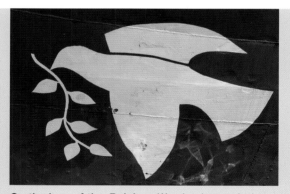

On the bow of the *Rainbow Warrior*, beneath the name, the dove of peace is depicted. Although the idea of painting a white dove on the bow – together with a rainbow – came from a Native American painting, the dove with an olive branch appears in the Old Testament (as a sign of life sent by God to Noah after the Flood) and was adopted by the first Christians as a symbol of peace. It more recently became popular and was adopted as a symbol for the peace movement after Picasso's lithograph of a white dove was chosen as the emblem for the *World Peace Congress* in 1949. The photo on the right shows the author touching up the ship's paintwork while in Lebanon.

Balance sheet of the war in Israel
• Hizbullah launched approximately 4,000 rockets into the north of Israel.
• 300,000 people were displaced and the attacks damaged many buildings.
• About 50 square kilometers of woodland and vegetation were burned.
• 165 Israelis died (43 of them civilians)

The divided island (Cyprus)

After leaving Israel, we carried out maintenance on the ship in Cyprus, the home of Stephen Nugent, the camera operator who had accompanied us in Lebanon and Israel. Some of us in the crew spent several days off in his company and he gave us an insight into the plight of his lovely island – another country suffering from the terrible consequences of armed conflict.

From the roof of Stephen's house, in the heart of the old city, we could see the great 'scar' that marked the border between the Greek and Turkish parts of the island, filled with trees along the stretch we could make out (see photo below). On the other side, the city of Nicosia continued, but instead of church bell towers there were mosque minarets. After the fall of the Berlin Wall, Nicosia (Lefkosia to Cypriots) became the only divided capital city in the world. In 1974, a great confrontation took place between the two ethno-religious communities that cohabited on the island of Cyprus. The Mediterranean island was divided in two, along with the capital. On a mountainside one could see in the distance an enormous flag had been painted. It was the Turkish flag with the white and red colors inverted.

A little later we walked to the Greek side of the 'scar'. We arrived at a street ending in a great barrier of sandbags and oildrums. We entered a labyrinth of abandoned houses that still had sandbags in their glassless windows. From these, 32 years before, the Greek-Cypriots shot at the

Between two worlds. The view over the Cypriot capital, Nicosia (Lefkosia), towards the Turkish sector, with the buffer zone marked by trees.

DMITRI SHAROMOV

Brief chronology

• In 1960 Cyprus became independent from Britain. There were 4.5 Greek-Cypriots for every Turkish-Cypriot.

• In July 1974, the Greek government sponsored a military coup and the Turkish government responded by invading a third of the island. In August a ceasefire was signed and the UN established a buffer zone, deploying a peacekeeping force (UNFICYP).

• In 1983, the Turkish-Cypriots proclaimed the Turkish Republic of North Cyprus, which has only been recognized by Turkey. Since 2004, the Republic of Cyprus has been a member of the European Union.

Turkish-Cypriots on the other side. In some parts of Nicosia, this front was scarcely three meters wide.

We went by car to the limit of the Greek-Cypriot zone so as then to cross Ledra Street on foot, the only 'bridge' that united both frontiers of the city. On one side of the street houses were beginning to be occupied and, on the other, a great expanse of 'no-man's-land' opened up, consisting of a landscape of green fields and woodland vegetation watched over by a blue tower of the UN. The UN force dominates the separation barrier of the buffer zone, but Cypriots call it the Green Line or, much more dramatically, the Death Zone.[4]

We arrived at passport control on the Turkish side, at the other end of the street. As soon as we entered, we were met by a big placard saying: 'Turkish Republic of North Cyprus. Forever.' There was much less bustle of traffic and we met many children on the street, who gathered round with curiosity. We arrived at another dead-end street, the Green Line closing it off. On the façade of a house was another placard conveying at least some hope: 'For those who are looking from the wall of shame. This is the bridge of peace.'

An environmental upside

Apart from a handful of inhabited villages and small farms within the territory, the demilitarized corridor has converted itself *de facto* into an enormous nature park where wild life and vegetation rule. Nature is the only thing that has benefited from the creation of this barrier that cuts Cyprus in two.

To this day the Nicosia wall and the separation territory across the island still stand. It is, of course, easy for someone passing through to say it, and much more difficult to achieve, but I look forward to the day when Cypriots break down this barrier and find a way of living with the mutual pain of the past so that the two communities can coexist in peace.

The strength of a wind (Croatia)

It was a very tranquil night. We had anchored in a bay north of the Croatian port of Split that afternoon. I was on watch from midnight until four in the morning. For at least a couple of hours the whole ship had fallen silent, with all the crew worn out by the eight-day passage from Larnaca in Cyprus.

Far away, on the port side, a storm was brewing, with lightning illuminating the low horizon. 'Good, it's a long way

The 'Green Line' or buffer zone, looks on the map like a river winding through Cyprus for 181 kilometers. At some points it is almost eight kilometers wide.

away,' I thought. I returned to measuring wind speed and the position of the ship without radar. All well, all quiet. Scarcely 10 minutes later, however, a gust of wind made the ship list terribly while rain began to strike the decks violently. I was calling Mike Fincken, the captain, by telephone when he appeared, bounding up the stairs three at a time. We turned on the deck lights, put on oilskins and went to the bow enveloped in the storm. You could feel the entire ship tremble with each gust of wind: the anchor was dragging. While Mike released almost 60 meters of chain, I tried desperately to lower the anchor signal and light, which were gyrating frantically and striking against the rigging of the bow sail. Within a few minutes several colleagues were around us lending a hand. Stumbling and holding on to fixed parts of the ship on our way across the deck, we returned to the bridge, which was now full of people. The whole crew had been shaken out of their placid dreams by the repeated heeling and sharp movements of the ship. Only time would tell if, with all the chain out, the anchor would stop dragging across the sea bed.

The Bora is a cold, strong wind that whips across the Adriatic Sea, especially in winter. It owes its name to Boreas, the Greek mythological figure who represented the north wind.

Some gusts of wind were stronger than 100 kilometers an hour and the 'old lady', as the second *Rainbow Warrior* was affectionately known, seemed to be weathering the onslaught. There would still be a couple of hours to suffer the lashes of the Bora wind, which had given us its particular welcome to this corner of the Adriatic. But when calm returned we found ourselves in the middle of the great bay.

The wild and violent onslaught of the Bora wind reminded me of the extremely violent attacks and assaults on cities and villages that took place during the bloody war in the 1990s in Croatia and the other regions that once formed 'Yugoslavia'.

A few days later we were contemplating the walls of Dubrovnik. UNESCO[5] declared this city-state (once known as the Republic of Ragusa)

Shadows of peace. At sunrise, the *Rainbow Warrior* is silhouetted against the ancient walls of Dubrovnik, in Croatia.

CHRISTINA MARIA SHOWASSER

a World Heritage Site in 1979, and the city was demilitarized so as to protect it from the war. Sadly, neither of these things spared Dubrovnik from a pitiless bombardment by the forces of Montenegro, which laid siege to it by land and sea for six months from 6 December 1991.

The *Rainbow Warrior* mission

The *Rainbow Warrior* went to Dubrovnik because it was hosting the annual meeting of ICCAT, the International Commission for the Conservation of Atlantic Tunas. The experiences related to our 'battle' to protect the bluefin tuna are covered in Chapter 9.

One of the first people who visited us when we opened *Rainbow Warrior* to the public was an amiable old woman who had been a professional guide and offered to give the crew a tour. What

CHRISTINA MARIA SHOWASSER

Crew members with their volunteer guide in the streets of Dubrovnik. The author is second from the left.

The Balkans War

The war that blighted this corner of Europe at the start of the 1990s left almost 100,000 dead, about a million displaced and involved the shameful practice of systematic 'ethnic cleansing'. During the siege of Dubrovnik, about 90 civilians died and 16,000 refugees were evacuated by sea. A total of 11,425 buildings suffered damage.

a marvellous present! With her we visited every corner of the medieval city while she told us about its glorious times as a city-state, taught us about its emblematic buildings and detailed the disasters of the latest war – the sad final chapter added to its history. Climbing to the high part of the city, we could clearly see the effect of the attacks: the vast majority of the roofs were new. Only the thickness of the walls in the houses and the other buildings spared them from even greater destruction.

Among the Croatian volunteers who were on the ship helping us with the tuna campaign was Toni Vidan, who was at the time a member of the International Board of Friends of the Earth.[6] Toni told me that after the bloody inter-ethnic conflict the environmental organization he belonged to – then called Green Action – published a report on the war and its effects. The conclusion it reached was that the environmental cost dwindled into relative insignificance beside the crushing human impact of the violence suffered by the different communities.

1 Noam Chomsky and other international experts have argued that the 'Arab Spring' actually began with the protests that took place in Western Sahara in October 2010. **2** The Guardia Civil is a national Spanish security force that exists alongside the police and is military in nature. **3** The US Coastguard is part of the US Armed Forces. It operates under the Department of Homeland Security but in times of war can be transferred to the Department of the Navy. **4** It is said that a British authority drew a green line to mark the trail of the 'scar' in Nicosia and the whole strip dividing the island has come to be called 'the Green Line', especially in the English-speaking world. **5** The United Nations Organization for Education, Science and Culture. **6** Friends of the Earth is the largest world environmental federation, with 76 national groups and around 5,000 local groups. It has over two million members and supporters all over the world.

9 **Pirates!**

On piracy
Ship pirates • **In the pirates' sights (Middle East, 2007)** • **Navigating pirate waters (in transit, 2010)**
Fishing pirates • **What gets thrown overboard (Tasman Sea, June 2004-June 2005)** • **The sleeping kids (Italy, 2006)** • **Stories of bluefin tuna (Mediterranean Sea)** • **The expulsion from Marseilles (France, 2006)** • **A white lily (Croatia, 2006)** • **Encounters on the high seas (north of Libya, 2007)** • **Red hot (south of Malta, 2010)**

On piracy

This chapter on piracy is divided into two parts.

The first part, 'Ship pirates', concerns 'traditional' piracy in which ships are attacked while sailing, something that has been happening at sea throughout history, right up to the present day. However, modern pirates do not conform to the stereotype of the pegleg, eyepatch and parrot on the shoulder. Today's pirates have traded the pistol and the cutlass for assault rifles and even grenade launchers; they use powerful outboard engines and sometimes sophisticated technology. This can be aimed at the theft of a cargo, as occurs in the Strait of Malacca and in the Gulf of Guinea, or the seizure of the boat and its crew to obtain payment, as has become common off the coast of Somalia.

The second part is devoted to the piracy of marine resources by the transnational fishing industry. These 'fishing pirates' are very different from the above: they still practice the plunder of the seas but those controlling the decision-making are usually dressed in suit and tie, courting respectability while seeking the greatest possible profit. For the sake of short-term enrichment, these pirates are putting species in danger of extinction (as was the case with bluefin tuna), causing the destruction of ecologically valuable treasures (through deep-sea trawling), slaughtering other species unnecessarily (the unwanted creatures caught up in driftnets) or hijacking the fishery resources of poor countries (as in Somalia and other parts of Africa).

If we do not curb the destruction of marine habitats and the wholesale plunder of the seas, there will be no ocean bounty for our children to hand on to future generations.

Ship pirates

In recent years piracy has hit the headlines as Somali pirates operating in the waters around the Horn of Africa have spread terror. The Horn is so named due to its triangular shape, and comprises Somalia, Somaliland, Ethiopia, Eritrea and Djibouti. This is an area of great economic, political and social instability, shaken by continual wars. It is of geopolitical interest because so many oil tankers and cargo ships have to pass through the corridor alongside it to reach the Suez Canal. Sporadic attacks in the early years of the century proliferated to such an extent that, since 2005, the waters off Somalia have been the most dangerous in the world.

Since the civil war broke out in 1991, Somalia has experienced two decades of fighting between different factions and clans. According to the United Nations Office on Drugs and Crime, those years of chaos also presented an opportunity for European and Asian fishing fleets that began exploiting the rich fishing waters off the Somali coast and having a fatal impact on the livelihoods of local fisherfolk. In addition to these trawlers, other foreign boats took advantage of the political vacuum in Somalia to dump with impunity toxic waste generated in the rich world.

When inland droughts caused terrible wars and famines that took the lives of over half a million people, destitute fishing communities decided to form 'control patrols', which began attacking foreign ships to ask for 'taxes' and ended up abducting hostages to demand ransom.

Somali piracy quickly became an enormously lucrative criminal enterprise that saw any passing boat as legitimate prey and attacked ships at ever greater distances. A financial-economic framework soon built up around the activity that has brought enormous benefits to warlords, arms dealers and even law firms and international insurance companies. In 2010 alone, Somali piracy earned a profit of $200 million.

In response, the provision of military security

Somalia has one of the highest rates of maternal mortality in the world and hundreds of thousands of Somalis are still dependent on international aid for food.

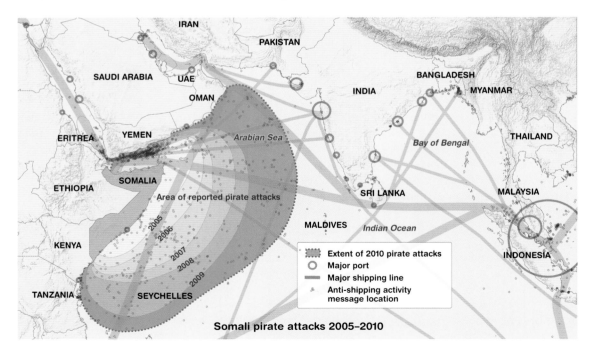

Somali pirate attacks 2005–2010

Lebanese crew member Randa Mirza with the *Rainbow Warrior* as the ship prepared for the voyage to Iran in 2007. Part of the preparation involved discarding copies of Western news magazines containing advertisements that would be considered offensive in iran.

for ships has become a lucrative transnational business. Ships crossing the most dangerous areas – particularly the Gulf of Aden – are organized in convoys and protected, since 2008, by the 'Task Force 150', a naval task force representing 25 countries.

In 2012, democratic institutions in Somalia were finally established and assaults began on the land bases of the pirates. As a result of this twin-pronged approach, Somali pirate activity has significantly declined.

In the pirates' sights (Middle East, 2007)

According to the motto of this tour the aim was to achieve a 'nuclear-free Middle East'. This was a tremendously complex tour in logistical terms. This was not just because of the nature of the campaign itself – tackling nuclear power and nuclear disarmament together – but also because of the great socio-political diversity that prevails in the region. In some cases, this was the first direct contact Greenpeace had ever made with those societies, which function very differently from those in the West.

The large region of the planet known as 'the Middle East' comprises the 17 countries in the western part of Asia, with the exception of the Caucasus but including Cyprus and Egypt.

Before the tour began, the *Rainbow Warrior* dropped anchor in Dubai, and there was a campaign training session on board. This kind of training is principally designed to bring the experience of people on the Greenpeace ships closer to those who work in the organization's offices, so they can learn how to use the ships as tools for campaigning. In practice, however, this particular example of campaign training was by no means standard. The local authorities did not really know how to deal with a ship that carried neither passengers nor freight and that belonged to an organization that used it to mount protests, so a lot of restrictions were placed on the *Rainbow Warrior*. For a start, the inflatables could not be put in the water, nor could the training involve simulated actions, as it normally would. In addition, one of the tour's logistics specialists, Lama Abdul, who was Lebanese, gave everybody an introduction to the Islamic culture of the countries the ship was to visit. It was vital that everyone on the boat learned to avoid any behavior or situation that might cause offense.

On 1 February 2007, in Abu Dhabi, the Greenpeace report *Energy Revolution* was launched on board the ship. This explored the viability of a Middle East free of nuclear technology, both civil and military. At the time, Iran was finishing the construction of its first nuclear reactor at Bushehr, with help from Russia, despite continual protests from the US and Israel, which claimed that the plant would make it possible for Iran to develop nuclear weapons.

The *Rainbow Warrior* headed for Bushehr after visiting the rest of the countries of the Persian Gulf. The intention was to visit Iran for the first time, carrying a message of peace, but, at the last moment, when the ship was about to enter the country's territorial waters, it was decided to abort the visit: the Iranian authorities had not given a definitive 'yes' to our entry at this delicate moment of great international tension.

The Bushehr nuclear plant was not officially opened until September 2011, in the same month as it started producing electricity for the Iranian national grid. Operational control of the plant was transferred from Russia to Iran two years later, on 23 September 2013. Israel and the US remain anxious that Iran's civil nuclear program could be used covertly to develop nuclear weapons and the risk of armed conflict over the issue remains high. As it stands, Israel is widely accepted as being the only country in the Middle East with a military nuclear program and it has refused to sign the Nuclear Non-Proliferation Treaty.

So instead the *Rainbow Warrior* headed for Aden, the Yemeni city that gives its name to the narrow gulf between the Red Sea and the Indian Ocean that has become the most dangerous place in the world for piracy. As they started to sail southwest down the coast of Oman, all those on board were on alert, with constant radar observation and special watches on deck at night.

It happened one morning that the *Rainbow Warrior* came across a large fishing boat, which came too close. This seemed a bit suspicious to the captain, Daniel Rizzotti, and others who were with him, but the boat maintained its course and eventually left the radar screen.

At two in the afternoon they were watching an approaching boat on the radar when they saw that two other points had appeared beside it, which suddenly headed directly for the *Rainbow Warrior*.

Most Yemeni visitors to the *Rainbow Warrior* had never heard of Greenpeace before but were keen to come aboard and learn; the women seemed particularly enthusiastic.

These were quickly located with binoculars. Daniel sounded the general alarm and sent out a Mayday on radio channel 16, which is always kept open on ships and is used as an international distress frequency. This was immediately responded to by a French corvette. All the fire hoses were connected, since high-pressure water was the only means the ship had of repelling boarders at that time. The two small boats, which each carried four or five men, began to circle the *Rainbow Warrior* slowly. Their occupants were clothed in black from head to toe – only their eyes could be seen – and were attentively studying the ship before them.

Minutes before they arrived, access to the living quarters from the deck had been blocked and all the portholes and hatches closed. All the women went to the radio room – the last bastion in case of boarding – and the men went on deck, carrying something in their hands to make them seem like 'tough guys'. The whole crew had its heart in its mouth during the long minutes of terror while they were in the pirates' sights.

Perhaps because they knew that the French warship was very near, or because the *Rainbow Warrior* did not seem to be worth the trouble – she wasn't exactly a luxury yacht – in the event the pirate boats ended up returning to their mother ship.

The *Rainbow Warrior* had the advantage that, long before Somali pirates were thought of, special measures had been taken to protect the ship against boarders following the seizure of the ship by French commandos in Moruroa (See Chapter 2).

At about eight the following morning, chief mate Olivier Lauzon went to wake up Bahadir Riza, who had been on watch from midnight until four o'clock.

'The captain has a problem. He has a strong pain here,' said Oli, indicating the right-hand side of the stomach.

The half-asleep medic opened his eyes wide on seeing this gesture. 'Wait for me to wash my face and I'll be with him shortly.' It looked like an attack of appendicitis, which can prove fatal. Immediately the course was changed for Salalah, the nearest port in Oman with a hospital.

The inflatable took Daniel off, accompanied by Bahadir, and soon after he underwent a surgical operation. Since the ship did not have permission to stay in Oman, the *Rainbow Warrior* had to continue sailing towards Yemen, with Oli taking command, and without any medic aboard. Those remaining miles to Aden seemed to last an eternity for a crew that had just had a close encounter with pirates and now had two crew-members fewer.

In Aden Mike Fincken came aboard as captain, as well as Bahadir, who had left Oman when Daniel returned home to Argentina. The tour then began its second phase, in the Mediterranean, with a visit to Egypt. From there, the *Rainbow Warrior* headed for Haifa, in Israel, and later Beirut, where she arrived at the beginning of April and was arrested for coming directly from an enemy country. In the middle of that month I embarked and we spent another two weeks detained in the Lebanese capital. This meant all the activities in

Between North and South. The view from the *Rainbow Warrior* as it emerges from the Suez Canal on the way to the Gulf of Aden.

Turkey that had been planned for the end of the tour – focusing on the two US nuclear bases on Turkish soil – had to go ahead without the ship.

Navigating pirate waters (in transit, 2010)

We were in transit from Cyprus to Bangkok and had scarcely been two days in the feared Gulf of Aden. It was a little after eight in the morning – I had just finished my watch – when a distressed voice sounding on channel 16 froze the blood of those of us who were on the bridge of the *Rainbow Warrior*. It was the captain of the *MV Suez*, desperately asking for help: his ship was being attacked by pirates. Just 12 miles away, we had the merchant ship perfectly located on our radar but, due to the prevailing haze in those waters surrounded by deserts, it was impossible to see it with binoculars.

A NATO ship, patrolling nearby, responded immediately, starting a frantic dialogue. From the warship, a female voice ordered the captain to undertake evasive maneuvers and maintain maximum possible speed, while the captain responded with cries that they had begun to open fire from the attacking pirate boats. As the words of both mingled, she ordered the whole crew to hide and lock themselves in a safe place, while the captain said that one pirate had boarded the ship, then another, then one more... 'Everyone hide,' were the last words heard before silence fell for several interminable minutes.

Binoculars in hand, everyone present scrutinized the off-white horizon, feeling the kind of anguish that makes you swallow hard. A helicopter appeared, flying in the direction of the ship, and was lost in the haze. A moment later, a hard voice broke the radio silence with a terrible threat: 'If you come close, we shall begin to execute the crew.' Next we heard the trembling voice of the captain repeating the same message: 'They say that if you come close they will kill us all.' We saw the helicopter again, this time climbing and moving away.

We followed the movements of the *MV Suez* on the radar screen. We saw how the little dot that denoted its presence changed direction and, once close to the coast of Somalia, stopped and moved no more. In scarcely a quarter of an hour, the pirates had taken another ship hostage.

Some international organizations recommend methods for trying to repel pirate attacks, which have varied as the *modus operandi* of the pirates has changed. These include protecting the gunwales of ships with barbed wire, showing the maximum possible number of crew members, and keeping fire hoses connected.

As soon as we had left Cyprus we had begun to prepare the ship for her journey through pirate waters, taking all measures necessary to resist potential attack. Even so, it was hard to live with the terrible doubt about what would happen if pirates did capture us – and it was arguably hardest of all for the women on board.

The days passed, the barometer fell and the waves and wind grew, so that Poseidon and Aeolus became our greatest allies in averting that feared attack.[1] At last we made it beyond the danger zone, and left behind the tension that had gripped us ever since we had witnessed the plight of the *MV Suez* in such dramatic, horrible detail.

The *MV Suez*

This merchant ship, Panamanian-flagged and Egyptian-owned, was captured on 2 August 2010. The ship and its 23 crew (11 Egyptians, 6 Indians, 4 Pakistanis and 2 Sri Lankans) were freed on 13 June 2011, after paying $2.1 million in ransom.

About three weeks later we were crossing the last few miles of a natural maritime corridor that is also famous for pirate attacks: the Strait of Malacca. Less than 24 hours remained before we were to reach dry land and make a brief stop in Singapore. It was Sunday, the weather was calm and a splendid sun shone. It was the last day we would be sailing with several of our colleagues and it was the birthday of one of these – Andrés Soto, the outboard mechanic responsible for the inflatables. Everything seemed set for a good celebration.

At midday, Andrés – who was preparing pizzas with Marin Conc, the second mate – opened a

MAITE MOMPÓ

Liberating the ship. Crew members on the *Avon* trying to free the *Rainbow Warrior*'s propeller from the plastic that had incapacitated it. Andrés Soto is steering.

piece of plastic had wound itself innumerable times around the propeller shaft until it was immobilized. Several crew members had to free-dive in turn and, knife in hand, tear the plastic off in strips. Andrés spent most of the rest of the day at the wheel of the *Avon*, and the rest took it in turns to help with the operation. The sun had set before the captain, Derek Nicholls, gave the order to stop. Although plastic was still wrapped around the shaft, it seemed that the propeller was finally free enough to function.

Well past nine o'clock in the evening, a handful of crew members gathered to welcome Andrés into the ship's mess. Minutes after the Chilean had blown out the candles on a cake that had been waiting for him for hours, and he had opened his present, there were just two of us left to keep him company – the others had gone to bed, exhausted.

The invasion of our seas by plastic is causing, amongst other problems, millions of birds and marine animals (including fish, turtles and cetaceans) to die every year from ingesting it.

The gyratory currents of the north Pacific have accumulated such a quantity of inorganic waste – most of it plastic – that it has formed a kind of gigantic floating island that covers an area at least the size of France – and may be more than double that.[2]

Fishing pirates

What gets thrown overboard
(Tasman Sea, June 2004 - June 2005)

On both occasions, winter was arriving in that corner of the planet, as beautiful as it is isolated, called New Zealand by Europeans and Aotearoa by Maori. The *Rainbow Warrior* set sail from Auckland in June in both 2004 and 2005, headed for the Tasman Sea, where the waters of the South Pacific and the Southern Ocean mix, free from dry land for thousands of miles.

The sea mounts here were suffering irreparable damage. Their slopes were being devastated by the nets of large bottom-trawlers. These nets contain metal weights that, as well as preventing snags and

beer and took a swig for good health. Just as the dough was being stretched, the *Rainbow Warrior* shuddered and, moments later, Bob Wigt, the chief engineer, appeared in the galley with a wild face: the ship's propeller had stopped turning! Given that we were in a busy shipping lane and all too close to waters frequented by pirates, this was not exactly the best place for a ship to find itself adrift.

The *Avon* – one of the big inflatables – had to be launched immediately so we could investigate what had happened. It turned out that an enormous

MALCOLM PULLMAN / GREENPEACE

Locked up. The bottom-trawler *Ocean Reward* was unable to fish for ours thanks to this action in 2005. The activists used wire cables to stop the trawl doors from opening.

rips in the net, cause it to descend, and they drag across the slopes of the sea mounts, ripping them to shreds. In addition to the disappearance of these precious and irreplaceable marine habitats, there is another tragedy: as many as 50 per cent of the creatures caught in these nets can be returned dead to the sea, since only the most saleable species of fish are of interest. It defies belief that something as small as a boat amid the immensity of the ocean might be capable of producing such a great impact on the whole marine ecosystem (see Chapter 7).

The campaign in New Zealand/Aotearoa had reached a dead end: Greenpeace said that these trawling practices were causing destruction of the marine habitat and the fishing industry responded that they were not. The only way out of this stalemate was to bear witness to exactly what was happening. To do that, it was imperative to have a ship, and the *Rainbow Warrior* was that ship.

On both voyages the crews had before them the same uncertainty: would they find the trawlers in the immensity of the Tasman Sea? Then came the days on the open sea, one succeeding another until they seemed to merge, with a rhythm of work marked by the movement of the waves. They went in search of the trawlers but that was not the only thing they found. Tawhiri – the Maori god of wind and storms – also made an appearance and that

caused half the crew to succumb to a seasickness that gripped their bodies and from which sleep provided the only respite. Defeated by seasickness, Martin Steffens, the electrician in 2004, asked himself if the ship would be able to withstand the assaults of the sea since, from time to time, the 'Old Lady', as we affectionately called the *Rainbow Warrior*, seemed to dance as if she were mad, shaken in all directions.

Not only did the ship survive, but on both journeys she was fortunate enough to succeed in intercepting the offending trawlers. The first ship encountered was registered in Belize. When its great net was hauled in, activists in the inflatables went to collect as much of the by-catch as possible. A branch of black coral, a listed endangered species, appeared among all the creatures' remains.[3]

The rest of the deep-sea trawlers that the *Rainbow Warrior* encountered bore New Zealand flags and were discovered in a zone where the fleet owners had given assurances that they did not operate. When Greenpeace reported their presence, the reply came back that they were indeed fishing there but that their nets never touched the sea bed. Sadly, refuting that argument was relatively easy: among the 'discards' retrieved were large numbers of creatures that only live on the sea bed, including urchins, starfish and crustaceans.

Coral, a minuscule animal, lives by forming colonies which can be enormous in size. Corals have become the oceanic equivalent of tropical forests because they harbor such rich animal diversity, hosting as much as 25 per cent of marine species. Around a third of all coral reefs are in danger of extinction.[4]

Caught in the act. A crew member on the bottom trawler *Waipori* is captured on camera dumping a magnificent specimen of Paragorgian coral over the side.

In 2005, the idea was not simply to find the trawlers and document the destruction of the sea bed: it was actively to try to stop that destruction happening, thereby attracting international attention in the lead-up to a UN debate on the gravity of the problem. Halfway through the campaign, it was decided to make a risky gamble: to sail the *Rainbow Warrior* to Norfolk Island, where the sea bed was supposed to require effective protection following the study made by the NORFANZ scientific expedition two years before.[5] How sad it was once again to prove the dismal reality that belied the trawler owners' claims! Here were ships indiscriminately casting their nets into habitats that the scientists had described as a marine 'Jurassic Park', containing species as old as the dinosaurs.

Albatrosses hoping to benefit from a trawler's bycatch. There were so many of these beautiful, wide-winged birds on the trips to the Tasman Sea that the *Rainbow Warrior* and (as here) her inflatables often had to take care not to run them over.

165

There are times when a small decision marks a definite 'before' and 'after'. Despite the fact that it was late in the day and the by-catch of the latest trawler to be confronted, the *Waipori*, had already been collected, it was decided that the inflatables should stay to document one more time what was coming up with the net. What happened minutes after it was hauled in caught the activists' breath: one of the fishers threw overboard a piece of Paragorgian coral of impressive size and the moment was caught on camera. The question of whether deep-sea trawling caused damage to seamounts had been settled for sure with just one image – and this was another picture that flashed right the way across the world and has had a major influence.

During the long return voyage to New Zealand/Aotearoa, Carmen Gravatt, who was responsible for the bottom-trawling campaign on both voyages, repeatedly played Johnny Cash's songs over the bridge sound system, since his music seemed to provide the perfect formula for enduring a storm, with the movements of the ship resembling a wild horse trying to throw off its rider in a rodeo. Faced with bad weather and seasickness, good humor is always the best medicine.

Greenpeace – along with other organizations and thousands of scientists – has been seeking a worldwide moratorium on deep-sea trawling for more than ten years, and the evidence gathered by the *Rainbow Warrior* and *Esperanza* in 2004 and 2005 has played a vital part in presenting its case to international forums (see Chapter 7).

The sleeping kids (Italy, 2006)

There were many miles still to go before the *Rainbow Warrior* would reach her destination, Genoa, when captain Peter Sandison received a message containing an extraordinary request. A man called Alcedo had asked the Greenpeace Italian office if a group of children from his community, which was called 'Damanhur', could sleep on board ship.

For Alessando Gianni, who was responsible for the oceans campaign in Italy, the request was

totally unexpected. After initially resisting the idea, Alessandro was forced by the man's insistence to reply: 'Well... I can't say that it wouldn't be possible, but it concerns a ship and so, at the very least, I'll have to ask the captain.'

Simona Fausto, a volunteer from Turin, was waiting excitedly for the *Rainbow Warrior* because she was about to embark for the first time, as an assistant cook. It was she who a little earlier had been to the Damanhur community to explain Greenpeace's work to the children.

Both the occupants of the *Rainbow Warrior* and the Italian office people liked the idea and managed to convince Greenpeace International that having these children on board would not present a problem. When all was said and done, it was argued, the children symbolized the future generations for whom we are responsible, and the ship is not the property of Greenpeace but of all

The Damanhur ecological community in Italy presented the *Rainbow Warrior* with this symbolic painting picturing a ship sailing the universe carrying children of all races.

MIKE FINCKEN

Damanhur

An eco-community some 40 kilometers from Turin, and based on ethical and spiritual values, Damanhur was founded in 1975 and in 2005 was considered by the World Forum on Human Settlements to be a model sustainable society.

Its inhabitants produce ecologically sustainable food, use renewable sources of energy and have developed a unique artistic technique called Selfic. With their own hands they have made *The Temples of Humanity*, a work of underground art that covers more than 8,500 cubic meters, considered by some to be one of the great marvels of the world.

people who have an affinity with the cause she symbolizes.

The 60 Damanhurians, young and adult, who arrived with Alcedo received a special guided tour. For their part, they served the crew with food produced by the community (wine, olive oil, cheese, vegetables, fruit) and presented the ship with a beautiful painting (see left).

The six youngest students in the party, who were aged six and seven, stayed to sleep, together with their teacher and four adolescent helpers. Simona, the only person on board they knew, became their assistant in everything and they treated her as a great expert, when in reality the volunteer had only been on board for two days and went around pretty much lost, trying desperately to assimilate so many new things.

The chief mate, Naomi Petersen, was especially concerned that they should be comfortable and safe, and was charmed to live with children on the ship. In fact, all the crew were happy to share the ship and spend time with the 'sleeping kids', as they came to be called.

The first night, the children slept on the *Rainbow Warrior*'s forecastle deck. The next day, they undertook various educational activities on board and then went off to investigate Genoa. That night, the little guests slept in the hold to escape the humidity on deck.

The children of Damanhur returned to their community, leaving behind a ship immersed in the final preparations for the launch of its next campaign. The brief period of co-existence with

Breakfast at sunrise: the 'sleeping kids' on board in Genoa, Italy.

our little friends had gone perfectly. In the words of Simona: 'They were there when they needed to be and were no trouble when they didn't need to be'.]

The official start of the ship's 2006 Mediterranean Tour was the launch of the new Greenpeace report *A Desert Called Sea* on board on 17 June. To help the campaign get under way in Italy (to end illegal fishing with driftnets, and to document valuable locations for future marine reserves) Beppe Grillo turned up – the comic, actor and blogger who became famous when he was censured for denouncing the corruption of the political class. Grillo was later (in 2009) to found the Five Star Movement, which, remarkably, came from nowhere to end up with 25 per cent of the vote and the largest number of seats in parliament in the 2013 election.

Driftnets

In the 1980s Greenpeace began a campaign to ban driftnets on account of the alarming quantity of species that were dying in them, including cetaceans, sharks, turtles and unwanted fish. The number of victims was increasing, not least because of nets that had been broken or abandoned, which degrade only slowly because they tend these days to be made from fibers derived from oil, rather than the traditional biodegradable materials such as hemp.

In 1992 the ban on driftnets longer than 2.5 kilometers came into effect and, since 2002, the use of driftnets for specific species (among others, bluefin tuna and swordfish) has been prohibited in the European Union.

When Simona returned to Italy two months later, she went to Damanhur to tell the children and anyone else who was interested how the campaign had gone, taking videos and photos with her. She told them that the *Rainbow Warrior* had been sailing to the north and the west of Sicily for almost a month, where many dives were made each day to capture images of the ecosystems most in need of protection. On the other hand, the

search for boats using driftnets took place at night since this is when those boats normally operate – and the ship came across five boats using this type of net.

When the *Rainbow Warrior* first encountered these boats, their occupants began by throwing not just insults but also empty beer bottles. When these ran out, they threw full ones – and naturally the only bottle that landed intact on board was later drunk by the Greenpeace crew with a toast to the health of its donors. A few days later, a driftnet was pulled aboard. The boat that owned it threatened to ram them and a furious fisher tried to intimidate the Greenpeacers when a beautiful

Hauling confiscated nets on board was a complicated process. Using the capstan at the bow for this made it difficult for the ship to hold her position.

swordfish appeared, caught up in the net, providing irrefutable proof of the crime the fishing boat was committing at the same time as being valuable prey for them. Fisherfolk from another boat gave assurances that their net was legal because it did not exceed two-and-a-half kilometers in length. It was then discovered that the boat was carrying another one – a 'spare' – and, in the absence of witnesses, they could deploy both.

Simona also told the children that, one day, a precious turtle trapped in a net had been rescued, and that on another day they met bluefin tuna fishers who had allowed the Greenpeace crew to take pictures of their cage filled with fish.

One of the lucky ones. Volunteer Marta Orihuela holds a turtle that has been freed from a net.

The meticulously documented reports made by Greenpeace and taken to consecutive meetings of ICCAT (the International Commission for the Conservation of Atlantic Tunas) caused Italian regulation to become much stricter and, in addition, the country now faces a fine of several million euros for its transgressions. As a result, illegal fishing with driftnets has been almost completely eliminated in Italy.

Later on, Alessandro from the Italian office also visited Damanhur. A member of the community offered voluntarily to analyze water samples for Greenpeace for two consecutive years. Thanks to them, the organization was able to report on the great accumulation of organic human waste suffered by the Ligurian Sea in summer – coming from ferries and big cruise ships. This

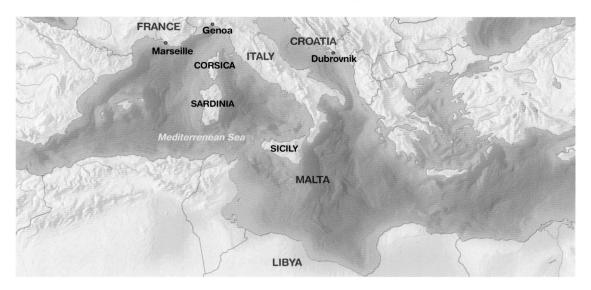

Industrialized slaughter. Rows of frozen tuna pictured before auction at the Tsukiji market in Tokyo, Japan – the largest fish market in the world.

contamination principally affects cetaceans – fin whales and various types of dolphin – which come to these waters in the same season and fall seriously ill.

For their part, the 'sleeping kids' of Damanhur started to visit colleges outside their community to recount what they had learned about Greenpeace and to talk about their experience of having *Rainbow Warrior* as their home for two days.

Stories of bluefin tuna (Mediterranean Sea)

The bluefin tuna is a magnificent predator, strong and fast, which can weigh over 450 kilograms and is at the top of the food chain in the seas it crosses. This species, fished in a traditional way for 3,000 years in the Mediterranean, aroused such crazy commercial interest at the dawn of the new millennium that it found itself on the threshold of commercial extinction in record time: 10 years.

The present and future of bluefin tuna is decided each year by meetings of the International Commission for the Conservation of Atlantic Tunas (ICCAT), which is responsible for the management and conservation of tuna and related species not just in the Atlantic but also in its adjacent seas (including the Mediterranean). For years,

Most tuna are transferred live to cages and transported in these to the coast. There they are fattened and then sent to Japan in enormous freezer ships – destined to be eaten in the raw fish dishes sushi or sashimi. Fattening a tuna in captivity by one kilogram entails feeding it 20-25 kilograms of other species.

conservation organizations (Greenpeace among them) have severely criticized the decisions taken by ICCAT, since the interests of the fishing industry have been prioritized over the conservation of the species and the future of traditional fishing.

The *Rainbow Warrior* has worked to defend bluefin tuna for several years both by bearing witness in the waters where the plunder takes place and by exerting pressure at ICCAT meetings.

The expulsion from Marseilles (France 2006)

The *Rainbow Warrior* entered the Bay of Marseilles with her four sails unfurled. But, just as she reached the entrance to the old city port, the whole bluefin tuna fishing fleet appeared at her bow.

The fishing boats surrounded the ship and impeded her forward progress. The captain had no alternative but to drop anchor and stay there for hours, with the ship effectively held as a hostage by the fishers, who never stopped throwing eggs and aiming jets of water from their fire hoses, shouting that the ship should turn around and go away. Surprisingly, at half past four in the afternoon the 23 French boats weighed anchor and returned to their port.

Just a week earlier the port authority had refused permission to dock, so the *Rainbow Warrior* had finally dropped anchor a mile from the entrance to the old port. The plan had been to open up the ship to the public and the media so as to explain the campaign for marine reserves. Even if the sailing ship could not enter, her inflatables could bring aboard all those who might be interested in visiting.

Marine reserves
Greenpeace has been campaigning for years for 40 per cent of the planet's oceans to be converted into marine reserves. If these were established, the biodiversity the areas once contained could be recovered, including the stocks of those commercial species, which are being exhausted by decades worth of industrial exploitation.

Mike Fincken's first thought, when he woke to the sound of the crane at 5.30 in the morning (winching the *Avon* into the water), was to wonder what would happen on his fourth day as captain of the *Rainbow Warrior*. The *Avon* had only just left to collect the first group of journalists when the ship's general alarm sounded: the French tuna-fishing boats had come back for more. This time several fishers even boarded the ship but then a French warship appeared on the scene and started negotiating. The fishers said they would leave *Rainbow Warrior* in peace provided the ship was towed out of French territorial waters, and then promptly withdrew – but only to a point where they were blocking the entrance to the commercial port of Marseilles (the third-largest in Europe) in an attempt to force the situation. As midday passed, with the aim of resolving the situation, the *Rainbow Warrior* crew decided to allow the ship to be towed.

The French tuna-fishing fleet had managed to expel the ship from their country. However, the incident led to something unexpected happening: the event was so widely covered in the national media that it prompted widespread discussion in France about the great crisis the fishery was experiencing, and public opinion at last began to question its own fleet. In the mighty battle these fishers launched against Greenpeace, the 'winner' turned out, against all odds, to be the bluefin tuna.

Blockade: around 20 tuna-fishing boats enclosing the *Rainbow Warrior* in Marseilles harbor to stop her entering port.

CHRISTINA MARIA SHOWASSER

A multi-agency press conference before the ICCAT meeting in Dubrovnik, Croatia, in 2006. Pictured from left to right are: Toni Vidan (Friends of the Earth), Zrinka Jakl (Sunce), Sebastián Losada (Greenpeace) and Raúl García (WWF).

A white lily (Croatia 2006)

November 2006. The alarm calls about the urgency of protecting the bluefin tuna so as to guarantee the survival of the species had already been set off. Approaching our berth in Split we saw a small group of people welcoming us. These were our new 'tenants' – workers and volunteers from the Greenpeace office in Austria, as well as volunteers from the Friends of the Earth branch in Croatia, and from Sunce, a local environmental organization that works on the creation of marine conservation areas, amongst other issues. The national volunteers (Toni Vidan, Luka Tomac, Zrinka Jakl, Ivana Carev, amongst others) not only lent us a hand in resolving day-to-day problems, they also became ambassadors for Greenpeace in their own country, guiding visitors around the ship, explaining what the organization does and why we were there.

After a couple of days we moved on to Dubrovnik – we were in Croatia to attend the annual meeting of ICCAT, which was taking place in that city; it was felt that the *Rainbow Warrior's* presence would reinforce the position of the conservationist groups at the meeting.

For two years running the World Wide Fund for Nature (WWF) had published devastating reports showing that some European fishing fleets were taking double the quota assigned to them – though even their quota was way above the levels recommended by scientists. There had been a big scandal in Europe and the powerful fishing magnates were a little nervous at the prospect of their piracy of bluefin tuna being exposed and challenged.

The Scientific Committee of ICCAT itself affirmed that the bluefin tuna catch in 2006 had been 50 per cent above the quota due to fishing piracy. The inefficacy of the measures adopted by the members of ICCAT was plain for all to see.

While the *Rainbow Warrior* was opened to the public, some Greenpeace members took part in meetings in the enormous convention hotel. Crew members also went there to invite delegates to visit the ship – and some even came. As the days passed, the situation became ever more tense between the fishers and all those who wished to put an end to their excesses: some country delegates were insulted and members of international environmental organizations such as Greenpeace and WWF became the objects of intimidation.

On one of the last days, a white lily appeared on the WWF delegation's table. The person who found it ingenuously thought that some gallant had left it there for her. It had nothing to do with romance but was a warning from the mafia aimed at the whole group. Two people in particular found themselves in a delicate situation: Roberto Mielgo (a former worker in the tuna industry and author of the WWF reports) and Raúl García (co-ordinator of fishing issues for WWF Spain), who had already been the object of several direct threats. The two men found they were staying in the same hotel as a group of troublesome fishers and, with the way things were going, they were becoming seriously concerned for their safety. So Sebastián Losada, the fisheries campaigner at Greenpeace International, proposed that they should move to the *Rainbow Warrior*. So it was that we welcomed two refugees for the last two days of the meeting – all in the cause of tuna.

When the ship started to sail around in front of the hotel, both men became – binoculars in hand – 'spies' from a distance on the conversations of the delegates. Our message to the meeting was written on two large banners strung between the masts, accompanied by a big black flag with a white tuna skeleton flapping in the wind.

Encounters on the high seas (north of Libya, 2007)

On my second voyage on the *Rainbow Warrior* (the 2007 Mediterranean tour) some unusual things happened, like ending up sailing with four captains, or my embarking when the ship was still detained in Beirut. In the midst of the bluefin tuna campaign in the western Mediterranean, we lived through a conflict between members of the crew that effectively paralyzed the campaign and forced

us to return to Malta to resolve it. Finally we went to sea again with a new captain, Frans van Dijk, and full of desire to start work again.

A great plundering of tuna was happening off the coast of Libya, where the government had declared a 60-nautical-mile area as a 'fishing protection zone'. Muammar Qadafi was then in power and, as Greenpeace had never been to Libya, we had no access to these waters. To enter the zone without the blessing of the authorities was highly risky – as had been proven the year before, when a Libyan coastguard had fired on an Italian tuna-fishing boat.

So we dedicated ourselves to patrolling the 'frontier', taking note of the boats we met (mostly Tunisian and Spanish). Occasionally we made contact and some even allowed us on board to document their cargo. We also located a refrigeration ship operating under a Panamanian flag, which we boarded with the intention of checking what its cold storage contained. Its crew would not let us do this, so we staged a protest with banners. It was plain that the cold-storage was full of tuna destined for the lucrative black market.

At daybreak one day the whispering voice of Lesley Simkiss, the ship's medic, shook me out of my sweet dreams. 'Maite, Maite, wake up! We have a Spanish tugboat nearby and the skipper says he's a friend of yours,' she said.

Boarding the Panama-flagged reefer *Daniela* to conduct an inspection: reefers often breach the ban on tranship-ments of tuna.

MARCO CARE / GREENPEACE

MARCO CARE / GREENPEACE

Hello, old friend! The author making contact with former Greenpeace skipper Peru Saban on board the *Zumaia 3*.

'Are you kidding?'

'No. No. Get up and put on your wetsuit. They're waiting for you in the *Avon*.'

Sleepy and dazed in semi-darkness – as my cabin mates were sleeping, I dressed without really knowing if I was dreaming or if it was real.

'Did she say "tugboat"? I don't know anyone who works on a tugboat!'

A smiling face looked overboard as we approached. 'Peru!' It was years since I'd seen the former skipper of the *Zorba* – a beautiful sailing boat in the service of Greenpeace Spain for several years – and now, here we were, meeting in the middle of the Mediterranean. How small the world is – its seas included!

They already knew we were in this area because they had heard us on the radio. Earlier that day, amid the dawn mists, Peru Saban had caught sight of the masts of *Rainbow Warrior* and, a little later, the silhouette of the *Avon* approaching.

'I have friends who work on the *Rainbow Warrior*,' he said at once, thinking of Sandra Fontanillas (then second mate on Greenpeace International ships, and also a former skipper of the *Zorba*) and me. They invited us for coffee on the tugboat, the *Zumaia 3*. My friend was working for a company that used to send tugboats every summer to take empty cages to the tuna-fishing grounds and, once

the cages were full of fish, to transport these to a place stipulated on the Spanish coast where they could be legally farmed.

When Peru and a friend returned the visit, we saw the possibility that they could give us a hand in finding out what was happening beyond the Libyan 'frontier'. In his first email, though, Peru didn't just tell us about tuna. While they were in the Libyan zone, they came across and rescued 26 migrants whose small boat had just sunk. They told the Libyan authorities and were ordered to take them to a port 50 nautical miles away. It took them almost two days to cover that distance, as the *Zumaia 3* was towing a cage, at which point a police launch came to pick up the castaways. The fear on the faces of the migrants turned to joy on seeing land and to fear again on finding out that it was

---

Hundreds of people from the Maghreb and sub-Saharan Africa attempt the dangerous journey to Europe in vulnerable small boats during the summer months. Many reach the south of Spain, Sicily, Malta or other shores, but many others perish in the attempt. On the *Rainbow Warrior* we routinely used to carry extra water and food in case we met one of these small boats.

Libya. How terrible it was to have no other option but to hand them over, despite the uncertainty as to what would happen to these people whose only crime was to bid for a better future.

For almost three weeks Peru fed us information, making himself our eyes and ears in the waters they sailed. As well as the joy of seeing an old friend, this fortuitous meeting proved to be a great help to the campaign.

Among the illegalities that we documented during this season were: the use of a spotter plane (registered in Italy) to search for tuna shoals; the transfer of tuna cargo from a French boat to a Panamanian-flagged one; and the presence of unregistered purse-seiner vessels.

Red hot (south of Malta, 2010)

Three years after the ICCAT meeting in Croatia, bluefin tuna were still heading for extinction – both because the fishing quota was far higher than

scientists had recommended and because piracy continued on a grand scale.

Greenpeace was keen to stage a spectacular action that might halt the fishing. But how could we stop an activity that takes place underwater? The answer we came up with seemed simple enough: liberate the tuna by attaching heavy sandbags to one side of the purse seine net and making it sink.

ICCAT had reduced the fishing season to one month: from 15 May to 15 June. The fishers met up south of Maltese waters and two Greenpeace ships, the *Rainbow Warrior* and the *Arctic Sunrise*, headed there to confront them. Just as the open season began, bad weather forced everyone to seek refuge. After two weeks of inactivity, both sides took to sea in a kind of desperation: the time to fish tuna was running out, but Greenpeace was also in danger of missing its opportunity to enhance tuna's long-term survival chances.

On 4 June, the Greenpeace ships met a French fleet consisting of five large fishing boats, several small ones (called 'skiffs') to tow and keep the nets open, and some supporting inflatables. When

Poetry in motion: the *Rainbow Warrior* and the *Arctic Sunrise* sailing together south of Malta to intercept the tuna-fishing fleet.

PAUL HILTON / GREENPEACE

the fishers saw the fast Greenpeace boats – three big inflatables and three small 'novis' – and the helicopter carried by *Arctic Sunrise*, they put all the small boats they had into the water (which amounted to some 15) and hurled themselves against the activists.

This scuppered our plan from the start, since the Greenpeace inflatables had to disperse and take evasive action while still trying to reach the net. The *novi* driven by Andrés Soto had barely touched the net when it was cornered against it by one of the fishers' skiffs and forced backwards, finally tangling its propeller in the rope used by the French boat to tow their net. An inflatable then hit them and climbed right up over their bow,

reaching halfway down the *novi*. The deckhand Ana Carla Martínez and a German volunteer had to throw themselves to the floor to avoid the blow. Even though the Greenpeace boat was already beginning to sink, this was not enough for the fishers. One of the men on another skiff threatened the crew with a knife, while another made to strike Andrés with a boat hook. Fortunately Ana was able to use one of the shields specially made for this campaign to protect Andrés.

When the fishers at last withdrew, three-quarters of the *novi* was underwater. For a few moments Andrés felt like the captain of the *Titanic*: 'Abandon ship!' he cried to his colleagues. The *Mermaid*, one of the *Arctic Sunrise*'s big inflatables, then appeared

Snapshots from a sea battle: (above) a French fisher swinging a gaff hook at Andrés Soto and Ana Carla Martínez; and (below) rescuing the crew of a Greenpeace inflatable that had been rammed and capsized.

BOTH PHOTOS: PAUL HILTON / GREENPEACE

Sunset south of Malta: the *Rainbow Warrior* on her way to confront tuna-fishing boats in 2010.

as if by magic and rescued them before going on to pick up the two occupants of another *novi* that had sunk.

> As far as the fishers saw it, they were attacking us for trying to steal their daily bread. They had legal legitimacy, since they were fishing during the official season. We considered ourselves as having ethical legitimacy in that we were fighting for the survival of bluefin tuna. From the point of view of Greenpeace, it should not be a case of bread today and hunger tomorrow – we want there always to be bread.

Not far away, a colleague had come out of the encounter greatly the worse for wear. Frank Hewetson was crewing the press boat, the *Hurricane*, which does not intervene in actions. Its driver, Luis Vasquez, had found it impossible to evade the fishing boats, which were everywhere. First, a fisher embedded his inflatable in the console of *Hurricane* and then another threw himself against them using the banner pole he had just taken from a *novi* as a 'pike'. Things got worse

still. From another skiff they threw a hook, which embedded itself in Frank's leg. Crying out with the acute pain, and worried that the fishers would pull on the hook, Frank reacted with great speed and cold blood, taking out his penknife and cutting the hook out of his flesh.

It was time to retreat. Frank was transferred immediately to Malta and into the operating theater. Fortunately the wound was between his shinbone and the muscle. One *novi* had been lost and two other inflatables had been severely damaged. Even the helicopter could have suffered a fatal accident because the fishers had set off distress flares aimed at it.

A couple of days later, the *Arctic Sunrise* tried to lift a cage-net full of tuna that was being towed by a Tunisian boat, using a four-point anchor and the bow winch to raise it. This maneuver also did not work, and the ship was repeatedly rammed by the fishing boat that accompanied the tugboat.

Returning to Malta after this tough campaign, the crew of *Rainbow Warrior* at least had a pleasant experience when they stopped for a swim. Suddenly a small shoal of tuna passed just beneath them as they swam. Would this shoal at least manage to escape the reach of human greed?

MARCO CARE / GREENPEACE

Fish-eye view: *Rainbow Warrior* crew members display a banner on the surface of the Mediterranean during the 2010 campaign.

Saving tuna: the latest developments
• In 2008, ICCAT established a quota of 22,000 tons (their scientists had recommended no more than 15,000).
• In 2009, the quota was 13,500 tons (their scientists had asked for a prohibition on international trade, since they calculated that only 15 per cent of the original population remained).
• In 2010, the quota was reduced by just 4 per cent (to 12,900 tons). A later study revealed that the quantity of tuna sold that year exceeded the quota by 141 per cent.[6]
• In 2011, Greenpeace and WWF continued to report on illegal fishing of bluefin tuna in Libyan waters and asked for effective control of the fattening cages.
• As of 2013, controls are much more rigorous and illegal fishing has declined enormously. It appears that stocks of bluefin tuna have recovered a little, although the situation remains unclear.

1 In Greek mythology, Poseidon was god of the sea and Aeolus was lord of the winds. 2 There are five great systems of gyratory ocean currents. The vast island of rubbish has formed in the North Pacific Gyre – a vortex in which there is very little wind. 3 It is listed in Appendix II of CITES (the Convention on International Trade in Endangered Species of Wild Fauna and Flora), which contains about 2,000 species of coral, including the whole order of black corals. 4 A 2008 study commissioned by the prestigious journal *Science*. 5 This scientific expedition investigated the surface habitats on seamounts and abyssal plains around the islands of Norfolk and Lord Howe. 6 The study was commissioned by the US environmental group Pew.

> 'In nature's economy, the currency is not money, it is life'
>
> Vandana Shiva

10 The planet we live on

This chapter is dedicated to the Arctic 30.

Humanity's greatest challenge (Earth, 21st century)
In the Land of the Long White Cloud (New Zealand/Aotearoa, March 2008)
Sails to be free (Netherlands, November 2008)
The Copenhagen experience (Norway & Denmark, December 2009)
The fingers of humanity (Israel, July 2010)
The story of the Arctic 30 (Russia, September-December 2013)

Humanity's greatest challenge
(Earth, 21st century)

The planet we live on, a place many species call home, is at a critical evolutionary stage. Millions of years ago, a perfect combination of gases in the atmosphere allowed for life on Earth. Unfortunately, certain human activities have changed this combination, shattering the equilibrium. The percentage of the so-called greenhouse gases, such as carbon dioxide (CO_2) and methane, in the atmosphere has increased rapidly, which has caused a rise in global temperatures.

Our civilization now faces its greatest ever challenge, with the survival of our own species in question. In a relatively short space of time, the combined effects of fossil-fuel burning, meat production and forest destruction have landed us at a crossroads.

The planet's temperature

The average global temperature is rising steadily. Scientists estimate that in order to avoid the worst effects of climate change we must keep world temperature increases below 2°C (compared with pre-industrial levels).

CO_2 is absorbed from the atmosphere by trees and forests through a process called photosynthesis. It can either then be converted into carbon, which is stored in wood and vegetation, or turned into oxygen, which is released into the atmosphere. It is calculated that forests and trees store more than one trillion tons of carbon. By destroying them, we add almost six billion tons of carbon dioxide yearly to the atmosphere.[1]

When we think of the causes of climate change, we think first and foremost of the burning of fossil

179

The atmosphere is in constant interaction with the oceans and the earth's crust. By altering its composition, humans have started a clock that is running against us. Each day that passes is another day lost in the race to avert climate catastrophe.

The burning of fossil fuels

CO_2 is estimated to be responsible for 77% of climate impact, most of it released into the atmosphere through the burning of coal, oil and gas. Burning coal alone accounts for a third of global greenhouse-gas emissions.

fuels but what many people ignore is the enormous impact that the rise in demand for meat has had on the climate. According to a 2006 study by the UN Food and Agriculture Organization, 18 per cent of global greenhouse-gas emissions come from the livestock farming industry.[2] However, a more recent report from the Worldwatch Institute has estimated the contribution of the meat industry to be far greater, responsible for 51 per cent of emissions – which, if so, would amount to more than the emissions from all the world's transport combined.[3] Whichever is the correct figure, it is clear that, if eating too much meat is bad for us, it is no better for our planet.

Worldwide meat production has almost quadrupled since 1961.

Meat production

Cows and other ruminants produce 37% of world methane, especially during their digestive process. Methane has around 30 times the effect of CO_2, and it stays in the atmosphere between 9 and 15 years.

Due to the mineral fertilizers used to produce compound feed, livestock excrement accounts for 65% of the nitrous oxide caused by human activities. Nitrous oxide's potential to produce global warming is 296 times that of CO_2. The production of compound feed also generates methane and CO_2.

The industrial production and transporting of meat release great quantities of carbon, while factory farming encourages deforestation and causes an overall degradation of land and water.

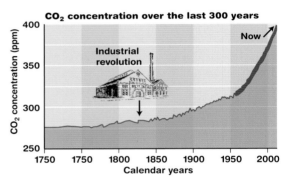

CO_2 concentration over the last 300 years

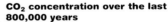

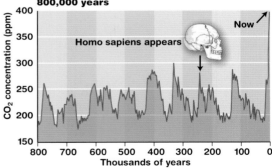

CO_2 concentration over the last 800,000 years

*Data from ice-cores until 1958 when records started at the Mauna Loa observatory in Hawaii.

Source: Scripps Institutio n of Oceanography – keelingcurve.ucsd.edu/

Carbon dioxide concentrations through the ages.

Scientists had long been warning about global warming before governments agreed that they needed to respond. The United Nations Framework Convention on Climate Change (UNFCCC) was negotiated at the so-called Earth Summit held in Rio de Janeiro in 1992 and the treaty came into effect in March 1994. The objective of the UNFCCC is to stabilize the concentrations of greenhouse gases in the atmosphere, and it has since been convening annual meetings under the name Conference of the Parties (COP) to advance this cause and reach a binding agreement for action. During the COP13 held in Bali in 2007 (see Chapter 5), world leaders decided that it would be in Copenhagen, two years later, when the necessary binding agreements to fight climate change would be reached. That is why the hopes of millions all over the world were invested in Copenhagen.

Bali marked the beginning of a two-year race. On the one hand, experts and specialists were to prepare all the information politicians needed to make the decision. On the other, social organizations – both environmental and humanitarian – would work together to raise citizens' awareness. During the months prior to the Copenhagen conference in 2009, an unprecedented social mobilization took place. Massive simultaneous public activities were carried out worldwide; thousands of individuals participated regardless of race, religion or language; and millions signed petitions asking politicians to reach an agreement fitting to the urgency of the global situation.

Operating under the slogan 'Quit Coal', the *Rainbow Warrior* spent 2008 campaigning on climate change in the Pacific (New Zealand/Aotearoa, the Philippines and Thailand), the Mediterranean (Israel, Turkey and Greece) and Atlantic Europe (United Kingdom, the Netherlands and Denmark). During the second half of 2009 she took up the torch again in Spain, United Kingdom, and finally Oslo and Copenhagen (during COP15 itself).

Scientific experts on climate have suggested that, in order to avoid the extreme changes in climate that could lead to our extinction, 350 ppm represented a safety barrier that should not be surpassed. On 10 March 2013, global atmospheric levels of CO_2 rose above 400 ppm.[4]

Number 350

Once carbon dioxide (CO_2) is released, it stays in the atmosphere and oceans for thousands of years. Before the Industrial Revolution, our atmosphere contained about 280 parts per million (ppm) of CO_2 – that is, for every million molecules making up the atmosphere, 280 were CO_2 molecules. Since the start of the 18th century, the amount of CO_2 (and similar gases) has risen steadily, and today it is increasing at a rate of 2.1 ppm every year.

'There Is No Planet B' was the slogan Greenpeace chose to take to the Copenhagen Summit, held between 7 and 19 December 2009. Most civil-society representatives present at the COP15 believed that politicians would finally be forced to take action but we were proved wrong. The great expectations that attached to the summit led to an even greater sense of disappointment, as all those arguing that effective measures had to be taken to address the climate crisis were completely sidestepped – when they were not actually beaten and sent to prison. During the summit's final days, Greenpeace changed its slogan to 'Politicians Talk, Leaders Act'. And, while politicians talked of the imperative need to act, the leadership necessary was entirely absent, as short-term political self-interest and the lobbying of corporate polluters won the day.

Years go by and time is slipping through our fingers. Faced by pressing day-to-day problems, we tend to forget to look at the big picture. We worry

Obama: 'No, we didn't.' One of the ads featuring older versions of heads of state placed all over Copenhagen Airport by the global coalition TckTckTck.org and Greenpeace.

The oceans

Oceans have absorbed around one fourth of all the CO_2 released to the atmosphere by humans since the beginning of the Industrial Revolution. The downside is that this process has increased the oceans' acidity levels by 26%, which has reduced their ability to absorb CO_2. In addition, acidification causes coral bleaching and makes it more difficult for new coral reefs to grow; it also has a negative effect on mollusks and certain types of plankton, which has a serious impact on the food chain. The rise in water temperature is increasing the number of invasive species and marine diseases, and causing changes in the distribution of species and weather patterns. The rise in sea levels due to the melting of the polar ice caps will cause the loss of habitat in many countries over the coming decades and produce waves of refugees.

about the state of the economy and about our families – and we allow politicians to prioritize the issues of the moment and pass the buck on climate change to the next generation. We know what needs doing. We know what is causing the rise in temperatures, the melting of the poles – including Tibet, the so-called 'third pole' – and the increase of major natural disasters such as droughts, floods, cyclones and hurricanes. We should not feel paralyzed by the vast challenge of climate change into thinking that there is nothing we can do. Big problems can be solved by our taking small steps, all together. We need to phase out our dependency on fossil fuels, to rely on clean energy sources and to reduce meat consumption. We should make countering climate change part and parcel of everyday life.

But we also need to let our leaders know that climate change is vital to us and force them to include it in their programs. COP21 in Paris in December 2015 is now being trailed as the next key point when a global deal on climate action might be struck. The future of humanity depends upon our not letting this opportunity slip by the way it did in Copenhagen.

In the Land of the Long White Cloud (New Zealand/Aotearoa, March 2008)

The line of police cars on the wharf started at the stern of the *Hellenic Sea* and looked as if it would never stop growing. I was watching the police arrive on the scene from a place that was, to say the least, unusual. I was literally below the bow of the *Rainbow Warrior*, hanging from one of her anchor chains, a banner in my hands. Was I protesting against Greenpeace?

We were on a six-week tour around beautiful New Zealand – or Aotearoa, 'the land of the long white cloud', as the Maori call it – working on climate-change issues and had several programmed stopovers. At this point we were docked at Lyttelton, the commercial port for Christchurch, the biggest city on South Island.

The *Hellenic Sea* had just finished loading 60,000 tons of coal into its hold and was getting ready to set sail when the *Rainbow Warrior* intervened. As fate would have it, the Port Authority had changed us from our initial location to one that was right behind our target, which made the initial steps of the action much easier to carry out. Leaving the wharf, we moved to the designated point and then performed a complicated double anchor maneuver – consisting of leaving one anchor at the bow and another at the stern – so that the *Hellenic Sea* was prevented from leaving. Immediately, I began to lower myself from the rail at the bow. As soon as I was safely sitting in the small bosun's chair, I unfolded the square banner that bore the campaign slogan and held it to the anchor chain. Finally, I was ready for the pictures which would immortalize the moment. I looked left and right; where the hell was Dima and his camera?

While I was lowering myself, the inflatable *Hurricane* took three climbers to the stern side of the *Hellenic Sea*. After securing her rope to the freighter's hull, Sheena Beaton began climbing it. 'This backpack is so heavy!' she thought as she started the ascent. She looked down and the sight of turbulent waters below made her hair stand on end – the *Hellenic Sea*'s propellers were turning! She was halfway up when the croll (a safety device used in climbing) got stuck and, to make matters

NICK YOUNG

Suspended animation: the author hanging from the *Rainbow Warrior*'s anchor chain in the action in Lyttelton.

overcome all the obstacles and were sitting pretty. Their eyes searched in vain for the photographer. Where the hell was Dima and his camera?

The aim of the tour

Greenpeace was asking the New Zealand government to commit to a 30% reduction in CO_2 emissions by 2020. Even though the country was taking theoretical steps to cut emissions, it was also allowing the development of the coal-mining industry and the expansion of dairy farming.

---

worse, every time Sheena turned her head, half of her face was buried in the hood under her helmet. The experience of the climb was as intense as anything Sheena had been through before. Once she and her climbing companions, Michael Simpson and Raoni Hammer, were in place, halfway between the ship's deck and the water, they started to unfold a large banner which kept jerking due to the strong wind. Finally they had

Dima Sharomov, the guy we were all looking for, had gone missing in the middle of the action. He was working as the tour photographer rather than as second mate this time around. Contrary to the golden rule when a Greenpeace action is under way, Dima had been told to leave the action scenario and personally hand over the photos he had already taken to someone waiting for him on shore. The photographer opposed the order but in the end had no alternative but to obey. The media boat took him to shore where, with all his photographic equipment on, he rushed to the place indicated to hand over the memory card. While he was gone, local journalists arrived at the

DMITRI SHAROMOV / GREENPEACE

Greenpeace climbers hang from the hull of the coal freighter *Hellenic Sea*. A few minutes after this image was taken, police from a large tugboat confiscated the banner and arrested the three activists.

media boat and asked to be taken to the site of the action. In the heat of the moment, the driver forgot about Dima and left. So it was that when the photographer made it back to where he had disembarked, he found that his mode of transport had evaporated. 'This can't be true!' he thought, wide-eyed in disbelief. He carried neither a radio nor a phone. 'What an absurd situation! How am I going to get out of this one!'... Well, he did. He told a local man who had just disembarked from his small motor boat that if he did not get back to his ship he 'would be left behind'. The man, unaware of what was going on, kindly delivered him back to the media boat. Dima arrived just in time to photograph the activists hanging from the *Hellenic Sea* and their arrest by a tugboat full of police.

The police tugboat then came for me, but the height of the ship's gunwale made it impossible for them to reach me. So instead the tugboat headed for the center of the *Rainbow Warrior* and made a feint to push her out of the way, a maneuver that would have placed me in an extremely dangerous situation. I climbed back on board to protect myself and immediately a violent ramming displaced the ship by several meters.

After almost four hours of action, we missed achieving one of our goals by a matter of just a few minutes: forcing the *Hellenic Sea* to wait for the next high tide. The media exposure was huge, covering both the action and our campaign, but we were also confronted with an unexpected issue. Because of our blocking of the cargo ship, all but one of Christchurch's police officers had come to Lyttelton – although most of them were mere spectators on the wharf – and the one remaining had been the victim of an attack, so that the local media held us responsible for leaving the city 'unprotected'.

The coal industry was by no means the only industry in New Zealand contributing to climate

The story of a possum

One early morning while I was on watch on the bridge, I saw it out of the corner of my eye. The possum was skipping along the jib's boom, at the bow. Binoculars in hand, I watched the animal running up and down the rigging and the deck. It was so cute! It was hard to believe that such a small creature could cause such destruction in the forests of New Zealand/ Aotearoa.[5]

After three weeks of repairs and maintenance, the *Rainbow Warrior* had just been put back on the water in Whangarei, North Island. The day came for the ship's half-yearly sanitation control inspection. Flavio Nakazono, the bosun, came on deck looking for help. 'Maite, quickly, follow me!' As we walked along the accommodation alleyway, he told me the situation. 'We have a possum in the mess! Right when the quarantine officer is doing the inspection! We need to push the animal out before the guy sees it!' So a number of us equipped ourselves with brooms and mops and made for the ship's mess brandishing them. As we entered, we found the quarantine officer there, sitting next to the entrance, checking some papers and waiting for the cup of tea Dima was preparing for him. No sign of the possum, though! We put on an act and left the mess.

I ran to the captain's cabin. 'Derek, we need to get the inspector out of the mess immediately!'

Two minutes later, while the captain engaged the inspector in a lively conversation over tea, several crew members extracted the animal from its hiding place, the corner behind the TV. A little push was all it took to set the marsupial running for an open porthole. It left the ship the same way it had entered it, skipping down a stern mooring line.

JOHN COWPLAND / GREENPEACE

Deforestation affects the rich world too, as with these areas in New Zealand/ Aotearoa cleared for large- scale intensive dairy farming. Agriculture accounts for 49% of the country's total greenhouse- gas emissions. In addition, palm kernel imports from Indonesia and Malaysia (to feed cattle) are rocketing.

change. The country's biggest contribution of all comes from one of the cornerstones of its economy – raising cattle for dairy products and meat. This makes it a thorny subject, since a high percentage of New Zealanders have worked for generations raising cattle in small family-owned farms. However, family farms have all too often turned to intensive farming and ended up being swallowed up by a huge industry that aims to maximize profit – including the government-owned company Landcorp. Even existing forest plantations for commercial exploitation began to be cleared to create more pastures for grazing. Although these were not native species, they were still trees, meaning that little carbon sinks were being destroyed to make way for more emissions of methane and nitrous oxide.

'If there is a way to get kiwis to listen to us, it is by speaking to them from the *Rainbow Warrior*.' I clearly remember these words by Bunny McDiarmid, the former deckhand who was by then Executive Director of Greenpeace New Zealand/ Aotearoa office. Thanks to the *Rainbow Warrior* tour, thousands of people took note and became more aware of the impact of intensive livestock farming on the environment. Sadly, the conversion of forest plantations to farmland continues.

Sails to be free
(The Netherlands, November 2008)

The *Rainbow Warrior* left Amsterdam accompanied by the *Beluga II* (a 34-meter-long sailing boat owned by Greenpeace Germany) and the *Argus* (a small vessel belonging to Greenpeace Netherlands). A patrol boat joined the small convoy in order to control its movements. The journey was to be short as Rotterdam was their destination. Europoort, its industrial and commercial port, is the largest in Europe, and up to a few years ago it was the busiest in the world.[6]

The *Rainbow Warrior* led the way as the ships entered the great inland waterway. They reached the breakwater that divides the waterway lengthways: on the starboard side (south of the channel) lies Europoort, while on the port side (north of the channel) the river leads to the city 30 kilometers farther on. The *Rainbow Warrior* held her position on the northern side till the last minute, then turned the rudder to head towards the commercial port.

At once the ship received a call from the port control tower ordering her to leave the restricted zone. Captain Mike Fincken tried to calm them down just as a big banner with the international campaign slogan 'Quit Coal' was being hung between the masts. Immediately the police arrived, arresting all the ship's inflatables that had been lowered to the water – including the media boat, which explains why there are almost no pictures of this action.

The *Rainbow Warrior* turned again to starboard, entering a cove where coal was being unloaded. The place was overshadowed by the two chimneys of a huge power plant. E.ON, the power company that owned it, was building a second plant on a nearby site that had been occupied by hundreds of Greenpeace volunteers since early morning.

Coal-fired power plants are the greatest single source of human-made CO_2 emissions.

A patrol boat tried to block the flagship on her starboard side while a big tugboat flanked her port side. The *Rainbow Warrior* managed to get away from both ships, heading deeper into the cove and dropping anchor in a spot where she obstructed the entrance and exit of ships. Even though she was anchored, the environmental ship kept her engines running. The *Beluga II* had also managed to display a big banner but had been immediately

arrested and removed from the action. The *Argus*, carrying several journalists on board, had long ago been taken away from the scene.

The patrol boat started to push the *Rainbow Warrior* very hard but the ship was able to hold her position with the help of the engines and the anchor. Now and then the ship heeled over so much that it looked as if she would capsize. Finally, the patrol boat gave way to the tugboat which started to shove from the other side and finally managed to push her out of the way. However, the tugboat did not stop pushing until the *Rainbow Warrior* came dangerously close to a dyke and then went aground.

The ship was now completely immobilized, 'sitting' on the seabed of the channel. It was so hard to believe that the entire crew went on deck to have a look. On the bridge deck, Mike felt a breeze caress his face. Wind was blowing from the North Sea. 'Just the perfect wind,' thought the captain, ordering the crew to set the sails. The wind filled the sails and the ship begun to heel. First they could feel the bow slowly start to move, and soon afterwards the stern came away as well. They were free!

After the crew's initial burst of jubilation, a frantic activity took over the vessel. While the

No smoke without fire. The *Rainbow Warrior* strategically posed in front of the E.ON coal-fired power plant in Rotterdam, the Netherlands.

WILL ROSE / GREENPEACE

WILL ROSE

Facing the music. *Rainbow Warrior* **captain Mike Fincken at the moment of his detention by the Dutch police.**

engines were turned on, the anchor chain was pulled up – the anchor had been dragged along the bottom of the channel as the ship had been pushed along – and the sails were folded. The flagship regained the position from which she had been forcefully removed, dropped anchor, and blocked the port again.

A few hours went by and it was starting to get dark when the police boarded the *Rainbow Warrior*. They found the ship locked and only one person on deck: Penny Gardner, the bosun, who was at the bow in charge of the anchor. From the wheelhouse the crew saw the police breaking in through an engine-room ventilation hatch. Realizing the game was up, it was decided to let them in. Mike happened to be alone with the police for a moment and a big police officer grabbed him and knocked him to the floor.

The ship was taken to a police area within Europoort where she joined the *Beluga II*. Mike was arrested and the rest of the crew were given five minutes to gather their things and leave the ship – with just three people remaining on board for safety reasons. The activists on land had managed to halt the construction of the new power plant for 10 hours before being arrested.

Although they were both held in the same prison, it was not until two days later that Mike met Uwe Linke, the captain of the *Beluga II*, at the moment when they were both released.

The Copenhagen experience
(Norway & Denmark, December 2009)

We were passionately engaged in conversation on our way back to the ship, analyzing the speech we had just heard. We were coming from the Nobel Peace Center in Oslo where we had watched Barack Obama's award ceremony live. The mobile phone of the *Rainbow Warrior* captain, Mike Fincken, rang.

2009 Nobel Peace Prize
Barack Obama – who had been elected President of the United States less than a year before – turned his acceptance speech into a case for war. He stated several times that 'war/force is sometimes necessary'. He glorified soldiers' courage, emphasizing that peace had been promoted all over thanks to their service and sacrifice, and although he quoted Martin Luther King – awarded the prize in 1964 – on several occasions, he proclaimed that he and Mahatma Gandhi were wrong because the nonviolence practiced by them 'may not have been practical or possible in every circumstance'.

He also stated in his speech: 'If we do nothing, we will face more drought, more famine, more mass displacement – all of which will fuel more conflict for decades.'

MAITE MOMPÓ

She appeared out of nowhere, dressed in the light clothes she would have worn in her Pacific island nation, Tuvalu, and immediately captured the attention of the hundreds of people gathered outside the hotel where Barack Obama was staying, just a few hours before the Nobel ceremony. It was very cold in Oslo and someone put a jacket over her shoulders. With her white homemade banner, its desperate message in large, irregular letters, she captured the urgent essence of the issue. The Tuvalu archipelago in Polynesia has a maximum height of five meters and so is more threatened by rising sea levels than any other country bar one.

The call came from Greenpeace International. Seeing Mike's face and hearing his part of the conversation made everyone go silent. When he hung up, he was stunned. 'They've decided that the *Rainbow Warrior* is not going to Copenhagen.'

'What?!' was the outcry from everyone. 'No way!'

It was precisely due to the Nobel Prize that we were in Oslo and not in Copenhagen, where the COP15 had begun three days before. We had gone to the capital of Norway to pressurize Obama into keeping climate change on his agenda.

Greenpeace was overwhelmed. Just for the climate summit, the organization had mobilized over 600 volunteers, three ships (the *Arctic Sunrise*, the *Beluga II*, and the *Rainbow Warrior*), the big Climate Rescue Station dome (installed inside the Bella Center, the place where the world event was taking place), in addition to climate campaigners from many countries, press people and logistics personnel. But we were drops in the ocean.

The city of Copenhagen was overwhelmed too. The Danish authorities were worried by the way the the summit had mushroomed. Tens of thousands of people from around the globe had come – collectively or individually – to demand a significant and effective agreement. The beleaguered Danish government decided to impose unprecedented repressive measures, passing a law that included preventive detention based on subjective criteria.

Under this law, police were arresting hundreds of people on a daily basis.

The arrival of the *Rainbow Warrior* was suddenly seen by Greenpeace people in Copenhagen as an additional complication in an already complex situation. We crew members could not have disagreed more. Fortunately, Mike was eventually able to convince the logistics people and the campaigners, and we set course for Copenhagen that same night.

Our arrival was pretty emotional. Our berth was right beside the main facility of the organization's volunteers ('Warehouse-A'), on the outskirts of Copenhagen. As we were approaching, young people started showing up to help us with the mooring lines, welcoming us with a big smile. The location was surrounded by trees and everything was covered in thick snow.

The long-awaited climate summit had started six days before and was already turning out to be a fiasco. The day before our arrival – Saturday 12 December – there was a Global Day of Action. In Copenhagen, around 100,000 people had gathered in a peaceful demonstration but the news headlines focused neither on the magnitude of the demonstration nor on the need to reach a global agreement, but instead on the detention of 900 people on the alleged grounds of 'violent attitude'. Nor did the media inform the public how the arrests had taken place: the police had burst into the demonstration from both sides, cutting off a section with fences. The people trapped inside the improvised cage had been shoved out and detained while the police had withdrawn until their next attack. The arrest of two guys wearing a cow costume – one serving as the head and the other as the tail – was enough to show the absurdity of the claim that those detained had threatened violence.

The *FAB* Agreement

At Copenhagen in 2009, over 400 social and environmental organizations (forming an alliance called *TckTckTck*) together with millions of citizens (over 17 million signed petitions were collected) demanded a **Fair** (for all the people in the planet), **Ambitious** (with significant emission reductions for industrialized countries) and legally **Binding** agreement to combat climate change.

In the nearby big warehouse, dozens of volunteers were constantly coming and going, setting up diverse activities around the Bella Center, taking part in small-scale actions, or otherwise going to the secret warehouse (the 'Warehouse-B') to prepare for a final full-scale action. Some crew members joined in these activities while the *Rainbow Warrior* herself welcomed on board many volunteers and campaigners, including the newly appointed Executive Director of Greenpeace International, Kumi Naidoo. It felt like the ship was fostering a spirit that united everyone in the organization.

On the other hand, the city itself was brimming with events. There were daily demonstrations, street exhibitions, NGOs' information canopies, a place for bloggers, and there were also discussions and debates with specialists and attendees of the Bella Center meeting in different places. And on top of it all was the Klimaforum or People's Climate Summit, the alternative conference

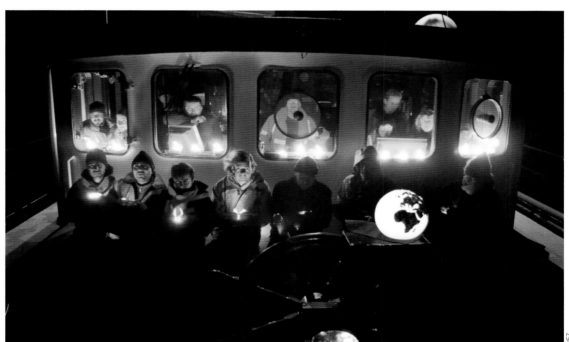

Flickering hope. On the middle Saturday of the COP15, the *Rainbow Warrior* crew took part in the global candlelight vigil for the climate while sailing from Oslo to Copenhagen. There were 3,241 such vigils held that day in 139 countries, most of them organized by the online campaign group Avaaz.

ANA CARLA MARTINEZ

attended by about 50,000 people that had among its participants persons as prominent as Vandana Shiva and Naomi Klein. It was really uplifting, this feeling of being part of such a global gathering of people, all of us working together to avoid catastrophe. But, as the days went by, it was also heartbreaking to see how our hopes were falling apart.

A People's Declaration was formulated before and during the Klimaforum calling for 'System change – not climate change' that was handed over to the COP15 on 18 December.

On Monday 14 December, thousands of accredited people were denied entry to the summit, and also admission quotas were established for the civil-society groups (with more than 20,000 people registered for the event): Tuesday and Wednesday 7,000 observers, Thursday 1,000, and Friday 90 people as a whole. The ones that had been thrown out of the Bella Center took refuge in the Klimaforum, which thus became definitively the place for social movements to meet, debate and mobilize.

The following day, Tuvalu submitted a protocol promoting deeper, legally binding emission cuts, and negotiations were suspended right after.

Civil-society groups immediately backed the tiny Pacific country, which maintained that as rich countries had caused global warming, it was their responsibility to fix it.

On Thursday 17 December, the heads of state started to arrive. That day, a number of Greenpeace activists positioned themselves on the route between the airport and the Bella Center. It was impossible for all the major politicians to miss people holding hand-banners or hanging bigger ones from different locations, all with the same message: 'Politicians Talk. Leaders Act.' These activists were arrested by the police at once and all of them were taken to a huge hangar that the Danish authorities had improvised as a detention center. In the words of Ilai Ben Amar, who belonged to a group that had climbed to the top of streetlamps: 'It was similar to the places where they keep homeless dogs. It was like a big cage divided into smaller cages, like compartments, each holding four or five activists.' Some hours later, well into the night, the sounds of whistles and laughter burst out all of a sudden. A lady in an elegant red dress had just walked in. It was Nora Christiansen.

That evening, the Queen of Denmark had been hosting a dinner party for the Heads of State who had come to the summit. As expected, Greenpeace activists displayed their banners on

The red-carpet activists rehearsing their gatecrash of the royal reception: Juan López de Uralde (left), Nora Christiansen and Christian Schmutz.

BAS BEENTJES / GREENPEACE

KRISTIAN BUUS / GREENPEACE

As negotiations at the COP15 Climate Conference approach an unsatisfactory conclusion, activists from Greenpeace and the rest of the TckTckTck coalition don masks representing various heads of state to protest the shameful outcome.

the politicians' route to the Royal Palace. But what nobody could have predicted was that a small Greenpeace convoy managed to follow the same route as the politicians' limousines and that three activists, dressed for the occasion, managed to make their way into the palace. Nora (Norwegian), her 'partner' Juan López de Uralde, or 'Juantxo' (Spanish), and their 'bodyguard' Christian Schmutz, or 'Chrigi' (Swiss) had been welcomed on the red carpet and directed to where they could be greeted by the Queen. They had no intention of meeting her. As soon as they found themselves in front of the media they unfolded their banners. This was the last chance to tell politicians to act – and images of them and their message went all over the world.

Friday 18 December was the last day of the summit – the decision-making day.

It was around midday when a few crew members left the *Rainbow Warrior* and headed for 'Warehouse-B', which was far away from Copenhagen in an inaccessible location to avoid police eyes. During the trip we had to take different trains, and at one train station Tuna Türkmen and Lesley Simkiss were left behind: the deckhand had a toilet emergency and the medic stayed behind to wait for him. As it turned out, these two were to be the only ones to make it to the warehouse.

We finally arrived at our destination only to bump into police agents asking for passports. The van that had been supposed to take us to the

warehouse instead drove us back to Copenhagen with the police hot on our heels. Initially frustrated that we could not take part in the final action, we ended up joining the rest of the crew in the Klimaforum so we could take part in activities organized by the TckTckTck Coalition. This at least meant that we experienced the sense of unity shared by so many organizations and individuals from all over the world. In the end, the politicians were not able to come to an agreement and the final decision was postponed for several hours.

The following day, the great disappointment hit us. The 'agreement' reached by our leaders turned out to be nothing more than a bunch of empty words. The economic interests of the big fossil-fuel corporations had been given more weight than the survival of humanity. I can't think of a greater crime that could be committed.

As had been the case with many of the protest activities planned for the summit, the big final Greenpeace action was cancelled at the last moment – and I'm afraid, for legal reasons, I can't reveal what that action was to have been, even now.

That evening, those of us still in the city gathered for a vigil at the entrance of the prison where the four people detained for the 'gala action' were being held (Joris Thijssen had been arrested afterwards). We left the place still not knowing when our colleagues would be released.

The rest of the Greenpeace detainees had already been released, including Dima Litvinov, who had

The COP15 endgame

On the last day of the summit, the US and 24 other powerful nations came together and tried to impose a new text on all the other countries (over 100 of them), making it impossible to reach agreement. The so-called 'Copenhagen Accord', of which politicians promised to 'take note', was not legally binding, and neither included specific and quantifiable commitments for emission reductions in the industrialized world nor guaranteed the aid that the Global North would provide to the countries of the Global South.

co-ordinated the different activities carried out by volunteers, and who had been taken from the *Arctic Sunrise* and kept under preventive arrest for four days. Dima's happy cries when his little cell's TV showed the images of Nora and Juantxo unfolding their banners at the Palace were heard all over the prison building. The following day, he actually met the pair in the prison courtyard.

The moment to relax had come at last, after two weeks of exhausting work, great expectations and immense disappointments – so many exciting moments followed by such frustration. The music filled the air in Warehouse-A, where the last Greenpeacers remaining in Copenhagen had come together for the last night, happy to be part of the global movement speaking up for the planet. The following day we were all due to leave the city, with volunteers and office people going back home, and the *Rainbow Warrior* setting sail for Amsterdam early in the morning.

I had been feeling a sick sensation in my stomach for hours, and suddenly I understood why. Four of our comrades were still behind bars. How could we be leaving? Christmas was around the corner and the *Rainbow Warrior* had no plans for the following weeks. Why couldn't we stay in Copenhagen and provide logistical support for the detainees? I talked the idea over with my friend Cornelia Ihl, Greenpeace International's action co-ordinator. When ship captain Mike heard the proposal, he thought it was brilliant. The three of us went then to talk it over with Mads Christensen, Nora's

In addition to the many detentions of Greenpeace members, the police tapped several of our phones, searched the apartments rented by those attending the Bella Center and had several people followed.

ANA CARLA MARTINEZ

From the author's blog, 19 December 2009. 'Tonight, I'm on port watch. All is quiet, with the silence of the white snow covering everything. I have just replaced Joris's candle, which had blown out. Then Nora's. From where I'm sitting in the wheelhouse, I can see our big banner calling for justice. Tomorrow, nearly a week into their detention, we'll continue to work tirelessly... Anything but stand still and be indifferent to injustice because, when one of us is imprisoned, we are all prisoners. I take a last glance before going to bed. Now it's the turn of Juantxo's candle. I go, leaving his face lit up.'

[Left] Ana Carla Martínez with Curdin, son of the detained Swiss activist Chrigi. The Argentinean deckhand became the on board 'children's nanny'. [Right] Chrigi's mother at the opening of a box containing dozens of letters supporting the detainees.

husband and Greenpeace Denmark's Executive Director. Lastly, the four of us went over to Kumi Naidoo, who also loved the idea. Not half an hour had passed since I had broached the subject with Cornelia before the final decision to stay had been taken. For the four detainees, knowing that the ship remained meant a great deal.

We took the *Rainbow Warrior* to the center of the city and she became a meeting place for us and the people from the Greenpeace Denmark office, all of us devoted to liberating and providing support for our friends, who were being held incommunicado. Lots of international media representatives came on board to cover the news from the ship.

Each morning we woke up thinking that this could be the day our colleagues were set free, but the days slid by and nothing happened. Kirstie Wielandt from Greenpeace International in the Netherlands came to act as back-up while Marco Weber, a Swiss volunteer during the COP15, stayed with us to help. We thought our comrades would be released for Christmas Eve, but on that day it was announced that they would stay in prison till 7 January. We then pinned our hopes on having them celebrating New Year with us, but that was not to be either. The 'family' on the *Rainbow Warrior* kept growing as the partners of several crew members also came aboard. With the coming of the New Year, I moved to another cabin to offer mine to some very special guests: Chrigi's one-year-old son, Curdin, his wife and his

parents would stay with us until his release. Later on, Juantxo's wife and brother also visited us and we took in Joris' partner, who was visibly pregnant, as well as various colleagues from Greenpeace national offices. The feeling of unity and solidarity in the *Rainbow Warrior* was something magical, as we all shared an experience we would never forget.

At last, on the night of 6 January, the so-called 'Red Carpet Four' were set free. That moment, and the subsequent celebration aboard the *Rainbow Warrior*, ranks among the most emotional experiences in my life. The following day, after a

Pure joy. The author hugging Juantxo López de Uralde, then Greenpeace Spain's Executive Director, on his release from 20 days' detention.

mass press conference held in the ship's hold, the *Rainbow Warrior* finally left Copenhagen, the city which had become the world's climate capital for two weeks.

On 16 December 2010, the Copenhagen City Court ruled that all the mass arrests during the summit the year before had been illegal, as well as all the preventive arrests from 11 to 16 December.

On 22 August 2011, that same court sentenced those involved in the 'gala action' to a 14-day suspended jail sentence while Greenpeace Nordic (the regional office for Norway, Sweden, Finland and Denmark) was fined.

The fingers of humanity
(Israel, July 2010)

We were full speed ahead, the *Avon* pounding into the waves. Although the sun had come up a while ago, we had not seen it yet as it was hiding behind the clouds. We were heading for our next objective, the unloading dock of the Hadera coal-fired power plant in Israel. Our bow was pointing towards a great cloud, which suddenly gave way to a magnificent fan-shaped spectacle of sunrays. Ilai Ben Amar, sitting next to me, said: 'They are known as the "fingers of God".'

Little by little, the three chimneys of the power plant began to appear on the horizon, growing taller and taller as we got closer. These were the fingers of humanity, pointing towards the blue sky that they were polluting and turning grey. Thus, before us, the 'divine hand' intertwined with the long concrete human-made fingers.

Orot Rabin, the Hadera coal-fired power plant, is the biggest power plant in Israel. It burns 18,000 tons of coal daily.

The Ukrainian cargo ship *Augusta* was unloading coal at that very moment. I and the other seven activists gained access to the dock using the stairs on its far side and then hung a large banner

from one of the cranes, halting the unloading. On board the *Rainbow Warrior* inflatables, our colleagues were painting 'Go Solar' on the hull of the freighter. Then they made it back to the ship, which continued her way to the port of Haifa. The police removed us from the cranes and took us to the police station, arriving there at around 10am.

Once we had been searched, they locked the women in one cell and the men in another. A few hours later we heard a commotion and the door opened to let in the colleagues who had painted the freighter's hull. All the female activists were now there – except one.

Three different types of police boarded the *Rainbow Warrior* as soon as she docked in Haifa. The entire crew was taken to the ship's mess, where they were amazed to witness the tension between the different security forces, all competing for the biggest say. One of the officers took out some photographs taken during the action, and so, one by one, all the activists in the inflatables were identified. All but Ana Carla Martínez. The police assault woke her up and she showed up in the mess with her curly lioness mane, which had been hidden beneath a headscarf and a helmet during

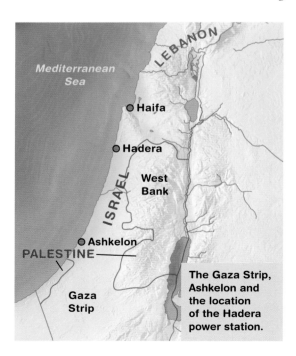

The Gaza Strip, Ashkelon and the location of the Hadera power station.

194

JIRI REZAC / GREENPEACE

Precarious protest. Activists display a banner with a message in English and Hebrew as they hang from one of the huge cranes in the coal port of the Hadera power station in Israel.

the action. The police were mad as hell because one of the activists – they thought it was a man – had escaped. Before leaving the ship's deck, the angriest police officer of all turned to Ana and her fellows and, signalling at them with his finger, blurted out: 'Tell your mate that he has been really very lucky!'

One by one, we were led out of our cell for our papers and belongings to be checked. When my turn came, a police officer asked me my name and country of origin, and began searching for my passport but couldn't find it. He looked at me and asked: 'Where is your passport?'

'Well, that is what I was about to ask you,' I replied. 'Where is my passport?' He became nervous, left, searched again through the papers, and finally my documentation appeared. We spent the whole afternoon up to almost midnight being taken from one place to another within the police station on an absurd pilgrimage.

Finally, those who had already made a statement were taken to prison. The remaining male activists were put back in their cell, but I and the last three women were left in a corridor, sitting on a small and uncomfortable wooden bench. Two of my colleagues were even handcuffed to each other at the wrists and ankles. It was cold, and we were given a single blanket for the four of us to huddle under. Impossible to sleep in those conditions.

At 1.30am I was taken for interrogation, and it was already 3.00am when I sat back down with my 'bench partners'. Finally, they decided to take us to Kishon prison, not far away from Haifa. I remember they left us standing in a courtyard waiting for our passports, which had been forgotten in Hadera. The four of us threw ourselves to the concrete ground to try to get some sleep, if only for a few minutes. Having hardly had any sleep in the previous three days, I was beginning to understand how terrible it is to be deliberately deprived of sleep when you are exhausted.

After a short stay in a cell, we were taken back to Hadera to appear before a judge. We (the activists on the cranes) were set free once Sharon Dolev, Director of Greenpeace Israel, had paid every individual bail and under the condition that the ship and crew left the country in the next 24 hours. A crowd of us were outside the building waiting for the rest of our colleagues to be released when a man wearing dark glasses required me to identify myself while momentarily showing something that resembled a badge. When I was about to show him my passport, he took it from my hands. Sharon and I went after him, asking him to give it back. We arrived at a car and the man told me to wait inside the vehicle while he confirmed my personal details.

'Don't even think about getting in that car! You would disappear!' said Sharon. The man belonged to the recently created Immigration Police and intended to 'kidnap' at least one of us. But why would Immigration get involved when we had already been sentenced to deportation?

The answer was obvious. The sentence setting us free had hurt the police in Hadera. This had been our second direct action under their jurisdiction in less than a week, and we had shown them up! They wanted a tougher punishment.

In the first action, three activists from the *Rainbow Warrior* had boarded a coal cargo ship, the *Orient Venus*, which had therefore ended up arriving at the Hadera power plant with the message 'Coal Kills' draped from its mast. Some of the media reports had portrayed this as Greenpeace demonstrating how to board a ship 'correctly', comparing it favorably with the Israeli navy's assault a month before on the ships of an international peace

Gaza peace flotilla

A coalition of organizations arranged a flotilla to take around 10,000 tons of humanitarian aid and medical supplies to the Palestinian population besieged on the Gaza Strip.

It comprised eight ships carrying approximately 800 volunteers of 60 different nationalities, including among their number members of the European Parliament and a Nobel Peace Prize winner.

The Israeli navy violently boarded the ships in international waters. Dozens of people were injured and nine Turkish citizens were shot during the assault on the *Mavi Marmara*.

flotilla heading for Gaza, which had left several people dead and dozens wounded. During our own second action, some of the newspapers again hounded the national and local security forces: we had entered with ease a high-security national area that was supposed to be under the navy's protection, while the police had been unable to find out about the plans despite having held the activists from the first action in custody for hours.

What the police did not know was that our action at Hadera had in fact been our Plan B. The priority for the local energy campaign was to stop the construction of Ashkelon's new coal-fired power plant, which was to be built beside the ones already there. The *Rainbow Warrior* could be

Riding high. Three activists, two Israeli and one German, board the *Orient Venus*, a massive 290-meter-long vessel carrying coal to the Hadera power plant, aiming to delay it from entering Israeli waters.

Open day on board the *Rainbow Warrior* in the Israeli port of Haifa.

of great help to the campaign, and local staff and volunteers had put a lot of effort and time into preparing for the ship's visit. But then the tragic assault on the peace flotilla took place. Due to the seriousness of what had just happened, the issues of pollution and climate change took a back seat. Although Greenpeace International decided to go ahead as planned, most of us on board the *Rainbow Warrior* were outraged and did not really want to go to Israel at that moment. The people we met from Greenpeace Israel, especially Sharon, made us change our minds when we arrived in Haifa. Most of them supported the Palestinian cause and regretted the despicable assault as much as we did, if not more. In countries like Israel, it is not easy to be a human rights activist, as you risk being seen as an enemy of your homeland.

In truth, there were reasons enough to take action, which is why the Israeli office had focused climate campaigning on this issue at local level, as Nili Grossman, the energy campaigner, explained to us. Ashkelon is located just a few kilometers from the Gaza Strip and its power plants are located in the south. The pollution from its chimneys reaches both the city and the Gaza Strip population, lowering everyone's quality of life.

Ultimately, the effect fossil-fuel burning has on the global climate puts everyone at risk, no matter if you are free, oppressor or oppressed.

After our open boat in Haifa we spent several days in international waters waiting to intercept any coal ship heading for Ashkelon, but none came. That is how Hadera became our next objective, as its coal supply had not been interrupted. So it was that our three activists boarded the *Orient Venus* while the *Rainbow Warrior* waited for the next coal ship.

A few days later, we heard a radio conversation that took us aback. An Israeli navy ship was threatening the *Amalthea*, a vessel carrying 15 human rights activists plus food and medicine for Gaza. An engine failure had left the ship adrift in international waters near the Egyptian coast. 'If you go to Gaza you will be responsible for any possible deaths,' the captain of the *Amalthea* was repeatedly told. What a terrible warning! The ship ended up going to Egypt to unload its aid material there, and we went back to preparing for the Hadera action.

In the end, Sharon managed to get my passport back. Knowing that the intention of the Immigration Police was to hold us by any means – not leaving Israel in 24 hours would have meant our possible detention and the lost of the bails, we kept out of

MAITE MOMPÓ

their way, though we were detained once more for while in one of the port buildings. Our relief was enormous when we finally made it to the ship and set sail. We had met so many wonderful people and, although we did not know it then, their seven-year fight against the Ashkelon plant was soon to be won. Gathered at the stern of the *Rainbow Warrior*, we drank a toast to freedom while the sun from which the fingers of God had emanated a day and a half before began to set on the horizon.

'Hostile entity'

The Gaza Strip runs along 45 km north to south being between 6 and 12 km wide. It is one of the most densely populated places on the planet with over a million and a half people living in just 365 square kilometers.

In 2007, Israel declared this a 'hostile entity' and completely isolated the Palestinian territory, controlling all its land borders, air space and sea access, as well as population registration, electricity, water, gas, and medicine supply, and the entry and exit of goods and people.

In 2008, a report from a group of respected NGOs, including Amnesty International, Oxfam, Save the Children UK and Christian Aid, declared the Gaza Strip to be effectively a prison.

The story of the Arctic 30
(Russia, September-December 2013)

Camila Speziale was excited by the SMS asking her if she could speak English. She had already been a volunteer in Greenpeace Argentina's climbing team for two years. 'It's for a three-week trip abroad, I can't say where. Could you go?' Camila said yes at once: to be on one of the organization's ships is the dream of every single Greenpeace volunteer. For two long months, the 21-year-old Argentinean kept her destination secret – she just said she was going to Europe. Although she was very excited, she was also full of doubts and fears. 'What if I am seasick? Will I be able to do it?' To climb a building was one thing, and to climb a structure from an inflatable boat in the middle of the ocean was quite another!

In Kirkenes, a Norwegian city some 400 kilometers north of the Arctic Circle, 14 people joined the crew for the next mission of the *Arctic Sunrise*: campaigners, communications and logistics people, volunteers, technicians, and two independent reporters (photographer and camera operator). On 14 September 2013, the Greenpeace ship departed with 30 people of 18 different nationalities on board, Camila being the youngest. Some had a long history within Greenpeace, such as Dima Litvinov (campaigns and logistics) and Frank Hewetson (actions specialist) as well as Pete Willcox (ship's captain), Colin

The Arctic is threatened

The Arctic, one of the planet's most pristine areas, is home to one of the most fragile ecosystems. Global warming is having a major impact on the region, and the increasingly accelerated ice melting is aggravating climate change in return. According to experts, the Arctic could be completely ice-free in summer in little more than 10 years. The loss of ice has brought about:

• The opening of new sea routes, which is threatening to pollute large areas that were previously inaccessible.

• The region, formerly a *de facto* marine reserve, is now in the crosshairs of the same industrial fishing fleet that has brought many of the fish stocks in other waters to the brink of commercial extinction.

• Several oil companies (mainly Shell and Gazprom but also Statoil, Cairn Energy and Exxon) have begun to drill for oil. Any oil spill, however slight, would have an irreversible impact on the Arctic ecosystem.[7]

• Five countries (the US, Canada, Russia, Norway and Denmark) aspire to seize the parts of the Arctic that do not belong to any state (including the North Pole) so as to exploit its resources. The militarization of the area has already started and there is a real threat of war in the future.

Russell (radio operator), Paul Ruzycki (chief mate) and David Haussmann 'Haussy' (electrician).

The aim of the trip was to draw world attention to the need to protect the Arctic while also peacefully preventing the *Prirazlomnaya* oil rig, owned by the Russian state company Gazprom (in partnership with Shell), from becoming the first to get oil in Arctic waters. The action ahead was a very complicated and highly risky one. It involved hoisting up the oil rig a 'safety pod' (measuring 2x3 meters) from where the activists were to communicate with the 'outside world' and be kept warm.

Technical and climbing preparations started in the port. It was essential that Camila and the other four climbers (the Finnish Sini Saarela, the Swiss Marco Weber 'Kruso', the Polish Tomasz Dziemianczuk and the British Phil Ball) succeeded in forming a consistent team.

DENIS SINYAKOV / GREENPEACE

GREENPEACE #SaveTheArctic

Ready for action. Activists Sini Saarela, Anthony Perrett, Phil Ball and Camila Speziale on top of the pod in Kirkenes, Norway, before confronting the Arctic oil industry. In 2012, Greenpeace started a worldwide campaign to get the United Nations to declare the Arctic's international waters a Global Sanctuary. More than five million signatures have been gathered and the campaign has the support of many celebrities and the European Union.

Phil was responsible for the proper functioning of the innovative electronic equipment incorporated into the pod (webcam, wi-fi phone, video and two laptops). He had been around when this equipment was being set up and, when its designer was injured, it was evident that he was the only possible replacement – which gave him only three days to get ready and travel to Kirkenes. It was a huge responsibility and the climber had to spend many hours testing and improving the electronic equipment instead of training with his teammates.

The *Arctic Sunrise* went first into a remote fjord to carry out – far from witnesses – several training sessions in which the whole action team and most of the crew took part. They practised towing the pod (which was provided with two longitudinal floats) and they also practised throwing from the inflatables to the ship's highest point the thin nylon lines that would enable them to attach the climbing ropes, climb the rig and hoist the pod. To prepare themselves for survival at sea, the activists also swam in the icy Arctic waters. The members

of the multinational climbing team got along perfectly with each other, so that an incredible fusion of climbing skills and personal experiences took place.

A few days later, the *Arctic Sunrise* headed to the Pechora Sea, an inlet of the Barents Sea. It was night time when the enormous oil platform began to be visible on the horizon, a giant construction in the middle of nowhere, packed with lights shining between the dark sea and the dark sky. The appearance of a threatening Russian Coastguard ship caused the action to be delayed for one day. The flat sea and the light fog filled the people on board with a strange feeling because, as everybody knows, after the calm comes the storm.

18 September. Camila managed only two hours' sleep, if that, before the wake-up call. Finally the long-awaited but feared moment had arrived. It was still dark when the first two inflatables left. Besides the two independent reporters, they were taking Sini, Tomasz and Kruso, who intended to climb the rig and set up the rope system for the

pod, assisted by Frank and Anthony Perrett. At the first light of dawn, the next three boats departed from the *Arctic Sunrise* carrying Camila and Phil – as well as the pod, which was being towed by the *Suzie Q*, the large jet boat. That day the sea was somewhat choppy and the pressure exerted by one of the strong swells cause the tugline to break. From the action scene, Frank told the boats to leave the pod and head fast for the platform. They had switched to Plan B: the aim now was to get the climbers on to the rig so that they could carry out a peaceful protest by unfurling a large banner.

Upon arrival, however, activists found themselves in the middle of a horror film. They started to be rammed by two inflatable boats of the Coastguard, the crews of which were threatening them with guns and knives and shouting at them in Russian. Their big, wild, scared-looking eyes were almost the only parts of their bodies that were visible.

Despite being continuously assailed by powerful streams of water from the platform's water cannons, Kruso had managed to climb several meters by hanging from a thick mooring line that made a loop on the rig side. Sini had just started climbing when she had fallen into the water but she had recovered to a point where she could finally hang in the air as well. At this point the Russian officers began firing their guns into the air and the water. How was this possible? With their arms raised at all times, it was clear that the activists intended no violence. The situation was so extreme that it did not seem real. The activists continued trying to attach the ropes to the rig structure but the Russian boats kept preventing them through their attacks.

The situation was becoming untenable and the activists decided to withdraw. The *Suzie Q* still remained beneath Kruso and Sini to protect their ropes but it also withdrew after a burst of gunfire from the platform hit the water just a few meters away. The climbers began to descend but Sini found that she could not do so because the rope she needed to use was being pulled from underneath. After a few tense moments, each shouting in a language that the other could not understand, the climbers landed on the military boats and were taken to the Coastguard. The other activists returned to their ship.

On the *Arctic Sunrise* they had also experienced a situation of great tension. They had just rescued the pod when the Russian Coastguards threatened them over the radio, saying that if the ship didn't stop, they would use their weapons to ensure that it did. Dima Litvinov sent the following answer to this: 'We are here in order to make the world a

The *Arctic Sunrise* approaching the Gazprom oil rig, which can just be seen in the distance. The ice-class *Arctic Sunrise* once provided supplies for seal-hunting. Greenpeace mounted two actions against the ship – and then bought it. Since starting its Greenpeace service in 1996, the ship has sailed all over the world, not only to both polar regions but also to the Amazon and Congo rivers.

DENIS SINYAKOV / GREENPEACE

DENIS SINYAKOV / GREENPEACE

[Left] Flashpoint. A Russian Coastguard officer points a gun at Greenpeace activists as other activists attempt to climb Gazprom's Prirazlomnaya oil platform.

[Right] Under arrest. Russian security forces abseil down from a helicopter onto the deck of the *Arctic Sunrise* to seize the ship at gunpoint.

better place and in response you are threatening to open fire on our ship... It is not just a legal matter, sir, I think this is also a matter for your conscience.' Accused of being terrorists, the pacifists counted up to 11 warning shots from artillery, as well as automatic gunfire.

When they lifted the inflatables on board, multiple punctures were found on their sponsons. The *Arctic Sunrise* started to move away from the platform with the Coastguard escorting it. At least the Russians allowed one of the Greenpeace inflatables to take some medicines that Sini needed on the Coastguard boat – by which means the team also sent food, books and notes encouraging her and Kruso.

The following day, normal routines were re-established on board. They had just finished dinner when, on a red-hued horizon, a black helicopter appeared, flying towards them. Going on deck, Phil (a professional camera operator) remembered the small digital camera that he happened to have on him and started to film as Russian security forces assaulted the ship's heli deck, pointing their weapons at the chests of people who had their arms raised. Aware of the importance of communicating these images to the outside world, Phil started running towards the radio room – only to find its portholes shut so that he could not pass on the camera. In the nick

of time, just before his arrest, he hid it inside his underwear and it was not found even when he was searched.

Within minutes, the Russians had seized the ship, which began to be towed. The captain was kept in his cabin and the rest of the hostages were taken to the ship's mess and galley area while the living quarters were searched. Phil took the opportunity to hide the little camera inside the extractor fan over the cooker. One by one, each crew member was then searched and taken to the lounge so that the mess and galley could also be searched. In the end, all communication devices were confiscated. But, to his great relief, Phil verified that his camera was still where he had hidden it. Afterwards he hid its memory card in the sole of his boot so that it would always be with him until he could deliver it safely.

Every time Pete Willcox went down to get his food, a few minutes of great excitement were shared. They all hoped that they would be released on arrival at port and, to kill time, they organized a championship of a card game taught them by Dima – the so-called 'Mexican Poker' or 'Widow' – though there was not enough time to finish it.

On 24 September, a beautiful rainbow welcomed them to the port of Murmansk. They spent two days in a detention center and, to everybody's

GREENPEACE

surprise, the 'Investigative Committee of Russia' opened a criminal case to determine whether they had committed the crime of piracy. Two months of detention would be required while the Russians conducted their investigation of the facts. The 30 people – now internationally baptized as 'the Arctic 30' – were placed in custody.

Two months in prison... and in such harsh conditions. Swallowing meals that made you want to vomit was such an immense effort. Small animals also resided in the cells, not just silverfish and fleas but in some cases also leeches and even rats. The cold, the worry and the uncomfortable beds made it hard to sleep. Just to survive in that infernal place, as is the case in many Russian prisons, it was essential to receive packages from outside, which finally started to arrive from the second week on, containing food, vitamins, medicines, sanitary products and clothes.

It was not at all easy to organize the team of people (Greenpeace volunteers and workers who were replaced on a rolling basis) that was to work in Murmansk providing support to prisoners and also ensuring there was media coverage of any event that affected their situation. The hearings before the Investigative Committee, despite being mere play-acting, were eagerly awaited as this was the only time when the support team could see their detained comrades and offer them their support by exchanging glances or sometimes even a few words. The prisoners' letters were extremely moving and many of them showed up the degrading conditions and inhumane treatment endured by almost 115,000 people in Russian remand prisons such as the one in Murmansk.

A woman called Irina

Irina Paichekova is a 60-year-old retired lawyer. She volunteers for a human rights committee and visits prisoners to secure improvements in prison conditions and campaign for freedom for political prisoners, something that greatly annoys the Russian authorities.

Irina visited the Arctic 30 on several occasions, especially Phil Ball. Aware that his voice would be heard louder than that of the average prisoner, the British activist made 10 formal complaints and also wrote to the director of the prison.

During the Arctic 30's detention in St Petersburg (after their transfer from Murmansk), Irina was arrested twice. Asked if she were not afraid for her life, she replied: 'I'm too tired of this, I haven't got the energy to be scared any more. I'm just going to keep doing it.'

Shortly after kick-off in the Champions League football match at the St Jakob Park stadium in Basel, Switzerland, Greenpeace activists unfurled this 28-meter-wide banner. It had a clear message for Gazprom, the Russian state-owned oil company that sponsors the Champions League, and called for the release of the Arctic 30. Among the climbing team was Christian 'Chrigi' Schmutz, who had been one of the Red Carpet Four in 2009. One of the Arctic 30, Marco 'Kruso' Weber, had then campaigned on board the *Rainbow Warrior* for his release and Chrigi was now doing all he could to help his friend.

Loneliness... Far from everything, even from their fellow crew members. The men shared their small cell with one or two prisoners, meaning there was a complete lack of privacy – and loneliness in company is arguably harder than being alone. The women were alone in even smaller cells. They were entitled to spend a daily hour in the 'exercise yard' pavilion – a filthy place with individual cells whose floors, black with dirt, were often flooded or icy. This was, however, the only place where they could communicate by shouting at each other.

Uncertainty... That was the hardest thing to bear – not knowing what would happen to you, your life being in the hands of others. In the arbitrary Russian legal system, two months could easily become many more and they had been charged with crimes (piracy first, hooliganism later) that could entail years of imprisonment (the maximum sentence for these crimes was 15 and 7 years respectively).

Hope... The only option was to survive by clinging to the hope that justice would be done, and what helped the Arctic 30 most was knowing that thousands of people were mobilizing to free them.

The *Arctic Sunrise* was seized in international waters, though within Russia's 'Exclusive Economic Zone'.[8] The Arctic 30 were neither pirates nor hooligans. The 28 Greenpeace members had only exercised the right to peaceful protest and, as regards the reporters, the photographer Denis Sinyakov declared: 'The criminal activity I am blamed for is called journalism.'

All Greenpeace offices worldwide (and the crews of the other two ships) became involved in the campaign to obtain the release of the Arctic 30, achieving an unprecedented mobilization. Hundreds of different activities were organized, from protests at Russian embassies and at offices of Gazprom and Shell, to projections and banners on emblematic buildings, concerts and protest marches. More than two million signatures calling for their release were collected and the cause won the support of many celebrities (actors, singers, writers), politicians (from heads of government to the UN Secretary-General), 13 Nobel Peace Prize laureates as well as social and human rights organizations.

On a personal level, I can assure you that it was very hard to think of my imprisoned comrades, among whom I had friends and many acquaintances – some of whom had shared in many of the other stories told in this book. Many of us could not help but put ourselves in their shoes because we knew that any one of us could have been in their situation. If, after the bombing of the *Rainbow Warrior* in 1985, the sentence 'You can't sink a Rainbow' encouraged Greenpeace

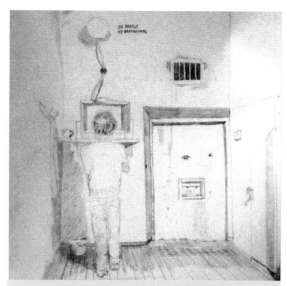

Phil Ball's drawing of his cell. Each cell contained a small and dirty toilet, a basin with cold water, a table and a bench (both screwed to the floor) and a bucket.

Greenpeace activist Faiza Oulahsen, from the Netherlands, continues campaigning even in the middle of her detention hearing in St Petersburg.

DMITRI SHAROMOV / GREENPEACE

people to continue, in 2013, the motto 'You can't seize a Sunrise' was born.

The very day they had entered prison, the men had learned about the *doroga* (which means road in Russian), the 'postal system' operating in jail overnight. This consisted of a network of ropes made from torn strips of bedsheet that had been twisted together and were wrapped around the window bars as if they were timing belts. Letters and packages, showing the name and cell number of both sender and recipient, were carried inside socks tied to these ropes. Delivery could even take place across the wide central corridor between the two rows of cells by utilizing the sewer pipes.

The women were outside this 'jail chat' but Alex Harris, Camila and Sini (in adjacent cells) created their own morse code by tapping on the heating pipes. Each letter of the alphabet matched a number of hits and they were able to make sentences and songs. Even if this means of communication was slow and tedious, it helped to make them feel they were not completely alone.

Just a few days before leaving that prison, Frank's cellmate urged him to put his ear to the pipe of the sink. He then heard Roman Dolgov's deep voice greeting him from the cell below. It was a shame not to have discovered this means of communicating before, as it would have eased the loneliness, especially for the women.

On 4 October, the Netherlands (*Arctic Sunrise*'s flag country) filed a lawsuit against Russia at the International Tribunal for the Law of the Sea for violating maritime law. A long month went by before the desperate Phil finally smuggled out of prison the images showing the assault on the ship, which were to form such an important piece of evidence in the trial.

As if they were in a spy movie, the Arctic 30 were secretly transferred to St Petersburg on 12 November and then distributed between several prisons. A week later, they finally started to be released on a bail of 45,000 euros, but they were forbidden to leave Russia.

On 22 November the International Tribunal for the Law of the Sea ordered the Russian Federation to release the Greenpeace vessel and its 30 occupants. However, it was another month before, on 18 December, the Russian parliament passed an amnesty law that included them and charges were finally dropped. The nightmare was over.

In the whole of Greenpeace history, the reaction of the Coastguard during the action and what

'You are my extended family,' said Arctic 30 member Alex Harris. In this photograph, Dima Litvinov, Sini Saarela and Camila Speziale hug each other having been granted an amnesty in St Petersburg. Phil Ball is in the background.

DMITRI SHAROMOV / GREENPEACE

Focus for global concern: 26 of the Arctic 30 in St Petersburg after their release.

happened subsequently in the Russian courts had constituted the toughest response by a government since the bombing of the first *Rainbow Warrior*. As a result of it, 30 people shared a dreadful experience and so became bonded forever. The Arctic 30 won their freedom but, as I write in April 2014, the *Arctic Sunrise* is still held in Murmansk and, of course, the Arctic is still in grave danger – a Gazprom tanker full of the world's first Arctic oil is on its way to Europe.

'This is not over yet. The Arctic is melting before our eyes and yet the oil companies are lining up to profit from its destruction. This is why I took action, to expose them and mobilize people to demand Arctic protection.' (Anthony Perrett)

1 Data from the UN Food and Agriculture Organization in 2006. **2** FAO, *Livestock's Long Shadow*, 2006. **3** Worldwatch Institute, *Livestock and Climate Change*, November/December 2009, worldwatch.org/files/pdf/Livestock and Climate Change.pdf **4** The data came from the Mauna Loa Observatory in Hawaii and was released by the US National Oceanic and Atmospheric Administration. **5** The possum is a small marsupial native to Australia (where it is a protected species) and New Guinea. Introduced in New Zealand/Aotearoa to produce leather, it has become a terrible pest as it has no predators – it is among the 100 most harmful invasive alien species in the world. Besides the enormous damage it does to trees and native wildlife, it transmits bovine tuberculosis. There are currently estimated to be 30 million possums in New Zealand/Aotearoa. **6** Betw een 1962 and 2004 Rotterdam was the busiest port of all. It was then surpassed by Singapore. Shanghai took over the mantle in 2010. **7** Evidence of this is provided by the *Exxon Valdez* disaster in Alaska in 1989. Eleven million barrels of crude oil affected 2,100 kilometers of coastline, and 28,000 square kilometers of ocean. Exxon spent $2 billion on a clean-up operation but could only recover some 10 per cent of the oil spilled and, 25 years later, oil still remains in many areas. **8** See Chapter 3.

> 'Big change looks impossible when you start, and inevitable when you finish'
>
> Bob Hunter

11 The circle of life

The last *Rainbow Warrior* missions (East Asia, 2011) • The voyage to Fukushima (Japan)
• The last campaign (South Korea)
Of Rainbows and Warriors • Farewell to a Warrior, welcome to a Rainbow • The circle of life

The last *Rainbow Warrior* missions (East Asia, 2011)

I arrived in Busan, South Korea, on the night of 15 March 2011, pretty exhausted after so many hours spent in planes and airports. Although I was very happy to see the *Rainbow Warrior* again, I could not avoid that feeling of sorrow that flashed through my body like lightning. This was to be the last time I was to sail on the ship, the last time I was to have her as my home.

In the plane from Madrid to Munich I had sat next to a young Japanese couple. Shortly after taking off, she started crying. I asked her what was wrong, and if I could help. Looking at me with desolated eyes, she simply said, 'Fukushima' and I could only reply 'I'm *so* sorry!'

Just four days before, on 11 March, northeastern Japan had been shaken by the strongest earthquake in the country's history, the fifth largest the world has ever recorded. It lasted for about six minutes and reached a magnitude of 9.0. Its epicenter was located in the Pacific Ocean, 130 kilometers east of the city of Senai. When the people of the northeast coast were just recovering from the earthquake,

Earthquake and tsunami

Tsunamis happen so frequently in Japan that the Japanese invented a word for the phenomenon: *tsu* means harbor and *nami* means wave.

According to the official count, the earthquake and the subsequent tsunami left nearly 16,000 dead and more than 2,500 people missing. The extensive damage included almost 130,000 collapsed buildings besides damage to a dam and to three nuclear power plants (including Fukushima Daiichi).

In the words of the Japanese Prime Minister, Naoto Kan: 'In the 65 years that have passed since the Second World War, this is the toughest and most difficult crisis for Japan.'

Scientists in protective suits inspect the Fukushima Daiichi nuclear power plant after the 2011 earthquake.

IAEA IMAGEBANK UNDER CC LICENCE

something even more horrific happened. A wall of water penetrated the mainland so fast and with such a ferocity that it swept away boats, cars and houses. In some places, the tsunami had reached a height of 40 meters. The breathtaking images of the water sweeping forward shocked the world.

But the worst was still to happen. The Fukushima Daiichi nuclear power plant was hit so hard by the wave that it overwhelmed the plant's seawall. Three reactors of the plant were in full operation when the earthquake struck. As the days passed, the scale of the disaster increased and there was talk of massive radiation leaks on the news.

When the disaster occurred, the *Rainbow Warrior* was actually in South Korea (north of Japan) finishing an oceans campaign tour in that region, centered on marine reserves and the protection of some marine species – mainly tuna. Given the scale of what had happened, the campaign was abruptly closed. The ship docked at the Korean port of Busan to disembark anyone linked to the campaign and to have a hasty crew change.

Two days after my arrival, we set sail for Singapore. The idea was to stop over there to remove all the valuable things from the ship, leaving only what was strictly necessary for the last mission to the Chagos Archipelago in the middle of the Indian Ocean. However, we had

The Fukushima Daiichi nuclear disaster

On 11 March, reactors 1, 2 and 3 (of six) immediately shut down at the detection of the earthquake. The emergency generators activated automatically to power the cooling and the control systems but these stopped when the tsunami flooded the installation. The emergency batteries started to fail within a few hours and the reactors began to heat up. As a consequence, multiple hydrogen-air chemical explosions took place in reactors 1, 2, 3 and 4, between 12 and 15 March. The spent fuel stored in the pools started to overheat and sea water began to be injected to cool them down.

Thousands of square kilometers were contaminated by radioactive fallout and will be for many decades to come. Unprecedented amounts of radioactive cesium ended up in the Pacific Ocean, significantly contaminating sediments and fisheries along the Japanese coastline. Many people were exposed to elevated levels of radiation and about 160,000 people were eventually evacuated. In the worst-case scenario presented to the Japanese government, an area with a radius of 250 kilometers would have had to be evacuated (including Tokyo), affecting around 40 per cent of the population or 50 million people.

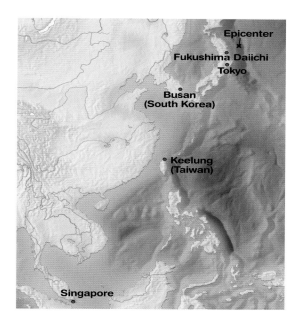

The voyage to Fukushima (Japan)

During the month we spent in Keelung, the news about the damage to the reactors of the Fukushima plant became more and more terrifying. The situation was made worse by the total lack of transparency on the part of the Japanese government and the TEPCO company, which owned the plant. Only two weeks after the earthquake, a Greenpeace team (the first of several to visit the site) took measurements of radiation in the district of Fukushima. They found out that the contaminated area extended far beyond the area evacuated by the government and that the levels of contamination were very high in some places where the population had stayed, thinking they were safe. After these results were made public, the Japanese government was forced to extend the evacuation zone to 30 kilometers (though, even so, many contaminated sites were beyond this new limit).

The next vital step was to conduct independent research into the impacts of radioactivity on the marine environment by taking water and algae samples from the sea close to the plant. Radioactive water was continuously pouring into the sea. Given that seafood (fish, crustaceans and

only been sailing across the channel between Taiwan and China for one day when we received orders to change course and head to the northeast of Taiwan, to a town called Keelung. The idea of bringing the ship to Fukushima was on the table.

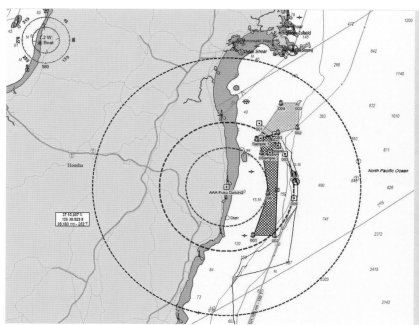

In the center of this nautical chart is the Fukushima Daiichi nuclear power plant. The smallest circle has a radius of 30 kilometers, corresponding to the Japanese government's exclusion zone; the second shows the 50-kilometer area that the *Rainbow Warrior* tried to stay beyond. The cross-hatched blue area is that covered by the *Avon* inflatable. The green line shows the ship's course and the green cross-hatching marks the area we sailed in on the last day. The places where the samples were taken are marked with a special symbol and numbered.

algae) is vital to the Japanese diet, it was essential that this information was made available to the population.

During the days we spent in Keelong, there was a buzz of expectancy in the air. Making the decision to go to Fukushima was extremely difficult – it not only meant a heavy responsibility fell on those working in logistics at Greenpeace International but it also of course offered potential risks to the health of all those on the ship. The first thing to establish was that the situation was stable enough for us to approach the area and work there. Then, no less importantly, we had to consider how we might protect the ship and ourselves in the event that new complications arose and the *Rainbow Warrior* was contaminated by fallout. After a lot of deliberation, we decided to go.

On 21 April we set sail and headed northeast. We received detailed reports on what was happening in the wrecked nuclear plant every day, with the possibility of having to turn around always present. The 25th anniversary of the Chernobyl nuclear disaster took place while we were in transit to Japan. Obviously, the lesson regarding the dangers of nuclear energy had not been learned in the intervening years.

We had two Radiation Safety Advisors on board:

Jacob Namminga (who had been part of the first Greenpeace team measuring radioactivity on the ground) and Ike Teuling (the nuclear campaigner in Greenpeace Netherlands). On the trip, we prepared ourselves psychologically and learned more about radioactivity as well as about how to protect ourselves by following a Radiation Safety Protocol. We all practised decontamination and learnt how to isolate our bodies totally from air contact (by using overalls, masks, gloves and boots). Two work teams were set to operate while we were at the site and the weather forecast was to be monitored at every moment.

After an eight-day transit, conveniently helped by tailwinds most of the time, we arrived in Tokyo Bay. Our intention was to dock there to announce our mission but this proved impossible because Greenpeace could not find an agent willing to represent us (big ships need such agents to carry out all the customs paperwork). In addition, the Japanese government had imposed two big geographical limitations on us: we could neither get into the country's 12-nautical-mile territorial waters nor could we enter the 30-kilometer 'exclusion zone' established around the damaged plant.

More than a month after the accident and just

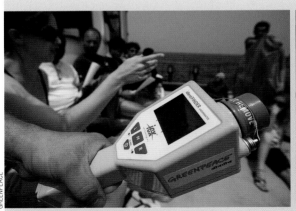
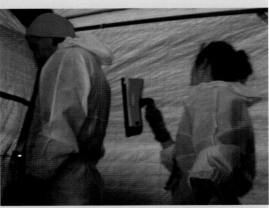

We installed special filters on the air intakes of the ventilation systems, and a radiation detection equipment on deck. We also had personal dosimeters and gammaspectrometers to measure radiation. We established two decontamination areas – one beside the wheelhouse and the other on the main deck. The hold was isolated and its access restricted. There, the water and seaweed samples were to be kept in special containers and a small laboratory was assembled.

JEREMY SUTTON-HIBBERT / GREENPEACE

MAITE MOMPÓ

a few days before our arrival, TEPCO announced the chilling results of a study on marine sediments near the plant: some radiation levels detected were between 100 and 1,000 times higher than those considered normal. There was now an urgent need to carry out an independent study on the situation outside the restricted area, where fishing had already resumed and the seaweed harvesting season was near.

We approached Fukushima Daiichi fully aware that the risks had not disappeared, as the situation in the reactors was far from being under control. A Japanese Coastguard vessel escorted us every part of the way.

On 2 May we were finally in front of the nuclear plant. For safety reasons, the *Rainbow Warrior* was going to keep at a distance of 50 kilometers. Our two teams were to collect samples of seawater and algae floating on the surface within the area between the ship and the limit of the 30-kilometer exclusion zone set by Japan, using our largest and fastest rigid inflatable boat, the *Avon*. We also met fishing boats that gave us fish for analysis. Thus, we stayed for three days – sailing in a semicircle or drifting – with the nuclear plant always visible through binoculars.

During the last night, we headed north, closer to the area that was hardest hit by the tsunami. At dawn, we saw that we were surrounded by remnants of the tragedy. The *Rainbow Warrior* had to weave in and out to avoid colliding with all the objects floating on the surface: wooden planks of all sizes (remains of fishing boats or houses, perhaps?), carpets, lamps, even refrigerators. The destruction wreaked on material things was obvious, while the human death toll had already reached about 15,000.

However, the real death toll from the Fukushima disaster will never be known. The lethal diseases (thyroid and other types of cancer, among others) and birth defects will take years, even decades, to appear and will also affect future generations. With just a few exceptions, including the so-called 'Chernobyl liquidators' (the squads required to clean up after the disaster in Ukraine), the thousands of deaths that nuclear energy has caused so far tend to be silent (or even, in some cases, silenced) victims. But nuclear accidents can mean that, without warning, people lose everything and forever: their homes and lands, their businesses and belongings, and their health.

None of the world's 436 nuclear reactors are immune to the possibility of disaster. However, the nuclear industry benefits from a liability system that shields it from bearing responsibility for the risks it takes and the damage it does – there are no independent regulators, no accountability, and profit is prioritized over people's protection. It is unknown when and where the next nuclear catastrophe will happen but we can be pretty certain that there will be one. Millions of people remain at risk.

It was on the very last day that one of our teams picked up a bunch of seaweed that we had spotted from the *Rainbow Warrior*, more than 50 kilometers from the nuclear plant. The seaweed turned out to have the highest concentration of radiation we had found so far – 50 times higher than the official limit. We headed south, taking with us multiple pieces of evidence that radiation was accumulating in sea life. After briefly stopping in Yokohama, we returned to Keelung to disembark and to prepare for Singapore and then Chagos.

I happened to be working on this chapter on the third anniversary of the disaster at Fukushima. Katsutaka Idogawa, former mayor of Futaba, a small town close to the damaged nuclear power plant, said: 'Our journey is like we are on a sunken ship without a paddle – or anything else.'

'Forgetting Fukushima makes it more likely that such a nuclear disaster could happen elsewhere,' said Tatsuko Okawara, one of the victims. Of the three most serious accidents involving nuclear energy, two were due to human error and system failures (Three Mile Island in the US in 1979 and Chernobyl in Ukraine in 1986) and one to a natural disaster (Fukushima 2011).

Dressed not to be killed. Greenpeace crew members, including radiation safety advisor Jacob Namminga, set off in the Avon inflatable to collect seawater and seaweed samples.

JEREMY SUTTON-HIBBERT / GREENPEACE

2014 – the third anniversary of Fukushima

The reactors are still not under control and huge amounts of sea water are still used to keep the nuclear fuel cool. There are ongoing leaks of contaminated water from the damaged reactors into the ground and ocean. The issue of how to reliably store the huge volumes of contaminated water and the massive amounts of radioactive material produced by decontamination efforts in Fukushima Prefecture is still unresolved.

Most of the 160,000 people evacuated are still displaced. Their lives are in limbo. The radiation levels are still very high in many zones that are supposedly 'decontaminated'.

The Japanese government and TEPCO are still covering up the levels of radiation to which people have been exposed and the health problems they face in consequence. TEPCO is driving the process of compensation, having been given the authority to decide the amount of money – if any – victims will receive.

As TEPCO was nationalized in June 2012, money the Japanese people paid in tax is being used to deal with a problem created by private companies. Not only have the suppliers who built and serviced the plant escaped responsibility, but some are even profiting from the disaster, being involved in the clean-up (including GE, Hitachi and Toshiba).

The last campaign
(South Korea, June 2011)

On 26 May 2011, we set sail from the port of Keelung in Taiwan and headed to Singapore for the second time on this trip. Our intention was to prepare the ship there for her last mission and most of the crew were very excited about it. We were going to take the ship to the Chagos Archipelago. The campaign had both a humanitarian and a pacifist side. First, we were to take a group of Chagossians from Mauritius to their former homes (now uninhabited atolls) so they could check on current conditions there – but also as a statement of support for their legitimate right of return. The second part of the mission was to take the ship to Diego Garcia as a protest against the military base there. Since this was the last mission of *Rainbow Warrior II*, the ship could make a major contribution to raising awareness of the Chagossian cause worldwide.

Many Greenpeace crew members support this cause. In March 2008, Jon Castle and Pete Bouquet, two former Greenpeace captains and both crew members on the first *Rainbow Warrior*, managed to sail into the lagoon of Diego Garcia and anchor their sailboat (the *Musichana*) there. Both were arrested, and eventually deported to the UK and released – but their boat is still in custody. Pete was helping in the preparations for the mission and was going to join the *Rainbow Warrior* in Mauritius – together with Rob Taylor, who was responsible for the overall logistics.

The day after leaving Taiwan, we had shocking news: the Chagos mission had been definitively cancelled. Once we knew the reason, we totally understood the decision. Unexpectedly, at the last moment, a group of 'experts on resettlement' had convinced the Chagossians that a condition *sine qua non* for their feasible resettlement was the development of sustainable commercial fishing. 'Commercial' and 'sustainable' are incompatible concepts here. Greenpeace had celebrated the creation of the marine reserve in 2010 but had made it clear that it should be without prejudice to the rights of the Chagossians. The organization had already offered to help them to develop small-scale, low-impact, sustainable fishing but in no case could support the development of commercial fishing in such a valuable ecosystem (it is home to one of the healthiest coral reefs in the world).

So what was the ship to do?

Diego Garcia and the Chagossians

The Chagos Archipelago consists of seven atolls comprising more than 60 tropical islands. Its legitimate inhabitants are descendants of former slaves brought in the 18th century by French settlers to work on the coconut and sugarcane plantations. Britain had colonial control from 1814 onward.

In 1965 the UK established the 'British Indian Ocean Territory' to ensure that the Chagos Islands were not included when Mauritius became independent. In 1966, Diego Garcia atoll was leased to the United States for 50 years (extendable to another 20 years) to house the US military base covering the Indian Ocean. In 1967, without warning, British soldiers bundled the Chagossians (around 2,000 people) onto boats and then left them to their fate, mainly in Mauritius.

In 2000, the British High Court ruled that the expulsion of the Chagossians was unlawful and conferred upon them the right to resettle but in 2004, royal orders banned anyone from setting foot on Chagos land. Then, two years later, the High Court overturned these orders. The case is currently at the European Court of Human Rights. In April 2010, the British government turned the Chagos Archipelago into the largest marine reserve in the world. According to Wikileaks CableGate documents, this was aimed at presenting the greatest possible impediment to the Chagossians' return home.[1]

The Diego Garcia US military base, which has nuclear capability, represents a threat to the local and global environment, as well as to world peace. Military facilities include, among others, a large naval ship and submarine support base, a military air base and a communications and space-tracking facility.

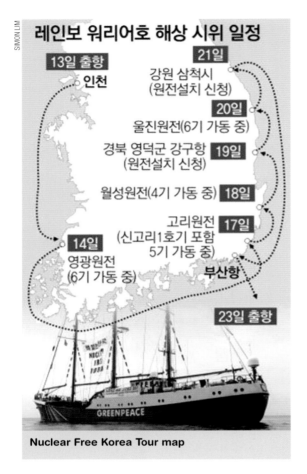

SIMON LIM

레인보 워리어호 해상 시위 일정

13일 출항
인천

21일
강원 삼척시
(원전설치 신청)

20일
울진원전(6기 가동 중)

19일
경북 영덕군 강구항
(원전설치 신청)

18일
월성원전(4기 가동 중)

17일
고리원전
(신고리1호기 포함
5기 가동 중)

14일
영광원전
(6기 가동 중)

부산항

23일 출항

GREENPEACE

Nuclear Free Korea Tour map

When Mario Damato, Executive Director of Greenpeace East Asia[2], was told that the *Rainbow Warrior* was available, he proposed bringing her to South Korea after consulting Rashid Kang, the Regional Development Manager based in Beijing. Rashid thought this was a fantastic idea, even if he had never organized a ship tour before and there was no local Greenpeace infrastructure to provide logistical support. Both of them had been in Korea for the first time just a month before to announce the upcoming opening of a Greenpeace office in Seoul. The ship could be used both to promote the new office and to raise awareness about the dangers of nuclear power, with the Fukushima disaster in Japan so close in time and space.

There was no-one who could speak Korean in Greenpeace yet, and there were no local volunteers, so Rashid called his friend Jun Kwon Song. They had met at an NGO meeting a few months before and Jun had already volunteered on open days when the ship had visited the country on the oceans campaign. Jun was to become the first employee of Greenpeace Korea, with the official title of 'Ship Tour Co-ordinator'.

The *Rainbow Warrior* arrived in the South Korean port of Incheon on 4 June, just nine days after leaving Taiwan. The norm is to start preparing a ship tour several months in advance. The last campaign of the ship as a 'Warrior' was to be a big exception, with everything organized in record time. While the ship was in transit, a shipping agent was found and contacts were made with various groups, including KFEM (the main Korean environmental organization, which had already worked with Greenpeace in the past, for instance in the whales campaign).

The *Rainbow Warrior* became the 'local office' and her crew turned into its spontaneous workers – along with other international staff who came to cover communication and Greenpeace campaigns. In order to get the tour off the ground by taking decisions at once, we had to be a very close-knit group. Actually, this way of working – the usual way in the 'old days' of the organization – greatly contributed to making this last campaign special in every way.

Just as the nuclear issue (for military use) had marked the second *Rainbow Warrior*'s beginning, so the nuclear issue (for civil use) was to take up the ship's last moments, first going to Fukushima and then launching a tour on the theme of a 'Nuclear Free Korea'. In Mario Damato's words: 'We want to visit places around nuclear power plants to show communities the deadly impacts of nuclear power.' A bit later, ship's captain Mike Fincken said: 'Only by phasing out nuclear-

South Korea currently has 23 nuclear reactors running, 1 under trials, 5 under construction and another 11 planned. Moreover, the country is dedicated to exporting its nuclear technology to other countries.

power plants and replacing them with clean renewable energy can there be real safety and energy security.'

A key person who definitely contributed to the success of the tour was Hye Jeong Kim, then in charge of the nuclear issue in KFEM, and who spent the tour on board ship. She was the one who co-ordinated the ship's different stops, spoke to the authorities and security forces, and mobilized local support and media coverage. Without the help of Hye Jeong and her organization, this fantastic tour would have been impossible.

6 June is a national holiday in Korea and it was the ship's second and last open day in Incheon. Sihnae Lee took the opportunity to come to the *Rainbow Warrior* and joined the last group visiting the ship, which I was showing around. At the end, Sihnae, who had worked in a local environmental NGO and had just quit her job, offered to help on the ship. The following day, she joined as assistant cook, though she was only to last one day in this position – it was obvious that she could be much more useful helping to prepare the future Korean Greenpeace office, researching other issues beyond that of nuclear energy.

Although the press conference to announce

Volunteers on board

As a general rule, there are always two volunteers as part of the crew – and so staying for three months – aboard Greenpeace ships. They come to help on deck but it is not a requirement to have any maritime knowledge. Then, when the ships are campaigning, volunteers from the offices involved also spend days on board helping both the ship and the campaign.

There are two ways to become a volunteer on board the ships. The normal procedure is to be already a volunteer in your own country and to be directly proposed by your office. The other way is to find yourself in the perfect time and place to join the ship, as was the case for Sihnae.

If you want to join Greenpeace ships as a professional seafarer, there is always a contact point on the Greenpeace International website.

the tour happened on 7 June, the ship was due to set sail on 13 June. All these days in-between were needed for preparation and to make the last crew changes. So it happened that my fellow crew

Crew members from the last voyage: from left to right, Amrit Bakshi, the author, Hye Jeong Kim, Sihnae Lee, Jun Kwon Song; and at the front, Grace Kawon Song.

MAITE MOMPÓ

SIMON LIM

The author with Runa Khan, Executive Director of the Bangladeshi organization Friendship, who visited the *Rainbow Warrior* to see whether the vessel could be converted into a hospital ship. Runa fell in love with the *Rainbow Warrior* as soon as she stepped on board. This was great news for the crew, who found it impossible to imagine a better future for the ship.

member Helena de Carlos had to disembark and I took her place, staying on for two more months so that I could finish the historical inventory – which meant a big change of plans for both of us!

A memorable thing happened on the evening before departure. We had already had dinner when the Italian national volleyball team appeared. They had heard that the *Rainbow Warrior* was there and, after playing a match against Korea, they decided to come to Incheon to meet the ship. The visit turned out to be very special. There was not the usual time limitation and the players were very excited about having the opportunity to be on board, to ask lots of questions and to listen to the stories of the legendary ship.

The tour agenda was very tight and there were times when the activities had to be planned on the hoof. In the course of the 10-day tour, the *Rainbow Warrior* visited four sites with operational plants and two others that were candidates for plants to be built. When we arrived at our first destination, the six 25-year-old reactors of the Yeongwang plant appeared semi-hidden by fog, which had a

rather scary effect. The second stop, Kori, was very important since Kori-1 is Korea's oldest nuclear reactor (it turned 33 in 2011) and its life had just been extended for another 10 years. The locals' opposition here was considerable.

As national media had pumped up the levels of expectancy, at every stop we met many people and local media representatives who wanted to come on board. The Korean security forces were a little nervous, not being sure exactly what to expect, and so two patrol boats escorted us throughout the tour (one at our bow and the other aft). A curious thing happened in one of the sites we visited. There were so many people wanting to come aboard that one of the patrol boats offered to transport them from the port to where the *Rainbow Warrior* was at anchor.

The fourth stop was in Yongduk, a beautiful fishing port where there are plans to build a new nuclear-power plant. There we found out that those who opposed its construction had been intimidated by the security forces and our visit enabled us to give our direct support to the victims of these threats. At every place, either locals came on board or we went ashore – as was the case in Samchuk, where we participated with a number of locals in a march demanding that the plans for a new plant be cancelled. It was fun to memorize

The *Avon*, full of local people and their banners, in front of Uljin nuclear power plant, which already has six nuclear reactors. As of 2011, there were two more reactors under construction and another two planned. At the bow is crew member Alexander Holmes.

SIMON LIM

JUN KWON SONG

None of us will ever forget the spectacular sunset we witnessed in the middle of the Korean tour, while at anchor in Pohang.

short phrases that we kept on chanting together with the locals at every place visited – for instance, *'chuisohara'* (meaning cancel), *'gaksunghara'* (wake up) and *'joong – danhara'* (stop).

Before the *Rainbow Warrior* left Korea, the ship gave a special gift to the new Greenpeace office that was to start operating in just a few weeks: one of the old ship's lifebuoys (which Jun had to keep at his home until the inauguration). The last tour of the

Rainbow Warrior had a very positive outcome. Prior to Fukushima, all South Korea's political parties and the majority of its population supported nuclear power, with just a few questioning it. Somehow, the ship acted as a catalyst for the Korean anti-nuclear movement and gave a definite boost to their national campaigning. In early 2013, Greenpeace office in Korea already had 18 workers, with Jun as its action co-ordinator.

Nuclear energy

• It is dirty. It generates waste that is also highly dangerous, with part of it (plutonium-240 and neptunium-237) taking thousands of years to semi-disintegrate. Nuclear waste therefore constitutes a terrible legacy for future generations.

• It is expensive. The construction, maintenance and decommissioning of a nuclear-power plant has a very high cost – with the expense of purchasing fuel and managing waste on top.

• It is dangerous. The risk of accident is always present in a nuclear-power plant and the direct victims of a nuclear accident lose everything forever.

• It is unnecessary. Clean and renewable technology is already available and could be scaled up enormously if there were sufficient commitment from governments.

SIMON LIM / GREENPEACE

The second *Rainbow Warrior* on its final campaign.

핵 없는 한국
NUCLEAR FREE KOREA

RAINBOW WARRIOR

GREENPEACE

Of Rainbows and Warriors

Farewell to a Warrior, welcome to a Rainbow

As we approached Singapore, the phrase 'This is the last time that...' started to be said or thought over and over again with the life of the second *Rainbow Warrior* truly coming to an end. Thus we had, for the last time, a swim stop in the middle of the ocean, jumping into the water from the bridge deck, and also a last Sunday barbecue on deck watching the sunset with a glass of wine in our hands. And of course there was the last time stopping the engine and sailing at the pace of the waves and the last time enjoying the sunrise while on night watch... All this was happening while crew members were involved in the colossal task of making inventories of everything on the ship.

Each department on board had to prepare conscientious lists which included everything from engineers' tools to books, bridge and radio room instruments, medicines and even things belonging to the galley. All cabinets, shelves and drawers were checked.

We had to know what we had so that we could decide what would be taken to the new *Rainbow Warrior* or to Greenpeace International and what would remain on board. I, for my part, finished my research on the origin of the 'historical objects' and then labelled all of them with their basic information.

We finally arrived in Singapore 18 days after having left South Korea. We had a month to accomplish the second phase, that is, to finish our

The author working on the Historical Inventory while in transit to Singapore.

MIKE FINCKEN

AMRIT BAKSHI

The last crew of *Rainbow Warrior II*
We were 16 men and women from 11 countries. One of the things we did – as a tribute to the ship and to commemorate this special trip – was to make a 2012 calendar with artistic photos of us on board. It was a limited edition of 20 copies, just to give to ourselves, to Elaine Hill (who helped us to edit it) and to the Ships Unit in Greenpeace International, and then to the *Esperanza* and *Arctic Sunrise*.

This photo was the back cover of the calendar. Its portrait of the last crew of the second *Rainbow Warrior* emulates the famous photo of the crew of the *Phyllis Cormack* in 1971, the first ever Greenpeace crew, as a tribute (see page 22). Between the one photo and the other 40 years had gone by.

inventories, arrange, dismantle, pack and put all the things, like pieces in a puzzle, inside large wooden boxes that would ultimately be taken to Europe. To finish on time was one concern; fitting everything into the boxes we had ordered was another. Penny Gardner, the bosun, played a key role in this race against the clock.

We had thought that it would be a bit sad to empty the bulkheads in the living quarters, especially the ship's mess. But when the time came, it was curious that despite the disappearance of all decoration, we could still feel the boat was our home, as if nothing had changed. Even when we had completely emptied her and the ship was carrying another name on both sides, the

particular energy of the *Rainbow Warrior* somehow changed not a whit – it continued to enwrap everything on board.

Dismantling the photos and pictures in the main alleyway, we got a surprise. Behind the silk-screen print of the *Rainbow Warrior* that was given to the ship in New York in 1989 (see Chapter 1), there was a chart with the names and ranks of the crew that took her to Moruroa in that mythical second voyage in 1995. It was the fire-alarm muster list and a crew member must have hidden it there before the French commandos stormed the ship.

At a personal level, it was funny to see how I started receiving messages from around the world, coming from members of the crew but also people

MIKE FINCKEN

Boxes on deck presaging the end.

When the moment came to paint over all the ship's identifying signs, Captain Mike Fincken suggested that all crew members played a part. I was assigned to erase the great Kwakiutl totem on the *Rainbow Warrior* stern. Having been so busy in the preceding weeks, I had not had time for sentimentality. However, as I started using the white paint roller, I was struck by a deep sadness. I felt how all these years aboard would now become just memories. With moist eyes and a bleeding heart, I watched the vivid totem colors disappearing bit by bit. I looked up and saw that Mike had stopped taking photos from the pier. I could not see his face but I knew that he was feeling the same – as he confirmed later on. After a few coats of paint and many tears, I stopped and looked at the freshly painted white square and smiled. The totem had refused to fully disappear. Its silhouette was still there as if it wanted to continue protecting that ship while she was sailing the seas, like a seal of good luck. Soon after, green paint was to cover the words Rainbow Warrior and Greenpeace completely, as well as the big rainbow and the dove with the olive branch.

from the office, reminding us not to forget about Dave... But how could we? The wooden dolphin had become the most symbolic and beloved object on board the second *Rainbow Warrior*.

On Wednesday 27 July, we celebrated our last dinner together. The two volunteer deckhands, Katie Furlong and Grace Kawon Song, cooked a superb menu for the whole crew. You could choose between *moules marinières* or *gazpacho andaluz*, mushroom and bacon pasta or pumpkin risotto, and we had cheesecake for dessert.

On the last Sunday, 14 August, something very special took place. Although it was not formally a wedding – the couple had already set a date for that – to all intents and purposes that was

AMRIT BAKSHI

Mike Fincken and Jemima Roberts in their Promise Ceremony on board the *Rainbow Warrior*.

what it was. Mike Fincken and volunteer Jemima Roberts promised each other love and respect in an intimate ceremony in front of the bridge. The chief mate Dan Binyon, master of ceremonies, opened the event with these words: 'Warriors of the Rainbow. We are gathered here today together, on one of the last nights, to witness two people's love for each other.'

The 'Promise Ceremony' was organized by the whole crew and included different elements from our varied cultures. The engaged couple were dressed according to Hindu tradition and Jem's hands and feet were henna tattooed. All the women had to make our hats for the occasion and beautiful invitation cards were also made. Raoul Kowsoleea moulded the brass rings (from a belaying pin) that the couple exchanged – a piece of the *Rainbow Warrior* was to be the symbol of their love. There was a wonderful buffet that the cook Wilindro 'Willy' Rodrigues prepared, including a large cake. The deck crew decorated the big awning with flowers and a white cloth that we had found in the hold, and Luis Vasquez, the chief engineer, chose the music. Everything was prepared to the last detail in record time!

It is highly probable that a few babies were conceived on board in the 22 years of the *Rainbow Warrior II*'s life. Gwynfi Fincken Roberts was the last of all of them and holds the title of 'Rongdhonu Warrior' on his own merit. The captain's son was also, even if just for a few days, the third generation of Roberts 'living' on board (being the grandson of Dave Roberts, a legendary logistician and action co-ordinator). It seemed that the ship did not want to say goodbye without spreading her last seed of love.

Two days after this ceremony, on 16 August, the Handover Ceremony took place. The Warrior that had fought for the environment for so long officially received a new name, *Rongdhonu* (which means rainbow in Bangla, the language the ship's bulkheads would hear from then on). Large letters announced on both her sides the name of the ship's new owner: the organization Friendship. The newborn Rainbow was undergoing a beautiful metamorphosis into a hospital ship for Bangladesh.

The Decommission Ceremony was attended by Lalita Ramdas, representing Greenpeace International, and Runa Khan, Executive Director of Friendship. The two women had met earlier the same year in Bangladesh, during a regional meeting on social issues. They just happened to sit next to each other at a dinner. Runa told Lalita about the organization founded by her and her husband, Yves Marre, and said that they were looking for a big boat. Then Lalita, former Chair

Mike Fincken gives the *Rainbow Warrior*'s lifebelt to Runa Khan to symbolize the handover of the ship. Lalita Ramdas of Greenpeace International is to his right.

ATHIT PERAWONGMETHA / GREENPEACE

ATHIT PERAWONGMETHA / GREENPEACE

Mike Fincken rings the ship's bell, a symbolic last act as captain of *Rainbow Warrior II*. The bunting in the background contain memories and good wishes from people all over the world.

of Greenpeace International Board, told her that they did not know yet what to do with the *Rainbow Warrior*. Runa replied that Yves had just written to Greenpeace International showing their interest in the flagship after the option of getting the *Sirius* (which then belonged to Greenpeace Netherlands) had proved to be unfeasible. Lalita committed herself to helping. 'I have to go to Amsterdam. I will talk to the new Executive Director and to the Board about your wonderful proposal. Let's see whether something happens...'

Another key person at the ceremony was Alain Connan, who in the early 1990s was captain of the *Rainbow Warrior* while being head of Greenpeace France at the same time. That country office finally revived when France cancelled the nuclear tests in Moruroa in 1992. Being a close contributor to Friendship from the outset, it was Alain who connected the two organizations. The *Rongdhonu Warrior* was going to be taken to Chittagong co-captained by him and Mike Fincken, and assisted by a minimal crew.

The formal farewell to the *Rainbow Warrior II* was very emotional but not sad at all. On the contrary, we were all overjoyed with the new destiny that awaited the ship. After the speeches, Mike, assisted by Lalita, presented to Runa an old lifebelt of the *Rainbow Warrior*, as a symbol of the handover of the ship. Then the ship's three most iconic objects

– still on board for the occasion, were taken out: the bell from the bridge, the beautiful steering wheel and the wooden dolphin on deck. The *Rainbow Warrior* crew also had a special gift for the *Rongdhonu*: a photograph of our beloved ship in full sail flying the Greenpeace flag.

In the handover contract, Friendship promised that, when the time comes for the *Rongdhonu* to be scrapped, this will be done to the highest environmental standards and, on the other hand, Greenpeace will provide financial assistance to make sure this happens. Greenpeace also has the right to approve any potential future owners so as to ensure that the commitment to these standards will be maintained.

I left the ship the following day. I had been on board on this last trip for five months. To say goodbye to the ship also meant seeing off a wonderful part of my life. On board I had spent many of my happiest moments and had been given the opportunity to meet so many amazing people from such different cultures. How lucky I was!

I remember walking though the whole ship on the previous night, finding memories evoked by every place, every corner. What a life for a ship!

Loved by thousands and having lived through so many adventures, she was to go from being at the service of the planet to relieving the suffering of the poorest who live on it. I was really happy that this great destiny awaited the ship and I held on tight to that feeling. It was my time to go. I went around the accommodation for the last time to say goodbye to my fellow crew members but in fact they were all waiting for me in front of the bridge. They had a gift and Mike gave it to me. As I opened the ship's flag, a gust of wind wrapped it around my body like a dress. My workmates had written short messages on the green cloth with the world map framed by a rainbow. The last hugs had the salty taste of tears. I left the *Rainbow Warrior* carrying both the ship and my colleagues in my heart.

'I stepped on the ship and I fell in love with it and I knew why... Because the past has a way of slipping through and talking to you. The fact that this is the *Rainbow Warrior* is that, in one jump, it is going to bring awareness of the people we care for to the whole world.'
Runa Khan, Executive Director of Friendship.

On 14 November 2012, the refitted *Rongdhonu* was officially launched in Chittagong, the new ship's home port. Along the coasts of the Bay of Bengal a rainbow was going to sail to provide the most disadvantaged people with primary and secondary healthcare (which so far includes specialized pediatric and women's healthcare, eye and dental care, laboratory and ward services), and to help increase awareness of health, nutrition and disease prevention. As was usually the case in the earlier stage of the ship's life, there would always be people on shore happy to see her masts appear. That old green-and-white metal shell will now bring hope to one of the most disaster-prone and climatically endangered areas in the world.

This time, the person representing Greenpeace was Pete Willcox, whose life has been so linked to all three *Rainbow Warrior* ships. In his own words: 'It was really good to see the boat. She feels very, very familiar.' Friendship has tried to preserve as much of the *Warrior* as possible. The masts have remained and the hull and decks are painted the same colors. There have, however, been major changes under the main deck, as the hold (with a new 'entry way' from the deck) and the adjacent area (where several cabins used to be) are now filled by two operating rooms. The outboard mechanic's workshop is now the pharmacy. The other parts have remained much the same except for the starboard side of the living quarters (the 'bosses' and the hospital cabins) that have been converted into consultation rooms.

MAITE MOMPÓ

**Rainbow Warrior II:
The 'Lala-ship'**
In recent years, *Rainbow Warrior II* was widely known as 'The Old Lady' but she also had another popular nickname, which came from the 1990s: 'The Lala ship boat.' The latter was 'invented' by two engineers (Tapio Pekkanen and Bart Terveil) joking about volunteers who hummed songs while doing their job (the 'lala people'). The ship herself was also full of 'lala' details, such as this old workboot that someone converted into a plant pot, which miraculously survived the conversion of the *Rongdhonu* and is still in the ship's mess.

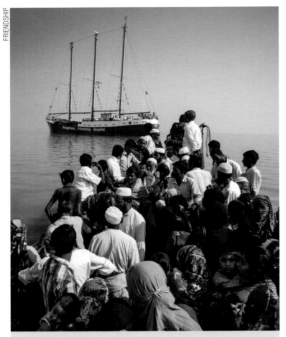

FRIENDSHIP

Friendship

Friendship is an organization with a holistic approach to development. It was founded in 1998 by Runa Khan and Yves Marre. It started with a project to deliver healthcare to the isolated communities of northern Bangladesh using an old barge, rebuilt as a small floating hospital and renamed *Lifebuoy*. Yves himself brought it from France. Subsequently, Friendship put up another small hospital-ship (renamed *Emirates*), and later on acquired the *Rainbow Warrior* to operate in the coastal belt.

The objectives of the organization have also been expanded, and in addition to providing healthcare, it is currently developing programmes in health, nutrition and population; education and good governance; disaster management and infrastructure development; sustainable economic development, and cultural preservation.

In the ship's first year of voyages alone, the *Rongdhonu* attended to 31,396 patients besides the 618 people who received treatment in the eight secondary camps supported by the ship.

On 19 January 2013, the *Rongdhonu* set sail to Kutubdia Island for her first humanitarian mission. May the fair winds go with you, Bangla rainbow!

The circle of life

'Maite, the chair of the [Greenpeace] International Board wants to visit the *Rainbow Warrior* – could you show it to her?' Lalita Ramdas – who had already been in that position for two years, came to meet the ship on 3 March 2009 in Amsterdam. The debate about whether or not to build a new ship (which required such a huge investment) had been going on for years but the issue had stalled. 'If anything convinced me that we deserved to give our activists and ourselves the new ship and give it fast, it was this visit,' said Lalita shortly after. The final decision to go ahead with building the third ship was taken at the following Board meeting. This is the first time that Greenpeace has built a ship from scratch, all the others being old ships either rebuilt or adapted to the organization's needs.

In October 2011, the final preparations before launching the *Rainbow Warrior III* were taking place in Bremen, very near Hamburg. I was put in charge of selecting the 'historical' objects that were to have a place on board. I loved that I was able to play a part in linking this ship to the spirit of the two that preceded her – to put in place these objects that served as cornerstones carrying the ship's legendary past.

We were just a few days from the ceremony and we were a little nervous because all the boxes from the *Rainbow Warrior II* had been held up at the German customs. The detailed lists we had made in Singapore did not correspond to the standards set out in international shipping and this had caused many problems. Imagine the customs officer's face while reading that a dolphin called Dave had been packed or that there was a box containing eight pairs of handcuffs. After much hassle, we got the seal lifted and everybody started to unpack and organize everything.

There were only two things that required a bit of a 'fight' to get them on board. The first one was the original *Rainbow Warrior*'s bell, which was wanted for the Greenpeace International office. In this case, Brian Fitzgerald, who had been with the organization since the early 1980s, helped me swing it. The second was the wooden dolphin. A few key people had said there was no space for it on deck and so I always got a 'no' for an answer. I left this little battle in the hands of those who were bound to ask after Dave as soon as they visited the ship. It only took a few weeks for the dolphin to regain its rightful place on board.

On 14 October 2011, the godmother of the brand new *Rainbow Warrior III*, Melina Laboucan Massimo – who belongs to the Cree Nation – smashed a bottle of champagne into the ship's hull. With this traditional act, the ship officially began her life as Greenpeace flagship. Thirty-three years had passed since the launching of the original *Warrior* in London. Two buses brought Greenpeace International and Greenpeace Netherlands people and many others came by other means. They did not want to miss the ceremony. Among those who gave speeches were Harald Fassner (the shipyard's owner), Ulrich von Eitzen (the Greenpeace project manager), Kumi Naidoo (International Executive Director), Grace O'Sullivan (crew member on the *Rainbow Warrior I*), Melina and captains Mike Fincken and Joel Stewart.

Rainbow Warrior III

The new *Rainbow Warrior* is the first ship designed and built specifically for Greenpeace – a purpose-built campaigning ship.

She is a sailing boat (a staysail schooner), almost 58 meters in length and little more than 11 meters in the beam, provided with a helicopter landing deck. Her two innovative 55-meter-high A-frame masts enable her to hoist five sails (covering 1,255 square meters of cloth).

The ship is one of the most environmentally friendly ships ever made, holding a green passport[3], with all engines following the highest environmental standards and carrying an electric drive system.

She was funded entirely by donations from Greenpeace supporters all over the world, with people from New Zealand/Aotearoa particularly involved.

Melina Laboucan-Massimo (the ship's godmother) at the launch of *Rainbow Warrior III*. Before the official ceremony, Melina performed a Cree First Nation prayer for the new ship.

Five days later, the *Rainbow Warrior III* set sail and started her first voyage. Like her predecessor, the new ship first toured Europe, visiting several countries and also entering the Mediterranean Sea, and then she crossed the Atlantic. New York was her first port of call in the Americas. After going into the Amazon, the ship headed for Rio de Janeiro to bear witness at a very important world meeting, the so-called 'Rio+20'. Exactly 20 years had passed since the *Rainbow Warrior II* had been in the same place for the previous summit, the first major global meeting on environment and sustainable development, known as 'The Earth Summit'. In 1992, the *Rainbow Warrior II* had had an exceptional visitor, the Dalai Lama, who had presented the ship with a '*kata*' (the Tibetan silk scarf). This was one of the items that disappeared when the French held the ship in custody for months in 1995 (see Chapter 2). However, the *Rainbow Warrior III* sailed from Bremen carrying a green *kata* that a crew member had taken to the Dalai Lama – the spiritual leader of Tibet and Nobel Peace Prize laureate – to be blessed just a few months before the launch.

The two Earth Summits

The Rio Summit in 1992 was unprecedented for a UN conference, in terms of both the scope of its concerns and its size. It was attended by 172 countries, there were about 2,400 NGO representatives, and some 17,000 people attended the parallel NGO Forum. It resulted in the Agenda 21 for Sustainable Development, the Rio Declaration on Environment and Development, the Statement of Forest Principles, the United Nations Framework Convention on Climate Change and the UN Convention on Biological Diversity Exchange. So the outcomes were very encouraging.

The Rio Summit in 2002 was, in contrast, a total fiasco. In the words of the Greenpeace Executive Director Kumi Naidoo, 'The Rio Earth Summit was over before it started... It has been a failure of epic proportions.' According to George Monbiot of *The Guardian*, 'The efforts of governments are concentrated not on defending the living Earth from destruction, but on defending the machine that is destroying it.'

MIKE FINCKEN

This child's painting was given to the *Rainbow Warrior* at the first Earth Summit in Rio de Janeiro in 1992. The water before the ship is dark and blood drips from national flags into it. But in the ship's wake the waters become clear blue and are full of flowers; the grey clouds turn white. The sails are unfurled in the opposite direction (from stern to bow), which is technically impossible.

When the *Rainbow Warrior III* arrived in New Zealand/Aotearoa for the first time in January 2013, the ship headed straight away to Matauri Bay, the place where the first ship of the saga rests. Tribute was paid not only to the original ship but also to the iwi Ngati Kura, the Maori people who take care of the Bay and are the 'guardians' of the waters where the wreck of the ship lies. As Bunny McDiarmid said, the place is like 'the *Warrior*'s spiritual home'. The first time the *Rainbow Warrior II* had visited the country, the ship also went to pay tribute to her predecessor. In both cases, the ships were blessed according to Maori tradition and so a sacred bond was created between the *Rainbow Warrior I* and the two ships that have come after her.

Over the years, the *Rainbow Warrior II* went to Matauri Bay several times. Her visit on 10 July 2005, the 20th anniversary of the bombing, was very special. Before leaving Whangaroa harbor, about two hours from the destination, the local 'kaumatua' (the most respected elders of the community) performed a brief Maori welcoming ceremony and came on board. It was the first moments of dawn and it was very foggy. Then the ship weighed anchor and headed out of the narrow harbor, which was about 40 meters wide and had very high hills on both sides. The sun rose just as the ship was going out to open sea. The fog cleared and a huge golden sun filled the air with golden and yellow hues. All on deck were left breathless. A beautiful memorial sculpture of a dove made of white marble was lowered onto the wreck of the *Rainbow Warrior*. There was a guest of honor on board: Marelle Pereira. The murdered photographer's daughter recalled, amongst other things, how when she and her brother were children, they had both helped to paint the rainbow on the original ship. The death of her father was of course not only a part of the Greenpeace story, but was also a family tragedy that scarred his children for life.

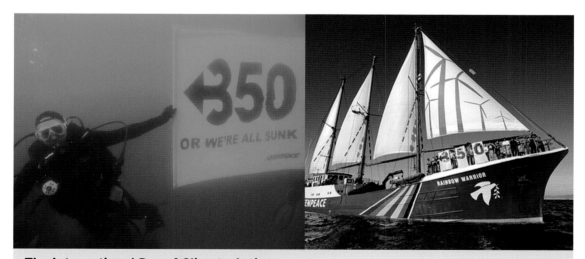

The International Day of Climate Action
24 October 2009 is an important date to remember. Thousands of citizens across the planet (in 181 countries) took part in over 5,200 synchronized demonstrations and other activities that depicted the number '350' (see Chapter 10) in a multitude of ways. The event was organized by the international environmental organization 350.org and supported by hundreds of organizations and groups, including Greenpeace. The aim was to pressure world leaders to address climate change. That was the most widespread day of political action in the planet's history.
It was also the only time that *Rainbow Warrior I*, from the sea bed in New Zealand/Aotearoa, and *Rainbow Warrior II*, from the Mediterranean, took part in a joint action despite being on opposite sides of the world.

REDSTAR IMAGES

William Willoya, with the *taonga* in his hands, Susi Newborn and Maori elders en route to the first *Rainbow Warrior*'s resting place.

It is funny how life puts back in front of you stories that you thought had ended. One day in 2008, the phone rang at Susi Newborn's home in New Zealand/Aotearoa. A male voice that seemed Maori asked her: 'Do you know William Willoya? I can give you his contact details.' Susi could not believe it! Such a long time ago she had given up hope of ever finding the co-author of 'Warriors of the Rainbow'! She had wanted him to give his blessing to the ship named after his book and to tell him that the dove and the rainbow symbols also came from it. Thirty years later, Susi finally could.

In February 2013, when *Rainbow Warrior III* was in a mission in the far south of New Zealand/Aotearoa, William Willoya came to the country. He had become the main character of a film called *The Eighth Colour*, based on an idea written by Susi, who is its executive producer. The Inupiaq, a prophecy collector and a sort of shaman, spent a few days with the iwi guardian of *Rainbow Warrior I*. In the middle of the month, a small boat went to the place in Matauri Bay where the ship lies. William and Susi were aboard, accompanied by a few members of the Maori community. They carried a '*taonga*' (Maori word for a treasured thing), that consisted of a woven basket containing a whale tooth, a small sculpture of a seal and an old 'Save the Whale' badge from the first *Rainbow Warrior* trip. Susi had given the diver instructions where to place it: in her cabin, the place where Bob Hunter had given to her a copy of the little yellow-covered book. While the diver was beneath the surface, Susi's mind went back to the first time the ship had set sail in London. Thirty-five years had gone by... She felt that a circle of her life was finally closed and the same was true for the ship's life. In this way, the continuity between the sunk *Warrior* and her successor in the battle for the planet was sealed.

A few days later, William went to Wellington and Joel Stewart received him on *Rainbow Warrior III*. The ship finally received the blessing of the person who somehow is her 'spiritual creator'. But the three *Rainbow Warriors* do not belong to William Willoya alone. They belong to anyone sharing the ideal for which they have been sailing the seas for nearly four decades – a world without war and violence, a world in which humans will finally stop destroying life in the name of progress. From the moment the first *Rainbow Warrior* set sail in London in 1978, the name has been an icon of hope for the world – and it remains so today.

'Such a special platform for so many environmental campaigns. A sea of people from all walks of life stood on her decks, all connected by a common goal. My time spent at sea on the *Rainbow Warrior* was the happiest of my life. I am sure all that have set foot on her have felt the same energy. A special, special heap of metal. Long live the *Rainbow Warrior*! I can't wait for number 3.' (Garbologist[4])

'...I also sailed for just a few days on the short trip from London to Edinburgh in November 2009. The crew were fantastic and made me so welcome... The *Rainbow Warrior II* will live with me forever and I wish her fair winds and following seas in her new life.' (Rachel)

'... While having a cup of coffee in her lounge we were lectured on the achievements accomplished by the crews of this ship. Some of the most remarkable stories were told, which impressed us all.' (Lover of animals)

'To hear the name *Rainbow Warrior* has always meant to me that there are still people who love nature and try to keep it alive for our children and the people who come after us.' (Jouko)

[Taken from bunting containing the memories and good wishes that people had sent for the farewell of *Rainbow Warrior II*, and currently displayed on the third ship.]

---

1 According to a senior officer of the UK Foreign and Commonwealth Office, 'the BIOT's former inhabitants would find it difficult, if not impossible, to pursue their claim for resettlement on the islands if the entire Chagos Archipelago were a marine reserve.' **2** The Greenpeace East Asia regional office includes China, Taiwan, Hong Kong and Korea. **3** A green passport is a document that covers the whole life of a ship, from construction, throughout its operating life to preparation for scrapping at the end of its useful life. The point of the passport is to enhance ship safety, protection of human health and the environment. **4** The 'garbologist' is the person in charge of recycling aboard Greenpeace ships. It is usually one of the volunteers.

NIGEL MARPLE / GREENPEACE

Historical curiosities

The 'stickers wall'

The bulkhead behind the stairs leading to the lower forecastle and the hold became a very special corner of the second *Rainbow Warrior*. Along the years, this wall was filled with stickers which in the end told the story of the ship. You could learn about the different campaigns in which she had worked, starting with the stickers about the nuclear tests in Moruroa. Other NGOs – such as WWF and Amnesty International – and other related issues also made their way onto this wall of history.

The 'stickers wall' became such an iconic part of the ship that Runa Khan – executive director of the Bangladeshi organization Friendship – personally made sure that the wall was preserved during the conversion of the *Rongdhonu* so that it remains intact as a witness of the hospital-ship's past.

The mystery of the wooden steering-wheel

For many years, it was believed that the beautiful wooden steering-wheel placed on the bridge deck

was the original *Rainbow Warrior*'s wheel. When I started my historical research, Pete Willcox, skipper on that ship and also in charge during the conversion of the second, assured me that this was actually the wheel of the *Grampian Fame* – the former fishing vessel that became *Rainbow Warrior II*. Last year, the issue was put back on the table when Pierre Gleizes (who crewed on the first *Warrior*) said he was convinced that the wheel was the original. Susi Newborn then corroborated Pete's opinion while many others said the opposite. In fact, both wheels are practically identical!

Which ship this wheel belongs to and where the other wheel is are the key questions. In the end, Susi, Pierre and myself started a research project trying to solve this mystery. It looks like the wheel was sent from Auckland to Europe, probably to Hamburg. Any help in solving this mystery will be greatly appreciated!

Nowadays, this wheel is at the entrance of the Greenpeace International office in Amsterdam.

Epilogue

WE ARE ALL living in a very important moment for humanity. Technological and industrial development have brought very good things regards quality in daily life for part of us but the cost of this "development" is too high regards nature and many other human beings.

As this book has shown, we do not live in a very healthy planet and it is an urgent matter to stop turning away from all the environmental problems we have created. We are our own biggest enemy because we tend to believe that we cannot do anything to reverse the situation. This is not true. We are very important as individuals. As the Dalai Lama says: 'If you think you are too small to make a difference, try sleeping with a mosquito.'

Before I starting sailing with Greenpeace International ships, I had a more pessimistic view about the future but I have changed my mind. In every corner of the planet you will find nowadays people who have stood up for Mother Earth, people from all races, beliefs and customs, in the cities and in the jungles – you will find these 'warriors of the planet' everywhere.

I have talked in this book about terrible things such as nuclear disasters, toxics and pollution, the over-exploitation of resources, climate change, the disappearance of forests and species being driven to extinction. Wherever you are, please believe that this can be changed and that your own acts can contribute to safeguarding the future of the next generations and of humanity as a whole. At the end of the day, the environment is the air we breathe, the water we drink and the food we eat. What happens to the environment happens to us. And if we do not change the world we live in, who else is going to do it?

Glossary of nautical terms

Accommodation: Living quarters of the ship.

Adrift: Without power, oar or sail to control the ship.

Aground (to run aground): The position of a ship when the hull is lodged on the sea bottom or on the shore and cannot maneuver.

Alleyway: Corridor.

Beam: The width of a ship at its widest part.

Belaying pin: A solid metal or wooden device used on traditionally rigged sailing vessels to secure lines of running rigging. Largely replaced on most modern vessels by cleats, they are still used, particularly on square-rigged ships.

Bilge: The deepest part inboard of a ship's hull, where any leakage collects.

Bollard: A heavy post, shaped wider at the top, mounted along a wharf, to which a ship's mooring lines are secured.

Boom: A long spar extending from a mast to hold or extend the foot of a sail.

Bosun's chair: A simple wooden bench seat in a rope sling that can be attached to rigging (usually a halyard or gantline) and hauled up or down from on deck.

Bow: The forward end or part of a vessel

Breakwater: A structure like a wall built in the sea to provide protection from heavy ocean waves for a harbor or beach.

Bridge: The wheelhouse and navigation station where the ship is operated, and where the ship's business is conducted

Bulkhead: Any vertical partition or wall in a ship

Bunk: A bed on board ship. A berth. The place where a sailor sleeps.

Cabin: A room used as living quarters in a ship.

Chart (Nautical Chart): a map designed to aid navigation by sea or air.

Crow's-nest: a lookout platform high up on a ship's mast.

Deck: Any of various platforms built into a vessel.

Drift: To float without direction on the surface of the water. To move with the wind and current, rather than with power, oar or sail.

Forecastle (Fo'c's'le): The part of a vessel at the bow where the crew may be quartered and stores, machines, etc, may be stowed.

Forepeak: The compartment under the main deck at the extreme bow, used for stowage of the anchor rode, ballast and other equipment.

Freighter: Cargo ship.

Galley: The compartment where food is prepared and cooked (there is no kitchen on board a ship).

Gangway: A portable bridge for boarding and leaving a vessel at dockside.

Gunwale: The top of the side of a boat.

Halyard (halliard): Rope for raising a ship's sail.

Hatch (hatchway): An opening in the deck of a vessel to provide access below.

Heel: To lean or tip under the influence of the wind on sails. Heeling is a normal characteristic of any sailing vessel, and is controlled by the ballast and underwater design of the boat.

Hoist: To raise or lift up, especially by mechanical means.

Hold: The space in a ship or aircraft for storing cargo.

Hull: The body of a ship between the deck and the keel.

Inflatable: A small boat made substantially of fabric that can be inflated with air pressure. They can also have a rigid hull and they are also called RIB and dinghies.

Jib: A triangular headsail mounted to the headstay.

Keel: One of the main longitudinal structural members of a vessel to which the frames are fastened and that may extend into the water to provide lateral stability.

Knot: A speed over the water of one nautical mile per hour.

Mess: The dining compartment on naval and big ships.

Mile (nautical mile): 1,852 meters.

Mizzen: The smaller aftermost mast (and sail) on a sailing vessel having more than one mast.

Novi: Short for 'novurania', the smallest inflatable boat on board most of Greenpeace ships because they are very easy to handle.

Pilot: A commercial ship operator who is especially qualified to operate ships in local coastal waters and into harbors. The pilot boards a visiting vessel and, for a fee, guides it safely into port or from port to open sea. Many ports require ships to hire the services of a pilot.

Pitch: The rotation of a vessel around a lateral axis as it heads into heavy seas.

Porthole: A small aperture in the side of a vessel to admit light and air, usually fitted with a watertight glass or metal cover, or both.

Port (port side): Left side of a ship.

RIB: A rigid inflatable boat.

Rigging: All of the wires, blocks, ropes, spars and other hardware installed above deck with which the sails are hoisted and trimmed.

Roll: The rotation of a vessel around the fore and aft axis.

Rounds: While sailing, there are two people in the wheelhouse from 8 pm to 8 am: a mate (including the captain) and a deckhand who are on four-hour watch. Every hour, the deckhand does a round around the ship to check everything is all right.

Schooner: A sailing vessel with at least two masts, with all lower sails rigged fore and aft.

Sponson: A sponson is any structure attached to a boat hull that aids in fendering, stability, or flotation.

Springline: A long mooring line run from the bow aft to the dock, or from the stern forward to the dock.

Strike: Smartly haul down sails or lower flags.

Starboard (starboard side): Right side of a ship.

Stay: A stout cable or rope used to support a mast fore and aft.

Stern: The rear or after part of a vessel, opposite the bow or stern.

Wheelhouse: See Bridge.

Winch: A mechanism employing sets of gears to turn a drum and provide a substantial mechanical advantage for taking the strain on lines. A few turns of the line are taken on the drum to achieve a purchase, then the winch is turned to bring the line taut.

Windlass: A machine for raising weights by winding a rope or chain upon a barrel or drum driven by a crank, motor, etc.

Chronological order of stories

1940s
Bikini, the lost paradise (1946): Chapter 2

1950s
Rongelap, the dawn of twilight (1954): Chapter 2

1970s
A book called 'Warriors of the Rainbow': Chapter 1

1980s
The great escape (*Rainbow Warrior I*, Spain, 1980): Chapter 7
Rise to glory (*Sirius*, 1982): Chapter 7
The birth of a myth (1985 on): Chapter 1
The return of a Warrior (1985 on): Chapter 1
Operation Exodus (*Rainbow Warrior I*, Rongelap, 1985): Chapter 2

1990s
Running away from Cuba (Caribbean sea, 1992): Chapter 6
The last trip to Moruroa (1995): Chapter 2
The story of Chile Willy (Chile, 1996): Chapter 6
To the beat of drums (Papua New Guinea, 1997): Chapter 5
A very tough campaign (Norway, summer 1999): Chapter 3

1999-2000
Toxic Free Asia Tour. (India, Thailand, Philippines, Hong Kong and Japan): Chapter 4

2000-2005
Crizel's story (Philippines, 2000): Chapter 4
The Djibouti boys (Middle East, 2001): Chapter 6
Bloodwood (Spain, 2002): Chapter 5
The oil-tanker disaster (Spain, 2002): Chapter 7
Action against the Iraq War (Spain 2003): Chapter 8
A question of *Honour* (Spain, 2003): Chapter 5
What gets thrown overboard (Tasman Sea, June 2004 - June 2005): Chapter 9
An assault (*Esperanza*, Spain 2004): Chapter 7
A hole in the hull (South Pacific, 2005): Chapter 6
The Great Tsunami (Indonesia, 2005): Chapter 6
Between the harpoon and the whale (*Arctic Sunrise*, Antarctica, 2005): Chapter 3

2006-2009
The sleeping kids (Italy, 2006): Chapter 9
Beirut under bombs (Mediterranean, 2006): Chapter 6
Mayday in the middle of the night (Mediterranean, 2006): Chapter 6
The expulsion from Marseille (France 2006): Chapter 9
Lebanon and Israel (Lebanon, 2006): Chapter 8
Israel and Lebanon (Israel, 2006): Chapter 8
The divided island (Cyprus, 2006): Chapter 8
The strength of a wind (Croatia, 2006): Chapter 8
A white lily (Croatia 2006): Chapter 9
Maite alarm (Cyprus, 2006): Chapter 6
Riots in Papua (Papua, 2006): Chapter 5
In the pirates' sights (Middle East, 2007): Chapter 9
Encounters on the high seas (north of Libya, 2007): Chapter 9
On the road to Bali (Indonesia, 2007): Chapter 5
In the Land of the Long White Cloud (New Zealand/Aotearoa, March 2008): Chapter 10
Sails to be free (Netherlands, November 2008): Chapter 10
Ten years on (Norway, 2009): Chapter 3
The Copenhagen experience (Norway and Denmark, December 2009): Chapter 10

2010s
The winds that blow these days (*Rainbow Warrior* II and *Arctic Sunrise*, Spain): Chapter 7
Red hot (south of Malta, 2010): Chapter 9
The fingers of humanity (Israel, July 2010): Chapter 10
Navigating pirate waters (in transit, 2010): Chapter 9
Voyage to Fukushima (Japan, 2011): Chapter 11
The last campaign (Korea, 2011): Chapter 11
Farewell to a Warrior, Welcome to a Rainbow (Singapore, 2011): Chapter 11
The story of the Arctic 30 (*Arctic Sunrise*, Winter 2013-14): Chapter 10

Other stories
Peace boats versus nuclear bombs: Chapter 2
Humans and whales: Chapter 3
Whales and the *Rainbow Warrior*: Chapter 3
Introducing Crizel: Chapter 4
Hope: Chapter 4
Humanity's greatest challenge: Chapter 10
The circle of life (*Rainbow Warrior I, II and III*, and *Rongdhonu*): Chapter 11

Index

Where a country is indexed, citizens are implied. **Bold** page numbers refer to main subjects of feature boxes and highlighted text. *Italic* page numbers refer to illustration captions. The following abbreviations are used for ship names: AS (*Arctic Sunrise*); E (*Esperanza*); PC (*Phyllis Cormack*); RW (*Rainbow Warrior*).

Abdul, Lama 159
Abdullah 119
Action Against Hunger 117, *119*
actions specialists *see* Hewetson, Frank *and* Roberts, Dave
Adams, Meredith 109
Adidas 83
Adriatic Sea 155
Aegean Sea (tanker) 132
L'Affaire Greenpeace 18, **19**, 42
African Queen (inflatable) 65
Alamar, Josevi 87, 88, *88*, 89
Alaska 9, 119, 206
Amchitka 20, 21, 22, 23, *23* (map), 40, 142
albatrosses *49*, *165*
Algeria 33
Amalthea 197
Amazon 85, *87*, 102, *201*, 228
Ambrós, Teresa 144, 146
Amchitka 20, 21, 22, 23, *23* (map), 40, 142
Amnesty International 89, 198
anchor maneuvers 100-1, 144, 182
ancient forests 85-6, *86* (map), *87*, 94
  see also forests campaigns
Andaman Sea 76
animals on board **184**
Anjain, John 36, 37, 38, 39
Antarctic 65-7
anti-driftnet campaign (*RWII*; Mediterranean; 2006) 168, *168*
anti-Greenpeace protests 62-4, 134-7, 138, 170-1

anti-military campaigns (*RWII*; Diego Garcia; 2011) 215
see also peace campaigns
anti-nuclear campaigns
  (*PC*; Amchitka; 1971) *21*, 21-3, 40, 49, 142
  (*RWII*; Muroroa; 1992) 42-4
  (*RWII*; Muroroa; 1995) 44-8
  (*RWII*; Middle East; 2007) 159-60
  (*RWII*; South Korea; 2011) *216*, (map), 216-19, *220*
anti-whaling campaigns 54
  (*PC*; 1975) *21*, 57, 64
  (*PC*; 1976) 23, *23*
  (*RWI*; Iceland; 1978) 56, *56*
  (*RWI*; Spain; 1978) 125-6
  (*RWI*; Spain; 1980) 126-8, 138
  (*RWII*; Norway; 1999) 56, 58-61
  (*RWII*; South Korea; 2005) 56-7
Anuva 137
Aotearoa *see* New Zealand/Aotearoa
Arctic **199**, *199* (map); *200*
'Arctic 30' 179, 198-207
Arctic Sunrise 13, 57, 65, *67*, 139, 143, 188, 192, *221*
  2010 bluefin tuna campaign (Mediterranean) *175*, 175-7
  2011 marine seabed campaign (Spain) 138-9
  2013 Save the Arctic campaign (Russia) 198-207
Ardhianto 99, *100*
Argentina 107, 122, 198
Argus 185, 186
arrests 41, 42, 46, *47*, 48, 60, *61*, 90, 126, 128, 161, *183*, 186, *187*, 188, 189, 190, 194, 215
Asia, southeast 71 (map), 85
  see also under countries
Ask that Mountain 49
Aspinall, Mariana 27, 28
Atlantic Islands National Park **133**, 139
Atlantic Ocean 111, 125, 129, 137
Atlantic Trench 129, **130**
Atomic Energy Commission 36
attacks, pirate 158 (map), **162**
Augusta 194

Augustine, Nerissa 80
Australia 33, 40, 45, 100, 135, 136
Australian Nuclear Science and Technology Organisation 33
Austria 172
Avaaz 189
Avon (inflatable) 42, *81*, 89, 90, *111*, 112, 163, *163*, 171, 174, 194, *211*, *214*, *218*
Aznar, José María 143, 145, 146
Azores 144

bail, bonds and fines 61, 92, 93, 126, 194, 195, 206
Baker, Al 48
Bakshi, Amrit *217*
Bali 99-102
Ball, Phil 199, 200, *200*, 201, 202, *205*, 206, *206*
Bangladesh 13, 16, 73, *218*, 223
Barents Sea *199* (map), 200
Basel Convention 73-4, 84
Batista, Fulgencio 106
Bay of Bengal 225
Bay of Biscay 29, 125
bearing witness 21, 142, 164, 170
Beaton, Sheena 182-3
Belgium 29, 143
Belize 164
Bell, Denise 24
bell, ship's 16, 224, *224*, 226
Belluga II 185, 186, 187, 188
Benetton 84
Bhopal chemical disaster 71, 72-3
Biedermann, Andy 17
Bifrost 45
Binyon, Dan 223
biodiversity 85, 94, **98**, **138**
biopiracy 110
birds on board 121-3, *123*
Birmingham, Dave 22
Bjuhr, Amanda 60, 112, 114
Blair, Tony 145
bluefin tuna campaigns
  (*AS*; Mediterranean; 2010) *175*, 175-7
  (*RWII*; Mediterranean; 2006) 170-3

(*RWII*; Mediterranean; 2007) 173
(*RWII*; Mediterranean; 2010) *175*,
  175-7, *177*, *178*
boarding by security forces 44,
  45-8, 60, 92, *92*, 144, 145, 161,
  171, 202, *202*
Bohlen, Jim 21, *22*
Bohlen, Marie 15, 21
bombing of *Rainbow Warrior*
  (Auckland; 1985) 9, 12, 16-19, 40,
  40, 42, 43, 49
books
  A Bonfire in my Mouth 30
  Ask that Mountain 49
  The Greenpeace Chronicle 30, 68
  Warriors of the Rainbow 9, 10, 15,
    20, 20-5, 230
Bora wind 155
bosuns *see* Gardner, Penny; Lloyd,
  Phil; Nakazono, Flavio; Patrick,
  Edward *and* Watson, Sarah
bottom trawling 135, *135*, 137, *137*,
  138, 157, 163-6
Bouquet, Pete 215
Bové, José 45
Bravo, Carlos 145, 146
Brazil 102, 181, 228
Breathed, Berkeley ("Berke") *124*
Britain 9, 24, 33, 43, 129, 143, *143*,
  181, 215, 231
Brookhaven National Laboratory
  36, 49
Brouwer, John *28*
Brown, Vinson 15, 20
buffer zones
  environmental benefits **154**
Buller, David 18
bunting *224*, 231
Burma 141
Bush, George 145
Butch *see* Turk, Lawrence
bycatch discards **59**, **136**, 164, *165*

C&A 84
Cairn Energy 199
Caister, Dave 112
Caixa Nova *139*
calendars *221*
camera operators *see* Ball, Phil;
  Ståhl, Jari *and* Nugent, Stephen
Cameroon 91
Campaign for Nuclear
  Disarmament (CND) *142*
campaign outcomes
  bluefin tuna fishing **178**

deep-sea trawling **137**, **166**
driftnets **168**
forest protection **102**
nuclear waste dumping 130
nuclear weapons testing **49**
timber trade 92, **93**
toxic contamination **84**
whaling **54**, 57, **64**, **68**
Canada 21, 22, 23, *23* (map), 64,
  102, 109, 110, 199
Cape Horn (US warship) 144
captains *see* Bouquet, Pete; Castle,
  Jon; Connan, Alain; Dijk, Frans
  van; Fincken, Mike; Linke, Uwe;
  Nicholls, Derek; Rizzotti, Daniel;
  Sandison, Peter; Stewart, Joel *and*
  Willcox, Pete
carbon dioxide, atmospheric *180*,
  180, **181**
carbon sinks *102*, **182**, 185
Carev, Ivana 172
Caribbean Sea 105-7
Carla Martínez, Ana 176, *176*, *193*,
  194
Carlos, Helena de 218
cartoons 122, **124**
Cash, Johnny 166
castaways 105-7, 111, 112, **174**
Castle, Jon 46, 47, 48, 111, 127, *127*,
  128, 136, 215
Castro, Fidel 106, 107
celebrations 95-6, 114, 115
ceremonies 9, 21, 22-3, 25, 99, 187,
  222, 222-3, *227*, 230, *230*
cetaceans
  human relationship with 51-4
  see also dolphins; porpoises *and*
    whales
CETPs *see* Common Effluent
  Treatment Plants
Chagos Archipelago 210, 213, **215**
chemical industry 70-3
Chernobyl 49, 130, 212, 213
children *16*, *39*, *59*, 81, 95
  from Damanhur 166-70
  see also Crizel
Chile 45, 68, 121, *121* (map), 122
Chile Willy 121-3
Chiloé Island 123
China 33, 43, 73, 103
China Sea 123
Chirac, Jacques 44, 48
Chomsky, Noam 110, 124, 156
Chrigi *see* Schmutz, Christian
Christian Aid 198

Christiansen, Mads 192
Christiansen, Nora 190, *190*, 191,
  192, *192*
Cies Islands 133
CITES *see* Convention on
  International Trade in Endangered
  Species
Clark Air Base, Philippines 79, **80**,
  82
climate change 179-80, 199, 207
climate change campaigns
  (*RWII*; 2008) 181
  (*RWII*; Copenhagen; 2009) 181,
    187-94
  (*RWII*; Indonesia; 2007)
  (*RWII*; Israel; 2010) 194-8
  (*RWII*; Mediterranean; 2009) *229*
  (*RWII*; Netherlands; 2008) 185-7
  (*RWII*; New Zealand; 2008) 182-5
Climate Change Conferences
  (COP13; Bali; 2007) 100, 101,
    102, 103, *103*, 181
  (COP15; Copenhagen; 2009) 102,
    181, 187-94
  (COP21; Paris; 2015) 102, 181
climbers *see* Ball, Phil; Beaton,
  Sheena; Dziemianczuk, Tomasz;
  Hammer, Raoni; Saarela, Sini;
  Simpson, Michael; Speziale,
  Camila *and* Weber, Marco
cluster bombs 150, *150*
CND *see* Campaign for Nuclear
  Disarmament
coal 181, 182, 183, *183*, **186**, 194,
  195
collisions 29, 58
Common Effluent Treatment Plants
  (CETPs) 75
Conc, Marin 162
Congo 85, *201*
Connan, Alain 224
Constantine, Texas 66
Convention on International Trade
  in Endangered Species (CITES) 54
cooking 60, 114, 222, 223
cooks *see* Bjuhr, Amanda; Mills,
  Margaret; Momeñe, Belén *and*
  Rodrigues, Wilindro
cooks, assistant *see* Fausto, Simona
  and Lee, Sihnae
Copenhagen Accord **192**
coral bleaching 182
coral reefs 215
corals **165**
  black 164

cold-water 61, 62, *62*
  Lophelia pertusa 62
  Paragorgia 165, 166
Cormack, John 22
Corsica 111
Cousteau, Jacques 42
Cree people 23, 227, *227*
crews
  Arctic Sunrise 67, 207
  Esperanza 67
  Phyllis Cormack 22, 221
  Rainbow Warrior 127, 127
  Rainbow Warrior II 28, *42*, *189*,
    221
  see also under names of crew
    members
crimes against humanity 83
Critical Mass of Valencia **93**, 103
Crizel 69, *70*, 78-82
Croatia 154-6, 172-3
Cuba 106-7
cultural values, respect for 56, 58
Cummings, Bob 22
cyclists 93, 103
Cyprus 114, *120*, 121, 146, 153-4,
  154 (map), 159, 162

Dalai Lama 228
Dallas 143
Damanhur community 166, **167**,
  168, 170
Damato, Mario 216
Daniela 173
Darnell, Bill 21, *22*
Dave the Dolphin **52**, 222, 224,
  226-7
deaths see Crizel and Pereira,
  Fernando
deckhands see Adams, Meredith;
  Aspinall, Mariana; Carla
  Martínez, Ana; Furlong, Katie;
  Kawon Song, Grace; Korman,
  Pablo; Marshall, Timo;
  McDiarmid, Bunny; O'Sullivan,
  Grace; Patrick, Edward; Petersen,
  Naomi; Pupuka, Phillip; Rarama,
  Kingsford; Riza, Bahadir; Simkiss,
  Lesley; Türkmen, Tuna and Ware,
  Sue
Decommission Ceremony 223, 224
deforestation see forest destruction
Denmark 68, 181, 187-94, 199
Detox campaign 83
Diego Garcia **215**
Dijk, Frans van 173

disputes, crew 22, 173
divers *148*, 149
Djibouti 107, *110* (map), 158
Dolev, Sharon 195, 196, 197
Dolgov, Roman 206
dolphins 52, 54, 68
  see also Dave the Dolphin
Don't Make a Wave Committee 21
dove symbol 24, 25, *152*, 229
Dow Chemical Company *71*
driftnets 57, 157, **168**
drinking water contamination 36,
  73, 75, 79, **80**, **82**
Dufay, Jo 109
Dunn, Phil 111, 112, 121
Dziemianczuk, Tomasz 199, 200

Earth Summit (1992) 106, 181,
  228
Earth Summit (2002) **228**
earthquakes **209**
ecology symbol 21
Edge, Brad 100, 102
Edwards, Davey 17
Egypt 110, *110* (map), 159, 161, 162
  The Eighth Colour 230
Einstein, Albert 31
Eitzen, Ulrich von 227
electricians see Caister, Dave;
  Haussmann, David; Pinto,
  Manuel and Steffens, Martin
electronics industry 83
emergencies
  hull damage 112-14
  medical emergencies 58-9, 161
  person locked in freezer 114-15
  propeller blockage 163
  rescues 111-12
  see also humanitarian missions
Emirates 226
Energy Revolution 159
engineers see Edwards, Davey;
  Pekkanen, Tapio; Sorensen,
  Hanne; Terveil, Bart; Vasquez,
  Luis and Wigt, Bob
entraining 10
environmental effects of war *146*,
  147-53
environmental standards **28**, **224**
E.ON 186, *186*
Eritrea **108**, 158
escape from detention 127-8
Esperanza 13, *67*, 111, *134*, 139, *221*
  2004 marine seabed campaign
    134-5, 166

Ethiopia **108**, 158
European Union 87, 93, 103, 109,
  134, 137, 168
eutrophication 138, 139
evacuation of Rongalap (*RWI*;
  1985) 11, 37
extinctions **85**
Exxon 199
Exxon Valdez oil-tanker disaster
  207

FAB Agreement **189**
Fabius, Laurent 19
FAO see Food and Agriculture
  Organization
Farias, Paula 73
Faroe Islands 68
Fassner, Harald 227
Fausto, Simona 166, 167, 168, 169
feathers, albatross 49
Fernández-Obanza, Mito 132
films
  The Eighth Colour 230
  Free Willy 122
Fincken, Mike 61, 100, 102, 111,
  155, 161, 171, 185, 186, 187, *187*,
  188, 192, 216, 222, *222*, 223, *223*,
  224, *224*, 225, 227
Fincken Roberts, Gwynfi 223
Fineberg, Richard 22
Finland 102
fisheries campaigns
  (*RWII*; Chile; 1996) 121
  (*RWII*; Pacific; 2004) 38
  see also anti-driftnet campaign;
    bluefin tuna campaigns and
    marine seabed campaigns
fishing industry
  bluefin tuna fishing 170-8
  bottom trawling 135, *135*, 137,
    137, 138, 157, 163-6
  bycatch discards **59**, **136**, 164, *165*
  coral reef damage **62**
  driftnets 57, 157, **168**
  fishing piracy 157, 163-6, **172**
  salmon farming **138**, 139
Fitzgerald, Brian 226
flags 23, *35*, 64, **132**, 136, 139, 224,
  225
flexibility 105
Fontanillas, Sandra 174
Food and Agriculture Organization
  (FAO) 85, 86, 180, 207
Forest Defenders Camps 94, *102*
forest destruction 86, 179, 184, *185*

Forest Rescue Stations 94, 98
Forest Stewardship Council (FSC) 103
forests campaigns
  (*RWII*; Mediterranean; 2002, 2003) 87, *89*, 91
  (*RWII*; Papua; 2006) 97-9
  (*RWII*; Spain; 2002, 2003) 87-93
Fort McHenry 81
fossil fuel burning 179, **180**, 197
France 29, 111, 112, 125, 182, 215
  bluefin tuna fishing 170-1, *171*
  bombing of *Rainbow Warrior* 9, 16-19, 42
  nuclear weapons testing 16, 29, 31-3, 40-8
Free Willy 122
freezer, person locked in 114-15
French Guiana 106
French Polynesia *41* (map); **44**
  Fangataufa 32, 33, 40
  Hao 19, 48
  Moruroa 16, 18, 20, 32, 33, 40-8, 161
Friends of the Earth 156, 172
Friendship organization 15, *218*, 223, 224, **226**
FSC *see* Forest Stewardship Council
Furlong, Katie 221
Furtado, Nelly 110

Gaillot, Jacques 45
Galeano, Eduardo 110, 124
Galicia 129-39
Galuh *97*
Gandhi, Mohandas 85, 141, 187
gangway sign **148**
garbologists 231
García, Raúl *172*, 173
Gardner, Penny 187, 221
Garnacho, Nacho 91, 92
Gaza Peace Flotilla **196**, *198*
Gaza Strip *194* (map), **198**
Gazprom 199, *202*, *204*, 205, 207
GE 214
Gem 129
Germany 27, 45, 52, *71*, *103*, 122, *196*
Gianni, Alessandro 166, 169
Gleizes, Pierre *127*, 130, 138
Gorter, Tim 46
Gotje, Martini 17
Gottschalk, Thomas *103*
Grampian Fame 27
Gravatt, Carmen 166

Greece 52, 153-4, 155, 181
Green Action 156
Green Line, Cyprus 154, *154* (map), 156
green passport 231
Greenland 68
Greenpeace (boat) *see Phyllis Cormack*
Greenpeace, MV (ship) 18, 42, 45, 47, 48, *48*, 128
Greenpeace Argentina 198
Greenpeace Austria 172
The Greenpeace Chronicle 30, 68
Greenpeace Denmark 193
Greenpeace France 224
Greenpeace International 17, 40, 106, 107, 116, 139, 143, 173, 188, 189, 193, 196, 212, 220, 224, 227
  Political Unit 108
  Ships Unit *221*
Greenpeace Israel 195, 196
Greenpeace Italy 166, 169
Greenpeace Korea 216, 219
Greenpeace Limited 24
Greenpeace Netherlands 212, 224, 227
Greenpeace regional offices
  Chile 121
  East Asia 216, 231
  India 78
  New Zealand/Aotearoa 12, 185
  Nordic 194
  Pacific 95, 96
Greenpeace Spain 89, 134, 136, 138, 174
Grillo, Beppe 168
Groenier, Willem 130
Grossman, Nili 197
Guevara, Ernesto ("Che") 106
Gulf of Aden 159, *161*, 162
Gulf of Guinea 157
Gulf of Thailand 76

Habib, Madeleine 60
Hadera power station, Israel 194-5, *195*
Hammer, Raoni 183
Hapsoro *97*
Hardingham, Mark 58-9, *59*, 60, 61
Harris, Alex 206, *206*
Hatton Bank 134, 135
Haussmann, David ("Haussy") 199
Hawkins, Sebia *20*
health problems
  from radiation **32**, 34, 35, **36**, 38, 39, 213

from toxic contamination 72-3, **74**, **75**, **76**, 79
heavy metals **75**, 77
helicopters 29, 45, *144*, 176, 202, *202*
Hellenic Sea 182, *183*
Hernu, Charles 19
Heulseman, Meike 116
Hewetson, Frank 177, 198, 201, 206
Hill, Elaine *221*
Hiroshima 34, 45
historical items **49**
  artwork and photos *16*, *19*, *20*, *48*, *57*, *59*, *70*, *76*, *80*, *97*, *124*, *166*, *228*
  inventory 15, 220, *220*, *221*, 226
  objects 15-16, 26, **49**, **52**, 62, **78**, *96*, **99**, *148*, 221-2, 224, *224*, 226-7, *228*
  poems 30, *30*
  ship's fittings 16, 28, 224
Hitachi 214
Hoare, Chris 136
Hoffman, Bene 27, *28*
Holmes, Alexander *218*
Hong Kong 70, 76-7, *77*, 84
Honour 91, 92
hooliganism charges 205
hope 82-3, 205, 230
Horne, Ann-Marie 41
hospital ship *see Rongdhono*
household products **76**
HP 83
hull damage 112-14
humanitarian missions **196**
  (*RWII*; Indonesia; 2005) 115-19
  (*RWII*; Lebanon; 2006) 120-1
  (*RWII*; Nicaragua; 1998) 121
Hunter, Robert (Bob) 9, 15, 21, *22*, *23*, 24, 30, 68, 209, 230
Hurricane (press boat) 177
Hurricane Mitch 121
Hussein, Saddam 144
Huxley, Aldous 69
Hvalur 9 56
Hynde, Chrissie 93, *93*

Ibsa I 126
Ibsa II 126
Ibsa III 126
ICCAT *see* International Commission for the Conservation of Atlantic Tunas
Iceland 56, 57, 60, 68, 135
Idogawa, Katsutaka 213

Ihl, Cornelia 192
IKEA 83
Ilai Ben Amar 190, 194
imprisonment 203-6
incineration, waste 74, 75-7, 128
India 33, 70, 71, **78**, 84, 116, 162
  Bhopal *71*, 72-3
  river pollution **75**
  shipbreaking 73, 74, *74*
Indian Ocean 68, 115, 210, 215
Indonesia 94, 97-102, 103
  tsunami relief 115-21
inflatables 56, *56*, 58-9, *65*, 66, 69,
  128, *128*, 130, 143, *165*, *176*
  see also *African Queen; Avon;*
    Mermaid and *Orca*
Iniupiaq people 9
injuries 58-9
International Commission for the
  Conservation of Atlantic Tunas
  (ICCAT) **156**, 169, 170, **172**, *172*,
  175, 178
International Criminal Court 83
International Day of Climate Action
  229
International Tribunal for the Law
  of the Sea 206
International Whaling Commission
  (IWC) 53, 54, 57
Inuit people 52
Iran 159-60
Iraq War (2003) 143-6
Ireland 135
Israel 33, 112, 120, 146-53, 160,
  161, 181, 194-8
Italy 149, 166-70, 174
IWC see International Whaling
  Commission

Jakl, Zrinka 172, *172*
James Bay 23
Japan 33, *33*, 45, 57, 60, 70, 74, 75,
  77, 84, 99, *100*, 102, 109, 126, 137
  bluefin tuna imports 170, *170*
  Fukushima Daiichi nuclear
    disaster 209-14, 216
  whaling *55*, *65*, 65-8
Jersey 127, *127*
Johnston, Emily 97, *122*
Jose, V.J. **75**
Juanito see Valle, Juan Antonio
Juda (Bikini atoll leader) 34, 35

Kan, Naoto 209
Kang, Rashid 216

kata scarf 228
Kato 60
Kawon Song, Grace *217*, 222
Kayopulau people 98, *98*
KFEM see Korean Federation for the
  Environment Movement
Khan, Runa 218, 223, *223*, 224,
  225, 226
Kim, Hye Jeong 217, *217*
King, Martin Luther, Jr 85, 141, 187
Klein, Naomi 190
Koettlitz, Athel von *127*
Korea 99, *100*
  see also North Korea and South
    Korea
Korean Federation for the
  Environment Movement (KFEM)
  56, 57, 216
Korman, Pablo 114, *148*
Kowsoleea, Raoul 223
Kristen 129
Kruso see Weber, Marco
Kumar, Sunil 72
Kwakiutl people 21, 23
Kwakiutl totem *21*, 25, **64**, 222
Kwon Song, Jun 216

Laboucan-Massimo, Melina 227,
  227
Lacoste, Pierre 19
Lafayette 43
L'Affaire Greenpeace 18, *19*, 42
Lala-ship *225*
  The Lancet 146
Landcorp 185
landfills 77, 84
languages 113, 124
La Ribaud 48
Lauzen, Olivier 161
Law of the Sea
  International Tribunal 206
  UN Convention on 54, 68
Lawrence, Elaine 116
Lawrence Livermore National
  Laboratory 38, 49
Lebanon 111, 112, 120, *120*, 121,
  146-53, 161
Lee, Sihnae 217, *217*
The Legacy of Bhopal 72
Lennon, John 105
letters of support *193*
Levi's 83
Liberia 87, 88, *88*, 89, 91, 103
Libya 141, 173, 178
Lifebuoy 226

Ligurian Sea 68, 169
Linke, Uwe 187
Litvinov, Dima 191, 192, 198, 201,
  202, *206*
livestock rearing 179, **180**, 183, 185,
  185, 207
Lloyd, Phil 145, 146
Lobi community 94
logging 94, 95, 96
  see also timber imports, illegal
logistics specialists see Abdul,
  Lama; Litvinov, Dima; Roberts,
  Dave and Taylor, Rob
López de Uralde, Juan ("Juantxo")
  134, 136, *190*, 191, 192, *192*, *193*
Lord Howe Island 178
Losada, Sebastiàn 137, *172*, 173
Louise 129

Macián, Óscar 113
Madsen, Jan *28*
Mafart, Alain 18, 19
mafia threats 172-3
Maisin people 94-7
Maitar, Bustar 97
Malaysia 94, 96
Malmgren, Sven *62*
Malta 174, 175, *175*, 177, *177*
Mango 83
Maori people 25, **49**, 52, 141, 163,
  164, 182, 229
Marcos, Ferdinand 79
Mariana Trench **113**, 124
marine pollution 75
  organic human waste 169
  plastics **163**
  radioactivity 42, 211, 213
marine reserves 215
marine reserves campaign
  (*RWII*; Mediterranean; 2006) 171
  (*RWII*; Norway; 2009) 61-4
marine seabed campaigns
  (*AS*; Spain; 2011) 138-9
  (*E*; Spain; 2004) 134-5, 166
  (*RWII*; Spain; 2011) 138
  (*RWII*; Tasman Sea; 2004-5) 163-6
Mark, Tim *127*
Marley, Bob 97
Marre, Yves 223, 226
Marriner, Tony *127*
Marshall, Timo *145*
Marshall Islands *35* (map)
  Bikini 31, *33*, 34-5, *35*, *36*
  Ebeye 39
  Enewetak 31, 32

Majuro 36, 38, 39
Mejato 37, 38
Rongelap 11, 16, 19, 31, *32*, 34, *34*, 35-9, 42
Marshall Islands visits
  (*RWI*; 1985) 11, 37
  (*RWII*; 1990) 38, 42
  (*RWIII*; 2010) 39
Mascareñas, Pablo 136-7
Massó family 126
Matauri Bay visits
  (*RWII*; New Zealand; 2005) 229
  (*RWIII*; New Zealand; 2013) 229
mates, chief *see* Binyon, Dan;
  Gotje, Martini; Habib, Madeleine;
  Lauzon, Olivier; Macián, Óscar;
  Petersen, Naomi *and* Ruzycki,
  Paul
mates, second *see* Conc, Marin;
  Fontanillas, Sandra *and* Sharomov,
  Dima
Mauritius 215
Mavi Marmara 196, *198*
mayday calls 111-12, 124, 160
McDiarmid, Bunny 11, 12, 18, 39,
  185, 229
McTaggart, Dave 40, 41, *127*
meat production 179, **180**, 183, 185
Médecins Sans Frontières (MSF)
  111, 116, 117, 120, 121
medics *see* Biedermann, Andy; Riza,
  Bahadir; Simkiss, Lesley *and* Turk,
  Lawrence
Mediterranean Sea 87, 91, 111-12,
  114, 120-1, 146-53, 161, *169*
  (map), 170-8, 181, *229*
  see also Adriatic Sea *and* Ligurian
  Sea
Meltemi 87-91
Mermaid (inflatable) 176, 182
Metcalfe, Ben *22*, 40
Mexico 68
Middle East **159**
  see also under countries
Mielgo, Roberto 172
military action
  environmental damage *146*,
  147-53
  see also nuclear weapons testing
military bases
  expulsion of local inhabitants 34,
  215
  toxic contamination from 79, **80**,
  82, 84
Mills, Margaret 17, 19

Mills, Stephanie 45, 46, 94
mining 95, 97, 99, 103
Mirza, Randa *159*
Mitterand, François 19, 43, 44
Moi, Sylvester 95
Momeñe, Belén 38, 97
Mompo, Maite 13, 65-7, *69*, 111,
  114, 114-15, 135, 136, *142*, *152*,
  156, 173-4, *174*, 182, *183*, 184,
  192, *192*, 193, *193*, 195, 196, *217*,
  218, *218*, *220*, 224-5, 226
Monbiot, George 228
Monker, Hans 100
Monkey Island *142*
Montón, Gonzalo 91, 92, 93
Moore, Patrick *22*
Morris, Noah 126
Moruroa 16, 18, 20, 32, 33, 40-8,
  161
Mosquito, Fred *23*, 24
Mount Pinatubo 79
multinationalism 11, 20
music 10, 61, 93, 97, 110, 126, 166,
  192
Musichana 215

Nagasaki *33*, 45
Naidoo, Kumi 189, 193, 227, 228
Nakazono, Flavio 112, 113, 114,
  184
naming
  Greenpeace **21**
  Rainbow Warrior 9, 11, 24
Namminga, Jacob 212, *214*
Netherlands 143, 181, *205*, 206, 226
  climate change action 185-7
New Zealand/Aotearoa 9, 18, 33,
  40, 45, 52, *103*, 110, 112, 119, 135,
  141, 163, 164, 181, 227
  bombing of *Rainbow Warrior* 9, 12,
  16-19, 40, *40*, 42, 43, 49
  climate change action 182-5
  deforestation 184, 185, *185*
  Matauri Bay 25, *25*, 229, 230
Newborn, Susi 9, 10, 24, 30, 230,
  230
Nicaragua 121
Nicholls, Derek 46, 47, 60, 163
nicknames, ship's *225*
night-watch **111**
Nike 83
9/11 attacks **107**
Nitto, Caterina 112, 113
Nobel Peace Prize laureates **187**,
  196, 205

Noble Bob Douglas 41
Nokia 83
nonviolence 9, 49, 99, **141**, 187
Norfolk Island 165, 178
North Korea 33
North Pacific Gyre 163, 178
North Sea *58*, *60*
Norway 16, *58* (map), 187, *188*,
  198, 199
  marine reserves campaign 61-4
  whaling 56, 57-61, 64, 68
nuclear campaigns *see* anti-nuclear
  campaigns
nuclear disasters
  Chernobyl 49, 130, 212, 213
  Fukushima Daiichi 209-14, 216
  Three Mile Island 213
nuclear energy **219**
Nuclear Non-Proliferation Treaty
  33, 160
nuclear radiation monitoring
  (*RWII*; Japan; 2011) 209-14
  (*RWII*; Moruroa; 1990) 42
nuclear reactors 159-60, 210, *210*,
  211, **213**, 214, **216**, 218, *218*
nuclear waste 219
  dumping at sea *128*, 128-30
nuclear weapons, number of 49
nuclear weapons testing 16, 20-3,
  29, 31-49, 142
  health problems from *32*, 34, 35,
  36
Nugent, Stephen 153

Obama, Barack *181*, 187, *188*
Ocean Reward 164
oil rigs 199, 200
oil spill monitoring (*RWII*; Spain;
  2002) 125, 131-4
Okawara, Tatsuko 213
Olivar, Mar 85
Oman 161
Operation Crossroads 34
Orca (inflatable) 65
Orient Venus 196, *196*, 197
Orihuela, Marta *169*
orphanages **119**
O'Sullivan, Grace 18, 227
Oulahsen, Faiza *205*
outboard mechanics *see* Dunn,
  Phil *and* Soto, Andrés
Oxfam 198

Pacific Ocean 16, 52, *53*, 112, *113*
  (map), **163**, 209, 210

see also French Polynesia *and* Marshall Islands
pacifism 142, 215
Paichekova, Irina **203**, 204
Pakistan 33, 73, 162
palm oil
    cargos 100, *101*
    plantations 94, 97, 99
Palmer, Louis *103*
Palmer, Stanley *19*
Panama 162
Papua *94* (map), 97-9
Papua New Guinea 33, *94* (map), 94-7, 98
Paradise Forests 94
Parmentier, Rémi 108, 138
Partial Test Ban Treaty 35
Patagonia 85
patents 110
Patrick, Edward 101, 143, 144, 145, *145*, *148*
peace campaigns (*RWII*; Spain; 2003) 143-6
peace symbols 21, **49**, *142*
peat *102*, 103
Pechora Sea *199* (map), 200
Pekkanen, Tapio 92, *225*
penguins 121-4
People's Declaration (on climate change) **190**
People's Task Force for Bases Clean-up 81, 84
Pereira, Fernando 9, 12, 15, 17, **19**, 29, 30, 38, 40, 42, 49
Pereira, Marelle 229
Periyar River Keeper *see* Jose, V.J.
Perrett, Anthony *200*, 201, 207
Persian Gulf 160
Persistant Organic Pollutants (POPs) **74**, 75
Petersen, Karsten *28*
Petersen, Naomi 27, *27*, *28*, 114, 167
Petro, Joe *20*
Pettersson, Pelle *62*
Philippines 33, 78, 82, 181
    toxic pollution 70, 73, 74, 75, 77, 78-9, 81, *81*, *82*, *83*, 84
philosophy, Greenpeace 9, 141-2
photographers *see* Pereira, Fernando; Sharomov, Dima *and* Sinyakov, Denis
Phyllis Cormack 21, 22, 221
    1971 anti-nuclear campaign (Amchitka) 21-3, 40, 49, 142

1975 anti-whaling campaign *21*, 57, 64
1976 anti-whaling campaign 23, *23*
Picasso, Pablo *152*
Pinto, Manuel *47*
Pip's poem 30, *30*
piracy 99, 100, 157-78
piracy charges 203, 205
Piwonka, Nicolas 123
plastics
    accumulation in Pacific **163**
Platinum II 84
pod, safety 199, 200, *200*, 201
poems 30, *30*, 19
Policomander 132
POPs *see* Persistant Organic Pollutants
porpoises 52, 68
portholes 28
Portugal 19, *111*, 125
possums **184**, 207
Prestige oil-tanker disaster 125, *131*, 131-4
The Pretenders 93
Prieur, Dominique 18, 19
Prirazlomnaya oil rig 199, 200, *202*
Promise Ceremony *222*, 222-3
propeller blockages 163
prophecies 11, 20, 24
public relations 64, *109*, 156, *160*, 172, *197*, 216, 217
Puma 83
Pupuka, Phillip *27*, 28

Qadafi, Muammar 173
Qatar 107, 109
Quakers 21, 30

radiation
    health problems from **32**, 34, 35, **36**, 38, 39, 213
radiation safety advisers 212, *214*
radio operators *see* Gorter, Tim; Hoare, Chris; Monker, Hans *and* Russell, Colin
radioactive contamination
    French Polynesia *44*
    Marshall Islands 33, **36**, 38, **39**, 42
    Japan **210**
radioactive waste *see* nuclear waste
'rafter crisis' **106**
rainbow symbol 15, 20, 23, 25
Rainbow Warrior (**first**; in service

1978-85) *17*, *24*, *28*, 67
1978 anti-whaling action (Iceland) 56, *56*
1978 anti-whaling action (Spain) 125-6
1980 anti-whaling action (Spain) 126-8, 138
1985 Rongalap evacuation 11, 37
1985 bombing in Auckland harbor 9, 16-19, 40, *40*, 42, 43, 49
1987 sea burial in Matauri Bay 9, *25*, 25-6, *26*, 230
and 2009 climate change campaign 229
Rainbow Warrior (**second**; in service 1989-2011) 13-14, 20, 38, 39, 42, *42*, *47*, *63*, 139
1988 preparation 27, 27-8, *28*
1989 launch and maiden journey *20*, 28, 28-9, 42
1990 Marshall Islands visit 38, 42
1990 nuclear radiation monitoring (Moruroa) 42
1992 Mururoa anti-nuclear action 42-4
1995 Mururoa anti-nuclear action 44-8
1996 fisheries campaign (Chile) 121
1997 Papua New Guinea visit 94-7
1998 humanitarian missions (Nicaragua) 121
1999 whaling observer mission (Norway) 56, 58-61
1999-2000 Toxic Free Asia Tour 70-84
2001 Qatar visit 109
2002 oil-spill monitoring (Spain) 125, *131*, 131-4
2002 research tour (UK) *59*
2002, 2003 Forests Tour (Mediterranean) 87, *89*, 91
2002, 2003 illegal timber imports actions (Spain) 87-93
2003 anti-Iraq War action (Spain) 143-6
2004 Fisheries Tour (Pacific) 38
2004-5 marine seabed campaign (Tasman Sea) 163-6
2005 anti-whaling tour (South Korea) 56-7
2005 humanitarian missions (Indonesia) 115-19
2005 Matauri Bay visit 229

2006 anti-driftnet campaign (Mediterranean) 168, *168*

2006 bluefin tuna campaign (Mediterranean) 170-3

2006 Forests Tour (Papua) 97-9

2006 humanitarian missions (Lebanon) 120-1

2006 marine reserves campaign (Mediterranean) 171

2006 war damage monitoring (Israel/Lebanon) 146-53

2007 anti-nuclear campaign (Middle East) 159-60

2007 bluefin tuna campaign (Mediterranean) 173

2007 On the road to Bali campaign (Indonesia) 99-102

2008 climate change campaigns (Netherlands) 185-7

2008 climate change campaigns (New Zealand) 182-5

2009 climate change campaigns (Copenhagen) 181, 187-94

2009 climate change campaigns (Mediterranean) *229*

2009 marine reserves campaign (Norway) 61-4

2010 bluefin tuna campaign (Mediterranean) *175*, 175-7, *177*, *178*

2010 climate change campaign (Israel) 194-8

2010 Marshall Islands visit 39

2011 anti-military campaigns (Diego Garcia) 215

2011 anti-nuclear campaign (South Korea) *216* (map), 216-19, *220*

2011 marine seabed campaign (Spain) 138

2011 nuclear radiation monitoring (Japan) 209-14

2011 transfer to new ownership 13, 15-16, *223*, 223-4

Rainbow Warrior (**third**; in service 2011-) 9, 20, 29, **227**, 230

2011 launch and maiden voyage *227*, 227-8

2013 Matauri Bay visit 229

Ramdas, Lalita 223, *223*, 224, 226

Rangkuti, Draga *119*

Rarama, Kingsford 95

Raukura **49**

REACH regulation 84

Réard, Louis 34

recycling 231

Red Carpet Four *190*, 190-1, *192*, 193, *204*

Red Cross 90

reefs, artificial 25, *26*

refugees 107, 108-10

renewable energy 84, 95

advocacy 77-8, *78*, 82

reporting of actions 43, 45, 46, 202, 206

reports

on bottom trawling 138

A Desert called Sea 168

Energy Revolution 159

on illegal timber trade 91

The Legacy of Bhopal 72

on tuna fisheries 169, 172, 173

rescues 111-12

research tours (*RWII*; UK; 2002) *59*

Rijnborg 128, 130

Rio+20 (2012) 228

river pollution 75

Riza, Bahadir 111, 112, 121, 161

Rizzotti, Daniel 107, 145, *145*, 146, 160, 161

Roberts, Dave 223

Roberts, Jemima *222*, 223

Robinson, Chris 18, *127*

Rodrigues, Wilindro ("Willy") 223

Rongdhono 13, 223, 226

Rongelap 11, 16, 19, 31, *32*, 34, *34*, 35-9, 42

Ross Kashmir 27

Russell, Colin 199

Russia 33, 43, 68, 119, *134*, 159, 160, *199* (map)

Arctic 30 action 198-207

see also Soviet Union

Ruzycki, Paul 199

Saarela, Sini 199, 200, *200*, 201, 202, 206, *206*

Saban, Peru 174, *174*, 175

sails and rigs 16, 28-9, 56, 61, *89*, 113

salmon farming **138**, 139

Samoa *53*

Samsung 83

Samud 107-10

Samui 76, 77

Sanchez, Gina 116

Sandison, Peter 166

Saramago, José 145

Save the Arctic campaign (*AS*; Russia; 2013) 198-207

Save the Children UK 198

Sawyer, Steve 17

Schenzle, Peter 28

Schmutz, Christian ("Chrigi") *190*, 191, 193, *193*, *204*

Schmutz, Curdin 193, *193*

Schullstrom, Jocke *62*

scientists *see* Alamar, Josevi

sea burial of *Rainbow Warrior* (Matauri Bay; 1987) 9, *25*, 25-6, *26*, 230

sea levels 182, *188*

seabed

oil contamination *148*, 149

radiation levels 213

for damage see bottom trawling

seamounts *135*, 163, 164

seasickness 164, 166

seawater analysis 169, 213, *211* (map), *214*

security forces

Danish 188, 189

Israeli 194-7

Russian 200, 201, *202*

Spanish 89-90, 92, *92*, 137, 143-5, 156

US 22, 107, 143, 156

Sepúlveda, Luis 14

Sharomov, Dima 111, 112, 115, **119**, *119*, 120, 121, 144, 182, 183-4

Shell 199, 205

shipbreaking 73-4, 84

Shiva, Vandana 110, 124, 179, 190

Siberia 56, 85

Sicily 174

Sierra Leone 89

Simkiss, Lesley 109, 173, 191

Simmons, Terry 22

Simpson, Michael 183

Singapore 13, 100, 115, 119, 162, 210, 215, 220, 226

Sinyakov, Denis 205

Sir William Hardy 9, 24, 25

Sirius 58, 59, 60-1, 224

1982 nuclear waste dumping action 128-30

skippers *see* Fontanillas, Sandra; Saban, Peru *and* Willcox, Pete

slogans

Coal Kills *195*, 196

Politicians Talk, Leaders Act 181, 190

Quit Coal 181, 186

Save or delete? 87

There is No Planet B 181
You can't seize a Sunrise 206
You can't sink a Rainbow 18, 205
solar taxi *103*
Solomon Islands 94
Somalia
  piracy 107, *158* (map), 158-9
Somaliland 158
songs 95, 110-11
Sony 83
Sorensen, Hanne 17
SOS Racism 89
Soto, Andrés 162, 163, *163*, 176, *176*
South Korea *16*, 123, 209, 210
  Nuclear Free Korea tour 215-19
  whaling 56-7, 68, 112
Southern Ocean *55*, 57, *65*, 65-7, 68, 163
Soviet Union 33, 57
  see also Russia
Spain 29, *126* (map), 174
  attitudes to Greenpeace 134-9
  Iraq War action 143-6
  oil-tanker disasters 125, *131*, 131-4
  radioactive waste dumping protests 129-30
  timber imports 87-93
  whaling 56, 57, 125-8
Speziale, Camila 198, 199, 200, *200*, 201, 206, *206*
sportswear companies 83-4
squisher device 43
Sri Lanka 116, 162
St Vincent and the Grenardines 68
Ståhl, Jari 63
Statoil 199
Steffens, Martin 38, 115, 164
Stewart, Joel 29, 92, *93*, 97, 106, 227, 231
stowaways 88-9, 90, 105-7
Stowe, Irving 21
Strait of Magellan 121
Strait of Malacca 99, 157, 162
Suez (merchant ship) **162**
Suez Canal 158, *161*
Sumatra *94* (map), 99, *101*, *115*, 116, 124
Sunce 172
Sunquist, Odin *135*
Suu Kyi, Aung San 141
Suwesnawa, Agus 118
Suzie Q 201
swim stops **113**, 177, 220

Switzerland *103*, *204*
symbols
  CND *142*
  dove 24, 25, *152*, 229
  ecology 21
  peace 21, **49**, *142*
  rainbow 15, 20, 23, 25
Syria 141, 151

Taiwan 123, 211, 215
tapa cloths 94-6, *96*
Tasman Sea 29, *41*, 163, *165*
Taylor, Rob 116, 215
TckTckTck *181*, 189, 191, *191*
Te Whiti 49
Temaru, Oscar 45
temperatures, global **179**, **182**
TEPCO 211, 213, 214
Terveil, Bart *225*
Teuling, Ike 212
Thailand 70, 76, 77-8, 84, 116, 162, 181
Thijssen, Joris 191, *192*, 193
350.org 229
Three Mile Island 213
Thurston, Lyle *22*
Tibet 182
timber imports, illegal 87-93
Tohu 49
Tomac, Luka 172
Toshiba 214
totems *21*, 25, **64**, 222
toxic contamination 70-82
toxic waste dumping 158
toxics campaign (*RWII*; Asia; 1999-2000) 70-84
trade negotiations
  Doha Round 107, 109
trade-related intellectual property rights (TRIPS) 110, 124
training, activist 59, 159
trials, activist 146, 205
TRIPS *see* trade-related intellectual property rights
Trumper, Liliana *28*
Trust Territory of the Pacific Islands 31, 49
tsunamis **209**, 210
  relief missions 115-19
tuna *see* bluefin tuna campaigns
Tunisia 141
Turk, Lawrence ("Butch") 80, 143, 144, 146
Turkey 120, 153-4, 161, 162, 181, 196

Türkmen, Tuna 191
Tuvalu *188*, 190
Tweety (helicopter) 45

Ukraine 213
UNCLOS *see* United Nations Convention on the Law of the Sea
underwater filming 42, 61, *62*, 64
UNESCO 35, 155, 156
unexpected events 105-24
UNHCR *see* United Nations High Commissioner for Refugees
UNICEF 118
Union Carbide 72, *72*
United Arab Emirates 108, 159
United Kingdom *see* Britain
United Nations 23, 89, 165
  Convention on the Law of the Sea (UNCLOS) 54, 68
  Food and Agriculture Organization 85
  General Assembly 41
  High Commissioner for Refugees (UNHCR) 108, 109, 110
  Office on Drugs and Crime 158
  peacekeeping forces 154
  Secretary General 205
  Security Council 31, 91
  Trusteeship Council **32**
  see also Climate Change Conferences; Earth Summit *and* Rio+20
United States 16, 20, 29, 33, 43, 45, 68, 99, *100*, 103, 106, 107, 109, 110, 121, 141, 160, 187, 192, 199, 213
  Iraq War (2003) 143-6
  military bases 79, **82**, **215**
  9/11 attack (2001) **107**
  nuclear weapons testing (Amchitka) 20, 21, *22*, 23, 40, 142; (Marshall Islands) 31, 34-9
Urquiola 132

Valencia, Jane Crizel *see* Crizel
Valle, Juan Antonio ("Juanito") 87, 89, 90
Vangal, Satish 73
Vasquez, Luis 177, 223
Vega 40-1 *41*, 42, 45, 64
Vidan, Toni 156, 172, *172*
vigils *189*, 191, *193*
Vila, Ánxel 129, 130
Villduen 58, *59*, *60*
volunteers on board **217**

WAHLI 118
Waipori 165, 166
war damage monitoring (*RWII*; Israel/Lebanon); 2006) 146-53
war wood 87-91
Ware, Sue 27, *27, 28*
Warriors of the Rainbow 9, 10, 15, *20*, 20-5, 230
waste incineration 74, 75-7, 128
water supplies *see* drinking water contamination
Watson, Sarah 111
weather, bad 155, 175
Weber, Marco ("Kruso") 193, 200, 201, 202, *204*
West Papua 94, 99
Westama 100-1, *101*
Western Sahara 156
Whale and Dolphin Conservation Society *59*
whale meat trade 57, **60**, **64**

whale-watching industry 56, 64
whales **52**, *53, 55*, 57, *58*, 64, 68
songs **54**
whaling campaigns *see* anti-whaling campaigns
whaling industry 53, **54**, 56-61, 65-7, 126, **127**
wheel, ship's 224
Whiting, Matt 48
Wielandt, Kirstie 193
Wigt, Bob 163
Willcox, Pete 17, 18, 27, *28*, 29, 37, 42, 81, 90, 112, 113, 114, 198, 202, 225
Williams, Heathcote 51
Willoya, William (Willie) 9, 10, 15, 20, 230, *230*
World Bank 75
World Heritage Sites 35, 61, 149, 156

World Trade Organization (WTO) 107, **109**
World Wide Fund for Nature (WWF) 24, 172
Worldwatch Institute 180, 207
WTO *see* World Trade Organization
WWF *see* World Wide Fund for Nature

Xurelo 129, 130

Yabem 107-10
Yashwant, Shailendra 78
Yemen 160, *160*
Yushin Maru 55, *65*, 65-6

Zamenhof, Lázaro 124
Zara 83
Zola, Emile *19*, 30
Zorba 174
Zumaia 3 174, *174*

GREENPEACE

Greenpeace is an independent campaigning organisation
that acts to change attitudes and behaviour, to protect
and conserve the environment, and to promote peace.
It comprises more than 40 offices across Europe, the
Americas, Africa, Asia and the Pacific.

greenpeace.org

New Internationalist

An independent, not-for-profit media co-operative,
New Internationalist is a voice that empowers. We tell
the stories that the mainstream media sidestep and offer
a platform for the people living those stories. Our award-
winning magazine, books and website set the agenda
for a radically fairer future, promote global justice and
campaign for the disadvantaged all over the world.

newint.org